Liu Xiaoming

SHARP
DIALOGUE

Collection of Interviews with Ambassador Liu Xiaoming

Sharp Dialogue:
Collection of Interviews with Ambassador Liu Xiaoming

Author Liu Xiaoming

Editor Victor Jiang
Designer Dorgel Chung

Published by Joint Publishing (H.K.) Co., Ltd.
20/F., North Point Industrial Building, 499 King's Road, North Point, Hong Kong

Distributed by SUP Publishing Logistics (H.K.) Ltd.
16/F., Tsuen Wan Industrial Centre, 220-248 Texaco Road, Tsuen Wan, N.T., Hong Kong

Printed by Elegance Printing & Book Binding Co., Ltd.
Block A, 4/F., 6 Wing Yip Street, Kwun Tong, Kowloon, Hong Kong

First Published in May 2023
ISBN 978-962-04-5137-9

尖銳對話：讓世界聽見中國聲音

著　　者	劉曉明	
責任編輯	阿　江	
書籍設計	道　轍	
出　　版	三聯書店（香港）有限公司	
	香港北角英皇道 499 號北角工業大廈 20 樓	
香港發行	香港聯合書刊物流有限公司	
	香港新界荃灣德士古道 220-248 號 16 樓	
印　　刷	美雅印刷製本有限公司	
	香港九龍觀塘榮業街 6 號 4 樓 A 室	
版　　次	2023 年 5 月香港第一版第一次印刷	
規　　格	16 開（170 mm × 240 mm）396 面	
國際書號	ISBN 978-962-04-5137-9	

本書中文繁體 / 英文版本由北京出版集團有限公司授權三聯書店（香港）有限公司
在中國內地以外地區獨家出版發行。

The traditional Chinese/English version of this book is exclusively published and distributed outside
mainlard China by Joint Publishing (H.K.) Co., Ltd., authorised by Beijing Publishing Group.

Highly Recommended

Following on his book of speeches delivered during his unprecedentedly long term of office as China's Ambassador to the United Kingdom, Ambassador Liu Xiaoming has now published a compendium of his interviews with British television under the title "*Sharp Dialogue*". As with his speeches, he takes no prisoners. The interviews are characteristically incisive. They are also concentrated on rebuttal, responding to what he regards as false claims and allegations levelled at China. Indeed the sub-title to the collection might humorously be "*The Empire Strikes Back*".

The interviews cover a very wide range of subjects from COVID, to Hong Kong, to China's relations with the UK. They pit Ambassador Liu against most of Britain's best known television interviewers. It is to his credit that he never shied away from a challenge. This gave him far greater exposure to television and the media generally than any other foreign ambassadors, and thus unrivalled opportunities to put across China's views.

He emerges as a formidable debater and someone who relishes a battle of wits, although he and his Chinese colleagues should not forget the adage that everyone is entitled to his own opinions but not his own facts. His is also a considerable achievement linguistically, reflecting a serious knowledge of English literature. "I hope we can have a bit more sense and sensibility rather than pride and prejudice." he reproves one interviewer at one point.

In short, one cannot but admire the professional media skills of a remarkable diplomat.

Lord Powell of Bayswater
Foreign Policy Adviser to Prime Minister Margaret Thatcher

Ambassador Liu Xiaoming's book is an unique contribution in the history of the evolving Sino-British relations over the last decade. Ambassador Liu was the longest serving Chinese Ambassador in Britain and his extended tenure of 11 years overlapped with the administrations of four prime ministers—Gordon Brown, David Cameron, Theresa May and Boris Johnson—as well as the whole journey of the Brexit referendum leading to Britain's eventual exit from the EU. During this special period in Britain, Ambassador Liu's long tenure enabled him to gain exceptional insights in the country's political, social and economic dynamics. He reached out enthusiastically to a broad spectrum of stakeholders to present the China story, oftentimes via mass media and multimedia communications. Ambassador Liu's approach has been highly effective—never one to shy away from difficult and complex issues, he would always confront them constructively, with typical articulacy and courtesy. This book is a treasurable collection of Ambassador Liu's interviews during his time in Britain—they represent a remarkable effort to mitigate the "understanding deficit" between the West and China at this crucial juncture of history.

Victor L.L. Chu
Chair of Council, University College London
Co-Chair, International Business Council, World Economic Forum

Liu Xiaoming's period of service as China's ambassador to the United Kingdom from 2010 until 2021 covered an extraordinary time in China-UK relations. Between 2013 and 2016 the two countries enjoyed the warmest ever relationship. The highlight was the UK's decision to join the AIIB in 2015, despite opposition from the Obama administration, which in turn encouraged many European countries to act likewise. President Xi Jinping's visit to the UK later that same year was widely regarded as a major success. This period was described at the time as a golden era in China-UK relations and for good reason. But it did not last. Prime Minister Cameron lost the Brexit referendum, and with his resignation in 2016, relations between China and the UK began to deteriorate and reached a new low point with the election of the pro-Brexit government of Boris Johnson in 2019. The golden era gave way to growing hostility towards China and rising tensions over Hong Kong. Liu Xiaoming's collection of articles and interviews provide us with a very valuable insight into the highs and lows of this period. He was at all times a powerful and articulate proponent of China's views and became a very well-known and respected figure in British politics.

Professor Dr. Martin Jacques
Political commentator & author

Sharp Dialogue captures the difference between two cultures and the two systems. Ambassador Liu used the media in the UK to help officials, leaders, business and finance to understand China and the fast emerging Chinese economic and social system.

Because of fault lines laid down in the 19th Century many in the West have the opinion that Socialists from Russia and China are committed to the downfall of capitalism. But that is not the case. China has large private sector and China faces many of the same problems of governance and sharing that are also evident in the UK.

In *Sharp Dialogue* you can see how the Chinese approach is to find win-win outcomes but the UK has concerns that make outcomes difficult.

Sharp Dialogue shows that this is not about propaganda, but it is about helping others see the facts and understanding the Chinese history and ways, and plans. Ambassador Liu was one of the first Chinese overseas to engage with the Western media systems and manage differences, and even sometimes, clashes of interest.

It is only through breaking from simple politeness that you can get to the real issues. Ambassador Liu is one of the few Chinese who have come to live in the UK who has been prepared to engage in this way.

Enjoy reading the media moments as Ambassador Liu travels across hundreds of years of few contacts to achieve real understanding of each other's position on key matters.

Stephen Perry
Chairman, 48 Group Club
Awardee of China Reform Friendship Medal

Liu Xiaoming's ability, and willingness, to communicate openly with the media was typical of his tenure as China's Ambassador in Britain. As his book's title suggests, he recognised the importance of an open dialogue with the BBC, and other news outlets, when China, Hong Kong, and latterly the COVID pandemic, were the focus of interest worldwide. Ever the optimist, Liu's understanding of complex issues such as globalisation and China-UK bilateral relations were a significant factor in his huge success as his country's Ambassador. His book "*Sharp Dialogue*" gives us further insight into how he was able to communicate so eloquently with an ever-inquisitive media at a time when China's position in the world was rarely far from the headlines.

The Duke of Richmond and Gordon
President of the British Automobile Racing Club

In the geo-politics of the 21st century one of the core challenges is to "Let the world hear the voice of China". This need has been recognised by President Xi Jinping since he was Chairman of the Committee that produced the 18th Congress Political Report in 2012. Embedded in that Report were policies to advance how to "Let the world hear the voice of China". The huge value of this book is it provides a unique case study of how Ambassador Liu Xiaoming made most valuable pioneering efforts from the Chinese Embassy in UK to make optimal impact to "Let the world hear the voice of China". When Ambassador Liu Xiaoming arrived in UK in 2010, he had gathered wide experience of communicating in many nations. His experience in the USA as the Deputy Chief of Mission had impressed on him the need for China to innovate in how it communicates. A careful study of the interviews in this book "*Sharp Dialogue*" will show the value of his great efforts to communicate in the best possible native English style used in the UK. Also, what comes across is the skill of Ambassador Liu Xiaoming to communicate in a style that has optimal impact in UK media. The passion of Ambassador Liu Xiaoming to explore new ways to "Let the world hear the voice of China" can be grasped by reading these many radio and TV broadcast interviews he made and the large number of media articles he wrote. I hope this collection of interviews provides a catalyst for the study of the approach of one of the most consummate of China's communicators in this century. Congratulations to Ambassador Liu Xiaoming!

Alistair Michie
Secretary General, British East Asia Council
Chairman, International Council, Centre for China and Globalization

Ambassador Liu Xiaoming served as the Ambassador of China to the United Kingdom for eleven years from 2010 to 2021. Within the context of Chinese history of over 5,000 years, his period of office coincided with one of exceptional change and progress in the history of China and its relationships with the United Kingdom.

Since the founding of the People's Republic of China in 1949 there has been a period of remarkable advance for China's interests including a strengthening of its economic and financial position, its investment in infrastructure, its importance to global trade, the self-sufficiency of its people and a strong work ethic, combined with a high level of education and the strengthening of its military power. We have witnessed China becoming astonishingly competitive in the world market; so much so that its share of world trade has risen to being comparable with the United States.

In addition, China has miraculously elevated some seven hundred million people out of poverty within forty years. Medical care now covers nearly one hundred percent of the population whose life expectancy has become longer and happier. The number of people travelling outside China has risen to about one hundred million. It was during this period that Liu served as Ambassador and he was, in one way or another, involved in all these areas of progress. It was a period which our then Prime Minister, David Cameron, referred to as "a Golden Time—a Golden Era in China/UK relations".

In his years here as Ambassador, trade between China and the UK in goods and services doubled while investment from China tripled. At the time of President Xi Jinping's state visit to the United Kingdom at the end of 2015, the Ambassador said in an interview with ITV in October 2015, that the rise of China presented an opportunity significantly more than a threat. The two countries saw the era as going beyond pomp, kind words and slogans. There was a wish and commitment to develop profoundly the relationship between the two countries. Inevitably there would be difficult moments but, in the round, during the Ambassador's term of office, China and the United Kingdom enjoyed a golden period in their relationship. The United Kingdom owes the Ambassador an immense debt of gratitude for all that he achieved and indeed for putting the relationship between China and the United Kingdom on a much stronger and secure footing.

Baron Jacob Rothschild
British Banker
Honorary Fellow of the British Academy

Sharp Dialogue is the second volume of Liu Xiaoming's series "Tell China's Story" based on the speeches and interviews he gave whilst he was China's Ambassador to the UK. This second volume covers a wide range of interviews he gave mainly on mainstream UK TV and radio. Quick, witty, on occasion combative, these interviews show him to be an accomplished diplomat explaining the position of China on a range of topics important for the world today. They give insights into a number of issues over which China and Western Nations do not always agree and the discussions are important if some these difficult problems are to be resolved. Read this book and get better informed about China and its position in today's world.

Sir Paul Nurse
Chief Executive of the Francis Crick Institute
Former President of the Royal Society
Nobel Prize Laureate in Physiology or Medicine

It is pleasure to say a few words about this collection of interviews, not least as it brings back sentimental thoughts for me of the brief exciting days of the Golden Era that I was part of. I recall the formal UK visit to China in Autumn 2015 where we took civic leaders from across the Northern Powerhouse along with an array of business and other civic figures on a frantic tour of the country, and of course, so after, the UK hosted President Xi here for his exciting trip. I still , to this day, cannot fathom , how I didn't manage to stop him visiting Manchester City instead of Manchester United—my own sporting obsession—and I will hold Ambassador Liu responsible for that as my lazy excuse. It was always a delight to meet with the Ambassador and I also reflect on that interview I did with him for my BBC documentary on the failings of globalisation that is featured in his collection. Two things spring to mind, firstly, he sowed the seeds in my and the BBC's mind for a possible long travel documentary that I might have done, travelling along the Silk Road, which alas didn't materialise, but would have been wonderful. And secondly, and more seriously, if policymakers would have heeded the general advise from my various interviewees as well as myself about the weaknesses of globalisation, we might have avoided some of the issues and mess the world seems to find itself in today, including the weaker state of global togetherness that seems to- hopefully, only temporarily-exist.

Jim O'Neill, Baron O'Neill of Gatley
The Man Who Coined BRICs
Former Commercial Secretary to the Treasury
Former Chairman of the Royal Institute of International Affairs

Contents

Hong Kong

President
Xi Jinping's
State Visit to
the UK

A Live Interview with Jon Snow on *Channel 4 News*

On 14th October 2015, I was invited to a live interview with *Channel 4 News* hosted by Jon Snow. I stressed the significance of the forthcoming state visit of President Xi Jinping, and answered questions about China-UK bilateral relations, bilateral economic cooperation and China's economy. The full text is as follows:

Snow: I'm joined now by China's Ambassador to Britain, Liu Xiaoming. He is with us right now. President Xi Jinping is coming all the way to the middle ranking European nation and nowhere else, and then going home. What's he hoping to get from Britain, Ambassador?

Liu Xiaoming: He will be here for promoting relations between China and the UK. You regard UK as a middle ranking country. We do not think so. We still believe the UK is a country with global influence. It's one of the powerhouses, and China and the UK have a lot to cooperate about. The UK now is China's second largest trading partner within the EU, China is the UK's second largest trading partner outside Europe, and UK is the largest recipient of Chinese investment. So in the past three years, China's investment is booming here in the UK.

Snow: But the backdrop in China is not an easy one: a 20% reduction in imports and of course this catastrophic fall in the stock market. Will the President be able to say that's all behind us now?

Liu Xiaoming: When you look at China's economy, you have to focus on the big picture. You have to see China's economy in the long-term view. I think fundamentally and basically China's economy is still sound and good. For the first half of this year, the growth rate of the Chinese economy is 7%. China is still a leading country in the world, in terms of the growth of its economy.

Snow: But don't you think these events have told us about a degree of tension between the idea of a Communist state and a free market economy. Can you really have that marriage?

Liu Xiaoming: I don't think your definition of China as a Communist state is a right one. China has its official name, People's Republic of China, and it's led by the Communist Party of China. Just like here in this country. Your ruling party is Conservative Party, does this...

Snow: But nobody could elect a non-communist party to run China.

Liu Xiaoming: But the Communist Party provides a strong leadership and enjoys the people's support. The people support the Communist Party as their leader to lead China from poverty to prosperity. So why should we rock the boat? And you just look at the past 30 years, China, turning from a relatively poor country to the second largest economy. It's a miracle.

Snow: So do you think Britain has talked too much about the human rights in China? Do you think they should stop talking about human rights in China?

Liu Xiaoming: I think we can talk about human rights. No country is perfect. But I think in your earlier video clips you gave the impression that once you talk about human rights in China, you always talk about the negative side of China. When you talk about human rights, you have to have a comprehensive view. What are the human rights? I think people have a right to a better life, a better education, a better job. I think everyone would agree that Chinese people live better, live longer. They enjoy their lives.

Snow: But the things which exercise people are executions and detentions. And there are detentions of very large numbers of people.

Liu Xiaoming: Very large numbers of people? Your video clips talk about 100 people. You have to remember China's population is more than 1.3 billion.

Snow: It might be rather more than 100 people.

Liu Xiaoming: I don't know how many prisoners here in the UK...

Snow: But they've all been tried.

Liu Xiaoming: They've all been tried through normal legal process. China is a country ruled by law. For those people who violate the law they have to be held accountable. So all countries ruled by law have to respect the law. We might be different with regard to how countries are run, but I think we agree that country should be governed by the rule of law.

Snow: Have you been to the Royal Academy to see Ai Weiwei's art exhibition?

Liu Xiaoming: To be frank with you, he is not my taste. There are so many beautiful museums here in the UK. But I've been so busy. I have to find time to...

Snow: But he is the most famous Chinese artist in the world.

Liu Xiaoming: I don't think so.

Snow: And his show is...

Liu Xiaoming: I think he is famous here because he is critical of Chinese government's policy...

Snow: Why do you bother with him? Why is he a problem? Why does the Chinese state have a problem with him?

Liu Xiaoming: He was under investigation because of fraudulent accounting. He was prohibited from leaving China. But now he can leave and put up his exhibition. That shows how open China is.

Snow: Let me ask you a final question. The new Labour leader, Jeremy Corbyn, has attacked China's free market philosophy, particularly regarding what happened to the victims of the fire in which a lot of firemen died and a lot of workers died. He specifically blamed China's free market for that disaster. Are you disappointed in this new apparently left-wing leader of the Party?

Liu Xiaoming: In fact, I just had a meeting with him this afternoon...

Snow: Oh, that's very interesting.

Liu Xiaoming: ... to prepare for the meeting that he is going to have with the President. We talked quite a lot. We talked about the contributions made by the Labour Party to the development of China-UK relations. And we talked about the party-to-party exchanges, the Labour Party and the Communist Party.

Snow: So the relation is good?

Liu Xiaoming: The relation is good. The incident you are talking about is a bad incident. It's a tragedy. And the Chinese government is investigating this. Those who are responsible will be held accountable and will be punished. There is no mercy about that.

Snow: Thank you very, very much.

Liu Xiaoming: It's my pleasure.

Channel 4 News is a flagship news programme of Channel 4, the third largest public television broadcaster in Britain. It is known for its international coverage and in-depth interviews, and has an audience of more than one million. Jon Snow is a senior presenter of Channel 4, having served as the broadcaster for nearly 30 years.

An Interview with Rageh Omaar
on ITV *News at Ten*

On 15th October 2015, I gave an interview to International Affairs Editor of ITV News Rageh Omaar on *News at Ten* programme. The full interview is as follows:

Omaar: What gives you the confidence and the feeling that this is indeed a golden period of China-UK relations?

Liu Xiaoming: My confidence comes from my contact with the British people from all walks of life, from top down. For example, from the Prime Minister's visit to China, the Chancellor's visit to China. They both said Britain wants to be the best partner for China in the West. Britain wants to be the strongest supporter for China in the West. In fact, the expression "Golden Era", the word "golden", was first used by Prime Minister David Cameron. At the beginning of this year, I expected a series of important events in China-UK relations. In my very first public speech in the Parliament for celebrating the Chinese New Year, I said that 2015 will be a "big year" in China-UK relations. We were expecting the visit by President and the visit by Prince William to China. This will be the most important royal visit to China in 30 years since Her Majesty's visit to China in 1986. Then when we celebrated the Chinese New Year, Prime Minister Cameron in his new year message used the word "golden year". He sees this year as a golden year. When I met with him in No.10 for the Chinese New Year Reception, I told him, Prime Minister, I think your "golden year" is better than my "big year", so we reached the consensus that this year is a "Golden Year". After the election, Prime Minister Cameron proposed that we should work together for the "Golden Time" for China-UK relations. And that idea was endorsed by Chinese leaders. So now we're not only talking about a "Golden Year", we are talking about a "Golden Time"and a "Golden Era" for China-UK relations.

Omaar: But it was only a short time ago that you were publicly saying that Britain was lagging behind other European countries in their relations with China. Has it really changed so much?

Liu Xiaoming: In fact, when I said the UK lagged behind the other European countries, I was talking about the political relations. I think my comment was not fully reported. The question put to me was about how I see China's relations with the UK, and China's relations with France and Germany. I said, each bilateral relationship has its strengths. I listed five to ten areas where China-UK relations are strong. But I said, we are still weak when it comes to political trust and political relations. Political relations are really the foundation of the overall relationship. The media however were interested in the negative side rather than positive side of my comments.

Omaar: But the positive side comes into this–even though you felt that a short time ago Britain was lagging behind in its political relations with China–that seems to have changed dramatically?

Liu Xiaoming: That was more than one year ago. Within this year there were a series of high-level contacts. The Prime Minister went to China. The Chancellor went to China twice. Immediately after the British election, the Chinese Foreign Minister was here to set up early contact with the new government. Then in June, two senior Chinese leaders came here. Between China and the UK there are three pillars or mechanisms, what we call, to support this relationship: the Strategic Dialogue co-chaired by a State Councilor of China and the UK Foreign Secretary, the Economic and Financial Dialogue co-chaired by a Chinese Vice Premier and the British Chancellor and the High-Level People-to-People Dialogue co-chaired by a Chinese Vice Premier and the UK Secretary of State for Health. All these three mechanisms had a meeting in September. This was a very intense exchanges of visits. All these lead up to this state visit of President Xi. So political relations between China and the UK are very strong and political mutual trust has very much been strengthened.

Omaar: The issue of human rights, China's human rights will be raised. I understand that the leader of the Labour Party Jeremy Corbyn has said that he is going to raise it. How does China react to criticism of its human rights record?

Liu Xiaoming: I think we are open to discussions about human rights as I said in the recent press conference. We don't shy away from discussing human rights. As I said, the important thing is to have the big picture. When talking about human rights, you have to approach this issue from a comprehensive perspective. Some westerners, politicians and media people, they only focus on some individual cases, but missed the big picture of the progress of China's human rights. In the past 30 years, there are enormous changes in China. I think any people who holds no bias would agree about the great advancement on China's human rights. What are human rights? When you talk about human rights, you talk about people's rights for better living, better education, better job, freedom of speech, freedom of assembly and freedom of travelling around. When some people talk about human rights, they try to dig out some individual cases which they think are a focus on, or concerns about human rights. What would you say about China elevating 700 million people out of poverty just within 30 years of time? It's a miracle. No country has done that. The medical care in China covers almost 100% of the people. Each year now, the number of Chinese people travelling outside China is about 100 million. The Chinese people are living longer and happier. They are enjoying their lives. I think that's a basic right of any human.

Omaar: But there will always be these cases of dissidents that are raised. Is it possible for China to have good relations with a country economically and otherwise, whilst at the same time these individual cases are raised? Can you have that relationship?

Liu Xiaoming: We can only agree to disagree. I think there are international norms countries should follow. The basic norm is non-interference in each other's internal affairs. If I see your system as not perfect, if I see you have cases I'm not happy about, then I hold the whole relationship hostage. Will that be in the interest of the UK or China? We have a channel to discuss our differences over human rights. As I said, no country is perfect. You have your concerns and we also have our concerns. I can give you a list of concerns of cases where we don't think human rights are perfect in the UK and US. But I think the whole purpose of a high-level visit and the main mission of the Embassy and Ambassador here is not to focus on human rights only. Human rights are one of the areas in relations between China and the UK. We have broad interests for collaboration. I think people in the UK care more about their jobs, about a better life, about their education. That's the same for the people in China. The government leaders have to find common ground how we can work together for common good. We can debate but we should not miss the big picture. If we spend all our time debating, I don't think you will have a winner from this.

Omaar: Can I talk about the growing economic relationship, which is an important part of this golden era of UK-China relations. The agreement for China to be involved in the

Hinkley nuclear power project was a significant moment. Is that a field where Chinese companies would want to be involved more in the UK?

Liu Xiaoming: I think Chinese companies are interested in all projects where they think they can get good returns and help promote their businesses. In China, your companies have the same aim.

Omaar: So they are looking at all different areas, nuclear power, housing?

Liu Xiaoming: Yes, of course. Infrastructure, Hotels.

Omaar: And Heathrow Airport, 10%, Chinese ownership?

Liu Xiaoming: Heathrow Airport, 10%, Thames Water, 8%, Weetabix, the City airport in Manchester, and...

Omaar: And there'll be a big business delegation coming with the President?

Liu Xiaoming: They will be here separately. They are not part of the entourage. When you have a state visit, which is quite different from other visits, it is really a big event that all sectors from both sides focus on, they want to use this visit to promote collaboration across the board. They want the President and the Prime Minister to witness the signing ceremony. It's a kind of pride and honour for their businesses.

Omaar: When you talk about it, describing it as a super state visit, it's almost like a restart of the relations between China and the UK. Would it be too much to say that? Not a restart, but sort of re-energisation.

Liu Xiaoming: Yes, that's exactly the word I used, to re-position, how we move from here to a higher-level. That's why I call it a "new milestone". It's a landmark linking the past and the future. So this is an important visit. We haven't talked about "Golden Time" or "Golden Era" in previous years. This is really the first time both sides have this consensus that we work towards the "Golden Era" for China-UK relations.

Omaar: Is it being reported widely in China, the state visit? How is it being seen there?

Liu Xiaoming: The Chinese people have high expectations for this visit. The Chinese people like the British people, just as the British people like Chinese people. I read a poll several months ago, that in the West, in Europe, the percentage of liking for China among Britain people is higher than many other European countries. I think the same can be said in China. When the British government decided to take the lead to join the AIIB, I was in China. It was well received and widely welcomed. They see that the British leadership has the vision. They see that Britain sees the rise of China as an opportunity, not a threat. The two countries see each other as partners earnestly. They really see opportunities for cooperation, not just for pomp, words or slogans. We really mean business.

Omaar: One of the issues that has been high on the agenda in the UK recently is that Britain used to be a very big steel-producing country. The Redcar steel mill has closed down because of the availability of cheap steel from China. Should communities in steel-making areas be worried about China?

Liu Xiaoming: When we are in the age of globalisation, every country has to make adjustment. In some areas where China is strong, others need to make adjustment, vice versa. China used to be very strong in processing of clothes, shoes and toys. I think China provides 80%-90% of the toys in the world. No more that is the case now. Some Southeast Asian countries are now very strong in these areas. Low cost of labour has made them more competitive. So you have to make adjustment. If you continue staying with your old and traditional business, you are losing money and opportunities. That's why China makes its own adjustment. That's why some people are concerned about the slowdown of the Chinese economy. In fact, it's a healthy slowdown. Even with the slowdown from double-digit to 8% or 7%, China is still the leader in terms of growth. China is making adjustment. Why not Britain?

Omaar: Prince William is making a television speech shown in China, talking about the illegal trade in wildlife. Is China cooperating with that?

Liu Xiaoming: Very much so. China is strongly supportive of the international efforts to fight against illegal trade in endangered species and to protect wildlife. In fact, China has taken its own initiative in this area. When Prince William was in China, I traveled with him. I also sat in a meeting he had with the President. They talked about how China and the UK can cooperate in protecting wildlife and fighting against illegal trade. President Xi told him about the efforts China has made, including destroying five tons of tusks, which shows the determination of the Chinese government. China has been an active participant in many international conferences. When Prince William and the Prince of Wales sponsored an international summit here for the protection of wildlife, China sent a large delegation to attend this conference. China is also hosting its own forums for the protection of wildlife. I believe there is a great potential of cooperation between China and the UK in this area.

Omaar: Thank you very much, Ambassador!

Liu Xiaoming: My pleasure.

ITV is the oldest commercial network in the UK. *News at Ten* is ITV's flagship news programme and one of the most watched evening news programmes in the UK with an audience of 4 million.

A Live Interview with Evan Davis on BBC *Newsnight*

On 16th October 2015, I was invited to a live interview with BBC *Newsnight* hosted by Evan Davis. I talked about the significance of the forthcoming state visit of President Xi Jinping, and answered questions about China-UK bilateral relations, bilateral economic cooperation and China's economy. The full text is as follows:

Davis: Well, I'm glad to say I am joined by the Chinese Ambassador to this country, Liu Xiaoming. Very good evening to you, Ambassador. Thank you for coming in.

Liu Xiaoming: Thanks for having me.

Davis: Do you think your country, if the tables were turned, do you think China would let a British contractor build a nuclear power station in China?

Liu Xiaoming: I would ask, do you have the money, do you have the technology to build nuclear power stations in China?

Davis: Suppose we did? Do you suppose the UK would get access?

Liu Xiaoming: Suppose? I am not sure about that. I think the reason why China is here, why you want China, is that you need Chinese investment. And also in term of technology, China is very advanced in terms of nuclear technology. I think China has more nuclear power stations than many other countries.

Davis: You are building lots of them and we can benefit from that. But I don't think we would. I mean, on your government website there is a catalogue of sectors prohibited for foreign investment industries. It is more restrictive than ours. I mean, No.6, exploring, mining and dressing of radioactive mining products. No.9, smelting and processing of radioactive mineral products; production of nuclear fuel. You wouldn't let us go anywhere near your nuclear industry. I wonder whether you think we are stupid to let you come near ours?

Liu Xiaoming: No, I think you are not stupid. In fact you are very smart, you know, using Chinese money to build your nuclear power station, and the British people will get benefit. If we can do that, we would love to do it.

Davis: All right. It is win-win.

Liu Xiaoming: It's win-win. I quite agree with you.

Davis: But there are lots of other things you don't do which we are really good at. I mean, air traffic control. We've got a great air traffic control company prohibited from foreign investment in China. Companies in postal services, auction companies, antique shops engaging in antique, construction of golf courses. Why can't we build golf courses...?

Liu Xiaoming: In fact there are several foreign investors building golf courses in China. What was the last time you were in China?

Davis: Well, I just got this catalogue of prohibited foreign investments industries...Is this an out of date one?

Liu Xiaoming: In fact there are many cooperations, joint ventures, between Chinese and...

Davis: Ah, joint ventures. But they can't go in, they can't go in and...

Liu Xiaoming: They can go in, as a joint venture...

Davis: Why don't you...

Liu Xiaoming: ... so that the Chinese partners can help foreign business to get a feel of the market. But you have to remember that China and the UK are at different stages of development. Just as your video clip said, you are more advanced in many areas and China is still a developing country. So we have to do things step by step. We have to learn your lessons. We try to avoid the mistakes you have made. So we have to be more cautious, when it comes to some of the areas of business.

Davis: But I mean, it is a win-win trade and that's why we welcome you in. And we will let you do all sorts of things here. Sometimes it looks like it's not reciprocal.

Liu Xiaoming: I don't think so. If we do not reciprocate, how could the UK become the second largest European investor in China, after Germany only? And your investment is also coming more and more. So I think it is win-win.

Davis: Let me ask you this one. There are a lot of concerns, security concerns. In fact, *The Times* newspaper today quoted security sources mentioning some of them, in relation particularly to nuclear power. There are fears that trap doors or back doors could be inserted into computer systems which might allow the Chinese to bypass British control of a nuclear plant, in the event of a diplomatic row. Now, how...is there any way the Chinese can assure those people in Britain who worry about that? Look, your plant is going to be safe and clean, but we won't have control.

Liu Xiaoming: We will do all this by following international standards. I think your intelligence people, your security people are not that stupid not to know all these things. You know, we are here for win-win cooperation, we are not here to try to control your nuclear power station. What will China get by controlling a British nuclear power station? I think you'd have to see there is a basic trust, when you are forging partnership. So I think if this bad media keeps playing up, China's business might be scared away from entering the UK. It would just be opposite to what your Chancellor has been saying the UK will be the most open western country to Chinese investment.

Davis: But basic trust? Is there a basic trust? I mean what about this People's Liberation Army Unit 61398 building in Shanghai, out of which a very large portion of the cyber crime reaches out of China...Is this nonsense?

Liu Xiaoming: I think that is a hyped rumour. First of all, I want to let you know that the Chinese government strongly opposes this kind of practice. During President Xi Jinping's visit to the United States, the two governments reached consensus that the two countries will work together to fight against this cyber crime. We are committed that none of the government agencies will be engaged in cyber espionage, and none of the government agencies will be in support of such activities.

Davis: We won't believe this. Look, I mean, it's a commitment...

Liu Xiaoming: If you don't believe us, how can we work together and build partnership?

Davis: But I have been reading your own book, *The Science of Military Strategy*, the PLA's own manual 2013 version, which was leaked out. This book did acknowledge that China has network attack forces. I mean, what is the network attack force?

Liu Xiaoming: I don't believe this. I don't think we have any cyber attack forces. China is more open for cooperation. In fact China itself is a victim of hacker attack.

Davis: Yah.

Liu Xiaoming: And in China, we have a saying. This is Confucius philosophy. I'm sorry to drag you more than 2,000 years back. Confucian said: "Do not do to others what you don't want them to do to you. " That is our philosophy. We follow this philosophy. Since Chinese are victims of hacker attack, we don't want to inflict the same attack onto others.

Davis: Look, very briefly, human rights. If Britain makes a big fuss about human rights next week–if there is a big protest, suppose the opposition leader, suppose the Prime Minister talks a lot about human rights and our version of it–will we have a price to pay in trade and investment?

Liu Xiaoming: First of all, I would ask you this: do you think human rights are perfect in the UK? That's number one. Secondly, do you think UK's model is perfect worldwide? I think every country has its own conditions–how to improve human rights, how to protect them. Do you agree with me?

Davis: Yeah, I do.

Liu Xiaoming: What is your definition of human rights?

Davis: I am not criticising your human rights. Sorry, my question wasn't about your human rights. The question was, if we criticise your human rights, and you can criticise ours, will we pay a price?

Liu Xiaoming: Is that what our President is here for, criticising each other on human rights?

Davis: No, no. If it came up, would there be a price to pay in terms of investment? 'Cause, I tell you why. I think if your President came and criticised our human rights, I think...

Liu Xiaoming: That is not our way of doing things.

Davis: He is not gonna do that, I know.

Liu Xiaoming: We respect the conditions of other countries. We think human rights are basically guaranteed by Chinese constitution, protected by the constitution, and it's really an internal matter to begin with. Of course, I hope you would have a big picture of human rights in China.

Davis: I am not getting into an argument about human rights. My point is about trade, and whether you use trade as a way to stop us talking about human rights.

Liu Xiaoming: No, we...

Davis: So there will be no price to pay if we spoke about human rights, and trade and investment...

Liu Xiaoming: So you think we use trade as a weapon to get things we want? That is absolutely wrong. Trade is win-win. We export what you need, and import what we need. I think it is a win-win.

Davis: So we should carry on trading even if we sometimes have a disagreement over human rights.

Liu Xiaoming: I agree. China and the UK are so different in social systems, both political and economic, in history and in culture, different stages of development. We differ. That is natural. But we can still do business. And we can reserve our differences and seek common good. Do you agree with me?

Davis: I do agree with you, I do. I am glad we agree. Just one, very quick last one. Our Health Secretary spoke about his Chinese wife, and the working values in Asia. He said we want to be a country that can work hard in the way the Asian economies do. Do we have a good work ethic here or do we have benefit levels that are too high?

Liu Xiaoming: I think the two countries can learn from each other. The Chinese people are working very hard, but the British people are very creative. So the two peoples can learn from each other.

Davis: We are not hard-working (laughing)...

Liu Xiaoming: Not as hard as the Chinese people. So that's how China can make a miracle, just in 30 years, to turn a relatively poor country into the second largest economy. I think we should give a credit to the hard-working spirit of the Chinese people.

Davis: In 40 years time do you think China will look more like Britain? Do you think there may be a democratically elected President?

Liu Xiaoming: So that's where we come to some of the basic of differences between us. You believe the UK is a democracy. We think our system is a democracy. We call it democracy of Chinese characteristics. When other people look at the UK, your system, the way you elect your national leaders, it's not a direct election. In China, it is also indirect election. We elect the county deputies, the county deputies elect the provincial deputies, then the national deputies, then the national leaders.

Davis: This is a bigger conversation...We'll get you back...We will discuss that one another day...

Liu Xiaoming: We can spend the whole evening talking about democracy.

Davis: Ambassador, thanks for coming.

Liu Xiaoming: Thank you. My pleasure.

Newsnight is a popular BBC 2 programme which specialises in in-depth analysis into current affairs and robust cross-examination with senior politicians.

Evan Davis, economist, is *Newsnight*'s lead presenter and economics editor, the most senior economics post at BBC.

A Live Interview
on BBC *The Andrew Marr Show*

On 18th October 2015, I was invited by BBC Andrew Marr to give a live interview. I talked about the significance of the forthcoming state visit of President Xi Jinping and answered questions about China's investment in nuclear power stations in the UK and human rights. The full text is as follows:

Marr: Ahead of the state visit by the Chinese President, I am joined by the Chinese Ambassador to the UK, Liu Xiaoming. Welcome, Ambassador, very nice to have you here.

Liu Xiaoming: Thank you.

Marr: First of all, about Britain's relationship with China. Are we in essence now a begging bowl economy, as far as the Chinese state is concerned, which doesn't have the right to raise issues like human rights?

Liu Xiaoming: First of all, I think China and the UK are partners. We call it a comprehensive strategic partnership, because our two countries are very important countries with global influence. We have so many areas for cooperation, for win-win.

When you talk about human rights, I think that is also an area where we can talk. But the important thing is how to approach human rights. When you talk about human rights, you should not miss the big picture in China. I hope people would realise how much progress China has made in the area of human rights.

Marr: So this is a changing picture, and the President won't be offended if it is brought up, for instance, at the state banquet by the Labour Leader Jeremy Corbyn, who says he will bring it up?

Liu Xiaoming: You think the Labour Party leader will raise this issue at a state banquet? I don't think so. I think President Xi is here for cooperation, for partnership. He is not here for debate about human rights. We all know that China and the UK differ very much because we have different histories and different cultures. We are in different stages of development. It's natural we have differences, even with regard to human rights. In China we care more about the rights for better life, for better jobs, for better housing. I think the Chinese people enjoy their happy life. On the other side, I think the Chinese people enjoy...

Marr: But there are a lot of dissidents who are in prison for expressing their views.

Liu Xiaoming: But I wouldn't say there are a lot of dissidents. All criminal are tried through a normal legal process.

Marr: But there are people who express criticism of the Chinese government and the state, whom we would not regard as criminals, who end up in prison in China.

Liu Xiaoming: No one would be put behind bars simply because they are criticizing the government. The criminals are put behind bars because they have a criminal record. They either incite or engage in organization to overthrow the legitimate government. Here in this country, I think, once you are involved in some activities that work against the interests of Britain and endanger the safety of the people, you will be put behind bars. Maybe we have some different opinions. In that case, we can talk to each other.

Marr: Well, let me give you a specific if I may, Ambassador. The most important and exciting art exhibition we've had in London for a very, very long time is the Ai Weiwei's exhibition at the Royal Academy. Here is somebody who is a global Chinese figure. And he is a Chinese patriot, very, very proud of his Chinese origins, and his father was close to Chairman Mao and all the rest of it. Yet he ended up in prison for a while. Do you regard him as a dissident, as a dangerous figure or as a patriotic important Chinese citizen?

Liu Xiaoming: I don't know how much you know about this so-called "artist". I was interviewed on one of your programmes. I told the presenter, he is not my taste. There are so many talented Chinese artists. Yet...and many are much better than him. Why is he so famous here? The reason is that he is critical of the Chinese government. He has never been put behind bars. He was under investigation because he was suspected about a crime. He was suspected of fraudulent accounting, destroying accounting documents. What about...if the same happens here in the UK, surely you investigate comparable criminal activities?

Marr: The only thing I could say is that we disagree about this. I think he is a great artist. I'll have to say it's a great exhibition. We can disagree about that and move on. Is the Chinese government offended by the Prince of Wales'decision not to attend the state banquet?

Liu Xiaoming: He will be with the President on several occasions. He might have a good reason if he is not available. But I know the Prince of Wales has made a lot of efforts. He even has to change his original schedule in order to meet the President. I think he will meet the President at least on three occasions...

Marr: Can I ask, I am so sorry to interrupt you, can I ask about the stories that British security and intelligence experts have warned our government that China is getting very, very close to the heart of state security through this nuclear contracts. And in a sense, they are opening the door to things that most governments, including the Chinese government, wouldn't allow.

Liu Xiaoming: I don't know where they get this information. I can only tell you that Chinese are here for win-win cooperation. We think it is in the best interests of Britain and also in the interest of partnership between China and Britain. I think that the UK needs Chinese investment here and UK people want to have a better life, want to have clean energy. I know you have to close the old nuclear power stations in the next dozen of years. You have to find resources for the new energy supply.

Marr: We certainly need the money, we need the expertise. But China wouldn't allow a foreign power to build her nuclear power stations surely?

Liu Xiaoming: Recently I was put the same question. I ask, do you have the money? Do you have the technology, do you have the expertise? If you have all these, we certainly would want to have cooperation with you. Like France, you know, the French nuclear services, we have some cooperation with France, because they have the technology. I think the UK is strong in other areas. Why do you always focus on building nuclear power stations in China?

Marr: We're expecting a big contract to be signed next week. Do you think it will be?

Liu Xiaoming: I certainly hope so, because it is a very important project between our two countries.

Marr: And finally, you said earlier on that you didn't think that Jeremy Corbyn would raise human rights at the state banquet. I mean, his people have been briefing that he will. If he does, what happens?

Liu Xiaoming: I think a state banquet is Her Majesty's banquet, it's her show. Either Jeremy Corbyn or others are there as guests. I think British people are very polite, very smart. They know how to behave on occasions like this. We do not shy away from discussions about human rights. In fact, I had a good meeting with Jeremy Corbyn last week. And I do hope...

Marr: So your advice is not to do this in public?

Liu Xiaoming: We are not interested in microphone diplomacy, just like we are not interested in TV camera diplomacy. We are more interested in candid discussion. If he has his concern, we can talk about it.

Marr: Yes. Ambassador, thank you very much indeed for joining me. And good luck with the state visit.

Liu Xiaoming: Thank you.

The Andrew Marr Show is one of the most influential political programmes on BBC, where the UK's Prime Minister and other Cabinet ministers give interviews. It has a TV rating of 5 million audiences.

Andrew Marr is a well-known British presenter who has interviewed many state leaders including US President Obama and Russian President Putin.

A Live Interview
on Sky News *Murnaghan Programme*

On 18th October 2015, I was invited to a live interview with Dermot Murnaghan on Sky News *Murnaghan Programme*. The full text is as follows:

Murnaghan: I am joined by the Chinese Ambassador to the UK, H. E Liu Xiaoming. A very good morning to you, Ambassador.

Liu Xiaoming: Good morning.

Murnaghan: A broad question first of all. Does UK have anything to fear from China?

Liu Xiaoming: Nothing to fear about China. China is a peace-loving country and the President will be here for cooperation and partnership. And I think China and the UK have a lot to cooperate about and we believe China and UK are two important countries of global influence. By working together, the two countries will help to build a better world, to promote prosperity and uphold world peace.

Murnaghan: Okay. I ask that question because I am sure you have had a look at it as well: Our security service, MI5, has opened an accessible website talking to the British public and that it has a question and answer page about the current biggest threats to national security. And then we have, at number two, Chinese cyber terrorism. MI5 are concerned about China.

Liu Xiaoming: China is very much opposed to cyber crime. China itself is a victim of hacker attacks.

Murnaghan: From where? Where do they emanate?

Liu Xiaoming: Everywhere, I would say. Cyber space is not a safe place. Countries should work together rather than criticising each other. During President Xi's state visit, he and President Obama reached consensus that the two governments will not support any cyber crime and we will not be supportive to any organisations to engage in cyber crimes.

Murnaghan: Well, that's loud and clear. But why would MI5 have come up with this analysis that China is one of the biggest global threats on cyber crime?

Liu Xiaoming: I'm sorry to hear this analysis. I heard quite a lot about these concerns about the nuclear power station. I think Chinese companies are here to build nuclear power at the request of the British business and government. We are here not for the so-called control of your nuclear power station. We are here for win-win cooperation. We will play by the international standard and follow the international rules. It is transparent. I think your security authorities, regulation authorities are not that unwise to let the Chinese companies control your nuclear facilities. I think these are things that have been hyped up by some media, by some people who do not want to see...

Murnaghan: The media and security services say, there it is on the MI5 website.

Liu Xiaoming: I think you should put this question to your MI5. But we are here, we are not spying on your nuclear facilities. I think we have more interest in doing something else: we are here for cooperation, for win-win. That is the whole purpose of Chinese investment here.

Murnaghan: And I know that President Xi Jinping is going to have long discussions about the Northern Powerhouse, which I understand doesn't translate very easily into Chinese.

Liu Xiaoming: Not that difficult. The Chinese language is very rich. I think Northern Powerhouse...do you speak mandarin?

Murnaghan: No, I am afraid not.

Liu Xiaoming: There are several translations, but at the end of the day we have found a very appropriate one.

Murnaghan: Okay. That's good to hear. But there are concerns about what's going on in the northern parts of Britain at the moment. When it comes to the steel industry, again, there are big concerns about China as a huge producer of steel. Do you accept criticisms of China that China has now got massive overcapacity in steel and is dumping it on global markets. Instead of a Northern Powerhouse, you are creating, as one of our newspapers says this morning, a "northern poorhouse"?

Liu Xiaoming: I think every country has to adjust itself to globalization, even in the case of China. China used to be a processing power for clothes, for toys, in the past. I think China exported maybe 90% or 80% of toys to this country and to the United States. But we are now faced with very competitive neighbours in Southern Asia and Southeast Asian countries. As their labour forces are more competitive and cost lower, business moves from China to those countries. So we have to adjust from processing to manufacturing. I think any country, every country, has to adjust itself. And we are here and, we should accommodate, looking for common ground between China and the UK. We certainly will address concerns here. We certainly will address concerns of your local communities.

Murnaghan: Don't you believe there is reason for, you must have seen it, you are the Ambassador, concerns about Chinese human rights records. Particularly things about the mass number of people executed in China and things like that. The Prime Minister said we oppose the death penalty everywhere and anywhere and we will raise it at all opportunities. Presumably the Prime Minister is going to do this with the President. Do you think that is rude?

Liu Xiaoming: I have been here for five years and I have heard a lot of comments about human rights in China. But I think more often than not, people miss the big picture of human rights in China. What are human rights?

Murnaghan: The right for a fair trial and not to be summarily executed.

Liu Xiaoming: The basic right is for people to have better living. I think people sometimes, when they talk about human rights, they miss the picture that China, in only 30 years, elevated 700 million people out of poverty. No other country has done that within such a short time. And Chinese people are living better, living longer and they enjoying their happy lives. Even in their political life, I think never before in the history of China did people enjoy the unprecedented dignity and freedom they do today.

You are talking about death penalty. China is a large country. To run a country of 1.3 billion will be naturally different from running a country of 64 million. The penalty has been handled in a very careful way, and the number reduced with each passing year. And it has to be approved by the Supreme Court so that such punishment comes through a very careful process.

Murnaghan: Last question: About the Labour leader Jeremy Corbyn. You will have viewed his election with interest. Have you had any substantive discussions between your President and the leader of the Labour Party, the leader of the Opposition?

Liu Xiaoming: President Xi will have a meeting with Jeremy Corbyn during the state visit at Buckingham Palace. We look forward to a productive and meaningful meeting between the President and Jeremy Corbyn as the Leader of the Labour Party.

Murnaghan: And do you think you will get on well with him? He is a socialist and you are a communist.

Liu Xiaoming: You know, socialists can debate. Socialists and communists can have a debate. But we are here for common ground. In fact last week I had an interesting meeting with Jeremy Corbyn, to prepare for the President's meeting with him. I think the Labour Party has made its important contributions to developing relationship between our two countries. And currently we have very strong party-to-party exchange relationship, with both the Conservative Party and the Labour. And I sincerely hope the Labour Party, under the leadership of Jeremy Corbyn, will continue to make its positive contributions to this important relationship.

Murnaghan: Your Excellency, we're out of time. It's great to see you. Thank you very much indeed. Here is to a successful visit.

Liu Xiaoming: Thank you.

Sky News is the second largest broadcaster after the BBC, providing 24 hours news broadcasting in the UK, with more than 7.5 million audiences in the UK and 115 million worldwide. *Murnaghan Programme* is the flagship current affairs programme known for its in-depth debate and discussions. Dermot Murnaghan is a senior presenter of Sky News.

Understand China

An Interview with Philip Dodd on BBC Radio 4

On 20th December 2011, I gave an interview to Philip Dodd, a well known presenter, at the studios of BBC Radio 4. I talked about the meaning of the giant pandas in Britain and the China-UK relations. The full text is as follows:

Dodd: Why are giant pandas so important to China? Are the giant pandas a "big present" from China to Britain?

Liu Xiaoming: Giant pandas are China's "national treasure" and an endangered species in the world. The reasons are they do not impregnate easily and are not good at taking care of their cubs. So wild giant pandas are small in number. To save and protect giant pandas, the Chinese government adopts many measures in policy making, legal construction and capital investment. These have helped to constantly improve the protection of this species. But even so, the population of wild giant pandas is only about 1600.

The coming of giant pandas to the UK cannot be simply regarded as a "present". It is an important scientific research project of China-UK cooperation and covers various fields such as field ecology, artificial breeding and rearing of giant pandas and study in cognition evolution and behaviour of giant pandas. Although many giant pandas came to Britain in the past, they never gave birth to a baby in this country. I hope that the cooperation of both Chinese and British scientists would help Tian Tian and Yang Guang to produce baby pandas as soon as possible, bring new results in the China-UK giant panda researches and further facilitate the release of artificially raised giant pandas into the wild.

Dodd: What is the message given by the giant pandas to the rest of the world as China's "image ambassador"? Does China believe that the coming of giant pandas to the UK will help to enhance China's soft power? It is estimated that by 2020, China will have 600 million middle class people and will become a true superpower. As Europe is deeply mired in the debt crisis, does China think that the affection of the western countries on giant pandas is out of their interest in expanding the Chinese market?

Liu Xiaoming: With their distinctive black and white colours and lovely look, giant pandas are very popular among the people both in China and in the world. The messages brought by the giant pandas to the UK can be summarized with 3 Ps: Panda Conservation, Public Awareness and Peoples' Friendship. The first aim and task of the cooperation on giant pandas abroad is with the study in the reproduction and survival of giant pandas in artificial and natural environments; The second purpose is to disseminate the knowledge on giant pandas, so that people of other countries can have a close look at them and directly learn about them, and then love giant pandas more and support the protection work; And third, it is to enhance the friendship between the peoples with the pandas as a messenger.

Tian Tian and Yang Guang's settlement in Edinburgh will be a tie for China and the UK to enhance mutual understanding, deepen friendship and expand cooperation, and will be a new story of the friendly exchanges between the two peoples.

It is impossible to learn about giant pandas without understanding their home country–China, China's culture, history, economy and society, the path of peaceful development pursued by China today, the country's will of achieving mutual benefit and win-win results with the rest of the world, and the enthusiasm and kindness of the Chinese people who are ready to get on with the people of other countries.

To promote the friendly exchanges between young people, the Chinese Embassy is working with some British universities to organize speech and painting contests revolving around giant pandas in 100 primary and secondary schools across Britain. The top prize winners will have an opportunity to visit the hometown of giant pandas–Sichuan, China.

China welcomes foreign businesses with open arms. It is true that China has made remarkable achievements over the past 30 years, but it is quite an overestimation to say that there will be 600 million people in middle class in China in 10 years. China's per capita GDP is still ranked over 100th in the world and there are 100 million Chinese people still living under the poverty line defined by the United Nations. China will remain a developing country for quite a long time and the country has still a long way to go in its development. It has been over 30 years since China's reform and opening up and 10 years since its WTO accession. China has an increasingly open market, and in the future, China is willing to expand the mutually beneficial cooperation with the rest of the world including Britain to achieve common development.

Dodd: Do you think the West does not know China well enough?

Liu Xiaoming: Frankly, there is indeed a lack of understanding or even misunderstanding of China in the West. With different cultures, China and the West handle things in quite different styles. The Chinese people emphasise modesty and peace and do not like taking a high profile. For example, when presenting a gift, a Westerner would describe how good the gift is and say "I hope you like it." But in the case of a Chinese person, even if his gift is very expensive, he would still say "This humble gift is not enough to show my respect. Please kindly accept it."

Enhancing understanding is a two-way street. The Chinese people should tell more about China to others and share its success story with the rest of the world. At the same time, the Western media needs to have a comprehensive and objective coverage on China and display China as it is. They need to let the Western public see that China's achievement is not limited to economy. Our success owes much to an all-round development and progress in politics, society, culture and other aspects. China and the West should work together to encourage a more comprehensive knowledge on China, and the BBC could make active efforts to this end.

Dodd: I fully agree.

In the UK, Philip Dodd is an award-winning broadcaster, writer, curator and cultured enterpreneur.

A Live Interview with Jeremy Paxman on BBC *Newsnight*

On 23rd January 2012, I had a live and one-on-one interview with Jeremy Paxman on BBC 2's *Newsnight* programme. The transcript of the interview goes as follows:

Paxman: Happy New Year! Mr. Ambassador.

Liu Xiaoming: Thank you.

Paxman: Let's try to define our terms. Are you a communist?

Liu Xiaoming: In China, the ruling party is the Communist Party. The Communist Party now has more than 80 million party members. But you have to remember China is a country with 1.3 billion people. So I don't think you can call China a communist country, just as you can not call the UK conservative UK.

Paxman: But you could call the UK a capitalist country.

Liu Xiaoming: And we say China is a socialist country. We could call China a socialist country with Chinese characteristics.

Paxman: Talking to the young people, in particular in Beijing, I very strongly got the impression that they were pretty optimistic about China's international role. They saw this as a century which was developing very much in a way that was going to make China a much more significant force in the world. Do you think that?

Liu Xiaoming: China will certainly contribute its part to maintaining peace and prosperity in the world. But we do not see China as a superpower. I would characterize China as the largest developing country with increasing international influence and responsibilities.

Paxman: But people look at what China does on the UN Security Council, for example, over the question of–you opposed the sanctions on Syria, sanctions on Iran, and they wonder, you know, what you are trying to achieve?

Liu Xiaoming: That's not the right impression. In fact, China voted four times with other members of the Security Council on the issue of Iran. China is strongly opposed to the Iranian nuclear weapon programme. But on the other hand, we believe diplomatic and peaceful solution is the most beneficial solution to the problem. It costs less and it's in the interest of maintaining peace and stability in the region.

Paxman: But do you accept that Iran is a potential threat to world peace, a nuclear armed Iran?

Liu Xiaoming: I would say, yes, Iran with nuclear weapons is not in the interest of peace and stability in the region. So that is why China made it very clear from day one that we are strongly opposed to Iran developing nuclear weapons. That has been reaffirmed by the Chinese Premier in his recent visit to the region.

Paxman: So why not impose sanctions, then?

Liu Xiaoming: There are already sanctions in place. But we don't think sanction for the sake of sanction serves the purpose. We also encouraged peaceful negotiations to engage Iran for a peaceful settlement of this issue.

Paxman: Do you think China has a moral role in the world?

Liu Xiaoming: I think China has a role to play, in terms of building a more peaceful, harmonious world.

Paxman: But what do you try to promote? The United States, for example, says it promotes, and will go to war, to promote democracy. What do you try to promote?

Liu Xiaoming: We are promoting a harmonious world. We believe the world will be more peaceful, prosperous, if all countries respect each other, rather than imposing their own ideas and systems onto others. We believe mutual respect, mutual accommodation and working together for the common good, common security is in the interest of peace and stability of the world. So we are strongly opposed to any military solutions.

Paxman: What about economic power? China sits on this mountain of trillions of dollars worth of foreign exchange. What's that for?

Liu Xiaoming: China is still a relatively poor country. Though China now is number two in terms of GDP, after only the United States. But in per capita GDP, China is still behind 100 countries. There are still about 700 million people living in the countryside. And there are about 150 million people living under one US dollar a day, that is the UN poverty line. So there is an enormous responsibility for the Chinese government to improve livelihood of those parts of the population of China.

Paxman: And let's talk a little bit about that difficult matter of human rights. Ai Weiwei, the well known artist, says that without free speech, you are living in a barbaric world. Do you understand what he's getting at?

Liu Xiaoming: I think Ai Weiwei has his freedom to express his view. Otherwise how could you get his opinion on this?

Paxman: Unfortunately, he has been in prison of course, isn't it?

Liu Xiaoming: No, he was under investigation on suspicion of evading tax, destroying his accounting books. In any country of rule by law, you have to respect and abide by the law. Nobody in a country ruled by law should be above the law. So even a so-called well-known artist has to abide by the law. When he violates the law, he should be punished. There's no doubt about that in China, I guess it's the same in Britain.

Paxman: He should be free to say what he likes, shouldn't he?

Liu Xiaoming: If he is forbidden to voice his opinions, how could you get to know them?

Paxman: All right, Mr. Ambassador, thank you very much.

Liu Xiaoming: Thank you for having me.

Newsnight is a weekday BBC 2 current affairs programme which specialises in analysis and often robust cross-examination. Jeremy Paxman, a well-known British journalist and commentator, has been its main presenter for over two decades.

A Live Interview with Evan Davis on BBC Radio 4 *Today* Programme

On 14th March 2012, following the closing of the annual NPC and CPPCC sessions in Beijing, I did a live interview with Evan Davis on BBC Radio 4's *Today* programme. The transcript of the interview is as follows:

Davis: As you've heard, China's National People's Congress has just finished its annual sitting. It is the world's biggest parliament, has almost 3,000 members and tends to meet a couple of weeks a year. This year Chinese Premier Wen Jiabao closed the congress with a press conference where he made some rather interesting comments about stepping up economic and political reforms to spread wealth wider. He also said that Beijing would allow the currency the yuan to float more freely.

With us in this studio, I am pleased to say we have the Chinese Ambassador to the UK, Mr. Liu Xiaoming. A very good morning to you!

Liu Xiaoming: Good morning!

Davis: Thank you for coming in. Can we talk about democracy? Do you think China is on a path to more western style democracy with more open elections, freer elections? I mean the parliament doesn't actually have any elections at the moment, does it?

Liu Xiaoming: Yes, we do have elections. But I think that's Chinese democracy. That means democracy with Chinese characteristics. I think many people focus on what Premier Wen has said about political reform. But Premier Wen basically reiterated the position of the Chinese government with regard to political reform. For the past 30 years, China has engaged in reform and opening-up, but some people in Western world only pay attention to economic reform. In fact this reform is all-round reform. It is not only about economics, but also about political reform.

Davis: How far can it go, do you think?

Liu Xiaoming: I think China has come a long way, if we compare China today with

China 30 years ago. When Mr. Deng Xiaoping started this reform and opening-up, one of the top priorities on his agenda was political reform. China had been ruled by emperors for thousands of years. It was not until after the founding of the People's Republic that we adopted what we call a socialist democracy system. But it is not perfect. So it is always on the road of practicing, searching for new methods, how to make our system more effective, more accountable, more democratic. But if you look at China today, it is quite changed, and is what we call "tremendous transformation".

Davis: But there are people in China, who perhaps are a little more middle-class, a little more affluent than they were a generation ago. Do you think they will like a little more say in the way the country is run? We had commune rebellion against bad actions of their leaders. People are beginning to say, " Look, we don't want to be bossed around and we're not going to be told. We like to have some say. " Do you think you can deliver that to the public on this gradual path that, as you said, has been changing already, without great crisis, rupture, or social disruption?

Liu Xiaoming: I would say political reform is already an ongoing process. No system is perfect. We have made tremendous progress and achievements, but there is still a lot of room to improve. I think the government has made a lot of efforts on how to make the government, both central and local, more accountable to the people and how to fight corruption, how to make people have access to information. For instance, the recent National People's Congress you mentioned has reformed the way people elect their deputies. In the past, the cities had more deputies than the countryside. Now we have it more evenly, more balanced. So, people will have their equal voice.

Davis: Now tell me this. Do you listen to *Today* programme in your role as Ambassador?

Liu Xiaoming: Yes.

Davis: What do you think when you hear my colleagues sitting next to me here berating a politician or interviewing him very toughly? Do you think that is a good thing or a bad thing?

Liu Xiaoming: It might not be a bad thing. That is a different culture. In fact I find it very interesting. I find Chinese people, Asians in general, show more respect to their leaders than the Western public. I am still trying to find out the answer, whether your politicians did a good job or maybe Chinese leaders and Asian state leaders have done a better job. But, they earned more respect from their public.

Davis: There are so many things we can talk about, because, there is Syria, there is North Korea. You were based in North Korea, I think?

Liu Xiaoming: Yes, for three and a half years.

Davis: I just want to ask you about North Korea, but I know I should talk to you about Syria. When is China going to–because it is all down to China. North Korea is a country where 25 million people have been held hostage, more or less, by a mad family. When is China going to pull the plug on that and just say, "Look, enough is enough. We need reform in North Korea as well?"

Liu Xiaoming: We see the DPRK as our close neighbour. We certainly would like to see them enjoy prosperity and economic development. And peace and stability are our top priority. So we want to have good relations with the country. We believe their people deserve a better future. So we think the best way to ensure stability in the Korean peninsula is to engage with them, rather than isolate them. That is why China engages very actively with what we call the DPRK. Now they have a new leader. We believe that he should be given the opportunity to carry out his duties. It seems to me there are good signs since the coming of the new leadership. The United States and the DPRK reached agreement on the nuclear programme, and on aid programme. We believe that if all countries work together, we will have a better future for the Korean peninsula.

Davis: It's about helping the people in North Korea though. We know a famine killed a couple of million people in the 1990s. It's about letting and encouraging, or indeed imposing reform on the leadership there, domestic reform of the kind China has engaged in so the population can have a...

Liu Xiaoming: China has always followed the principle of non-interference in the internal affairs of other people. We believe it is up to the people to decide the future of their respective countries.

Davis: We could talk for ages. Ambassador, we know now you listen to the *Today* programme. We can get you on and grill you again on many issues. Liu Xiaoming, thank you very much for coming in.

Liu Xiaoming: Thank you for having me.

Today, colloquially known as the *Today* programme, is a long-running BBC early-morning news and current-affairs radio programme on BBC Radio 4. It is the highest-rated programme on Radio 4 and one of the BBC's most popular programmes across its radio networks. Evan Davis joined the presenter team on *Today* in April 2008 following a six-and-a-half year stint as the BBC's economics editor.

A Live Interview with Gavin Esler on BBC *Newsnight*

On 21st December 2012, I gave a live interview to Gavin Esler on BBC *Newsnight*. I answered questions about the 18th National Congress of the Communist Party of China and China's development, cyber space governance and foreign policy. The full text is as follows:

Esler: Ambassador, when we think of a change at the top, we think of elections, we think about a whole lot of people swept away and completely new people coming in. This doesn't look like such a big deal to those outside your country. Has it been a big deal?

Liu Xiaoming: With regard to the 18th Party Congress, I think it's a big deal in terms of China's future development. I would say it's significant because it elected the new leadership which will lead the country for the next five years and even beyond. And this new leadership is young, energetic, and down-to-earth. They have a lot of experience with the grassroots, some of them even worked in the countryside and factories. And also this congress produced a new blueprint for China for the next five years and even beyond. That is to build China into a well-off society. The target is to double the GDP of 2010 by 2020.

Esler: So in 10 years you'll double GDP?

Liu Xiaoming: Yes, in 10 years, not only double the GDP, but also double the per capita income of the people.

Esler: What about that specific point that the new leader Mr. Xi made about corruption, which he knows really angers ordinary people? And you've got to crack down on it. But how you are going to actually do that, deliver, because it will make these people even angrier if you don't do it in these five or ten years.

Liu Xiaoming: I think corruption is, not a problem for China alone. Once you are in a period of social transformation, it's unavoidable you have all kinds of problems. Just like Deng Xiaoping once said at the beginning of the opening up in China. He said, "when we open the window and let in the fresh air, it is unavoidable that flies and mosquitoes will come in. " But the important thing is how the Party faces up to it and adopts measures to deal with this problem. I think the leadership is resolute and determined.

Esler: Do you see things like the Internet as being like flies and mosquitoes? I mean do you see it as a bit of an irritation. Because again, from our side, we don't understand what you are worried about, when you want to control how people exchange information.

Liu Xiaoming: I think there is a misperception about the Internet development in China. In fact, China is much more open in terms of the Internet. China has the most number of internet users.

Esler: But our correspondent can't even get onto Facebook when he's in China. I mean you can't get onto Twitter. It's not quite as you presented.

Liu Xiaoming: In China, every day, there are hundreds of thousands of comments made by bloggers and 66 percent of Chinese internet users make comments online. It is up to the government to regulate the use of internet in protection of the safety of the internet to ensure that healthy content is available and unhealthy content should be removed.

Esler: But isn't that really up to the ordinary people to decide. Looking at the history of your country, you've had thousands of years of creativity and we see creativity is based on the free exchange of information. And part of the reasons why people in the West think your crackdown has been very hard on bloggers and is very difficult for some people because you don't like certain ideas.

Liu Xiaoming: If you are in China and get connected to the Internet, I think you can get all kinds of opinions. It's much more open than you suggest and a lot of things can be debated including politics, economic, cultural affairs. I think you have to have a big picture of the internet development in China.

Esler: Ambassador, can you help us with the main point? China may become, with the ambition of doubling the GDP by 2020, the world's biggest economy, but what world role does China want to have?

Liu Xiaoming: China certainly wants to play a role as a responsible country. We call ourselves the largest developing country with global responsibility. We want to contribute to peace and stability of the world because we need a peaceful environment to develop our own country.

Esler: Because you couldn't have that economic development without peace.

Liu Xiaoming: That's right. And China's peaceful development in turn will contribute to peace and prosperity of the world. And I think China's growth is also a big contributor to the world economic growth.

Esler: How does that square with what seem to us as quite small problems which could become very big problems, for instance the potential for conflict with Japan over a bunch of rocks in the sea?

Liu Xiaoming: We certainly would like to have good relations with Japan. I know you are talking about the Diaoyu Islands. In fact, these islands have belonged to China since ancient times.

Esler: You know this is not quite how the Japanese see it. We are worried about it.

Liu Xiaoming: It was not until 1895 when China lost the first war with Japan that Japan illegally seized these islands. It was in 1943 when Churchill, Roosevelt and Chiang Kai-shek met in Cairo. They issued the *Cairo Declaration*. And in this *Cairo Declaration*, it declared in explicit terms that all territories seized by Japan from China should be returned to China without any conditions.

Esler: Does that mean you can resolve it peacefully, you think.

Liu Xiaoming: Of course, we want to resolve this peacefully with Japan.

Esler: One other issue which China has had a role which has been very controversial, which is the question of Syria. We've got President Putin saying that we are not concerned about the fate of the Assad regime. Is the Chinese government concerned about the Assad regime?

Liu Xiaoming: We are concerned about the fate of the Syrian people. I think it's up to the Syrian people to decide who will be their leaders. So the reason why China opposed some of the resolutions tabled by Western countries in UN Security Council is because these resolutions called for regime change.

Esler: Do you think it will be a bad thing if Assad went?

Liu Xiaoming: I think it's up to the Syrian people. If the Syrian people believe what is good to them, we will agree with them. It's not up to China to decide who should be their leader and what kind of the regime should be in place. I think it's up to the Syrian people.

Esler: But isn't it kind of obvious that most Syrian people want to rid of him and they would like help from outsiders. And that is a problem.

Liu Xiaoming: It depends on which side of the Syrian people you are talking to. I think Syria is in a civil war situation. You have opposition and you also have the people behind the government. So the important thing is to bring about a ceasefire and to immediately start this political transition process. I think that's the most important thing: to stop violence.

Esler: One of the big things we in the West have to get our head around is perhaps summarized by British writer Rudyard Kipling, who said that the East and the West will never completely understand each other. Do you think that's true?

Liu Xiaoming: I think there's a problem for Western countries to understand China. There's a strong bias against China. When it comes to China, some people are still haunted by this cold war mentality. They do not like Communist Party, so whenever they see China, they see China through the lens they use to look at the former Soviet Union. And that really prevented them from having a big picture of China. So I do hope that we have more sense and sensibility rather than pride and prejudice.

Esler: Right. It was a quote from another famous English author. I mean in terms of that, so much has changed since the Deng Xiaoping era, even the phrase Chinese Communist Party does not sound to outsiders as if it sums up where China is going. It sounds like a very uncommunist Communist Party.

Liu Xiaoming: I think there's a misunderstanding about the Communist Party in China. In China, the Communist Party still upholds the path of Chinese socialism. We call it socialism with Chinese characteristics. It has combined the Marxist theory with realities of China. The system suits China. It can deliver. It's successful. So why should we change this system when it's still effective and it can still deliver benefits to its people and is welcome by its people.

Esler: You've been very clear on how we might misunderstand you. Do you think you sometimes misunderstand us, which is in saying that when we talk about human rights issue, the internet, all those kinds of issues which seem quite important to us, it's not to be triumphant about that, it is to suggest actually you will be a more creative country if you have some of these?

Liu Xiaoming: We welcome criticism with good intention. Because we don't think China is perfect. Just like any countries, there's much room to improve. But we are strongly opposed to interference in China's internal affairs and the use of human rights as tools to change China's political system, to humiliate China. That is something we can not accept.

Esler: Ambassador...

Liu Xiaoming: Before we finish, I just want to mention one thing about how we have differences. Like the map behind me. There is one mistake. There is one important part of China that is missing. That's Taiwan. It's much bigger than the Hainan Island. We Chinese people hold territorial integrity dearly.

Esler: Indeed. Perhaps you'll come back and we can talk again about this. Thank you.

Liu Xiaoming: My pleasure.

> *Newsnight* is one of the best known current affairs programs on BBC TWO. It has built a reputation for the depth of its analysis and intensive cross-examination, with strong influence across the broad spectrum of politics and intelligentsia. Being a prominent author and correspondent, Mr. Gavin Esler joined the *Newsnight* in 2003 and has interviewed a broad range of world leaders.

A Live Interview with Jeff Randall on Sky News

On 14th January 2014, I gave a live interview on *Jeff Randall Live* on Sky News. I answered questions from Jeff Randall on a wide range of issues, including the Third Plenum of the 18th Central Committee of the Communist Party of China, China's economic reform, China-UK economic cooperation and trade, media and internet management, exchanges between the East and the West and China-Japan relations. The transcript of the interview goes as follows:

Randall: Joining me now is China's Ambassador to the UK Liu Xiaoming. Ambassador, lovely to see you. Thank you for coming in.

Liu Xiaoming: Thank you for having me.

Randall: It strikes me that this is a make-or-break year for the leadership in Beijing. In 2013, the President set out plans for fiscal reform, land reform, business reform. This year, he has to deliver.

Liu Xiaoming: That's right. Last year was very important for China. As a result of the Third Plenum of the Communist Party of China, the leadership launched a master plan on what we call "comprehensively deepening reform". In fact, the plan covers all the important areas of the economy. Not only economy, it includes the following major areas: economic reform, political reform, social, cultural and environmental reforms. So I think the country will be completely changed as a result of these reforms.

Randall: It seems to me that in order to maintain the confidence of the people, many more sectors will have to be opened up to private competition. Very soon, this is going to be a capitalist country run by a Communist Party.

Liu Xiaoming: No. That's not true. In fact, we call it socialism with Chinese characteristics. Just as Deng Xiaoping said, market and plan are just tools of the economy. In a socialist economy, you have a market. And in a capitalist market, you have plan. So I think it's a combination of the two. We try to make the best of the two systems.

Randall: Clearly China wants to be in cutting-edge industries, wants to lead the way in global business. One of the world's booming businesses is media. We saw that bid today for Time Warner Cable. And yet in China, the *New York Times*, Bloomberg, Facebook and Twitter are all blocked. What do you have to hide?

Liu Xiaoming: We manage the media according to law. The important thing is the media, whether foreign or Chinese, have to follow the law of China. And they have to serve the interests of the people. What we are concerned about is healthy content and whether it is in the interest of improving mutual understanding between China and the world.

Randall: Are you saying what you want is propaganda rather than the truth?

Liu Xiaoming: No. That's not true. We are looking for truth.

Randall: But what Bloomberg, Facebook and Twitter possibly publish that would damage your interests?

Liu Xiaoming: You should ask them. We would expect them to be a good citizen in China, rather than spreading rumours and biased stories against China. We don't think that serves the purpose of increasing mutual understanding between China and the outside world.

Randall: As China becomes increasingly a global force in the global economy, this sort of hermetic seal around the country will dissolve, will it not? Because Chinese people will travel increasingly to foreign countries and they will find out the truth.

Liu Xiaoming: China is a much more open country than you can imagine. Chinese people are all over the world. They know the outside world. But unfortunately, it is Western countries who don't know enough of China. There is a big imbalance between how much the Chinese people know the outside world and how much the outside world knows China. Especially in Western world, there are still some people haunted by the "Cold War" mentality. They see China through tinted glass and they see China through stereotyped mindset. I think especially for the Western media and Western journalists, they have to wide open their eyes to see a comprehensive picture of China.

Randall: What about two-way trade, that is part of this deal, the implicit deal? Chinese companies have done very well in the UK. They bought the famous businesses such as the Weetabix, property companies, fashion names, Rover the car company. We in Britain cannot go and buy Chinese companies. That has to end, does it not? It has to be a two-way street.

Liu Xiaoming: Yes, very much so. Trade is a two-way street. In fact, Britain is doing very well in terms of trade.

Randall: But we can't just go and buy a Chinese company.

Liu Xiaoming: Why not? Earlier this week, I was attending an inaugural ceremony, the so-called "ring the bell" for the first RQFII launched here in the UK. All British individual buyers can invest in these shares, in this fund in China. Talking about trade, I think Britain last year did very well in terms of export to China. Your exports to China increased by 13.8%, much higher, way higher, than the other EU partners of China.

Randall: Finally, what about foreign affairs as it were closer to your home. You have this dispute with Japan over uninhabited islands. Many see it as China flexing its military muscles and settling old scores. That is true. Isn't it?

Liu Xiaoming: That's not true. It is the Japanese Prime Minister who visited this war shrine where they honour Class A war criminals of Japan. That is Japanese equivalent of Nazi in Germany. What the British people will feel about if German leaders pay respect to Hitler and other leaders of Nazi? By comparison, you may have a better understanding of the feelings of Chinese people.

Randall: Ambassador, it's been a pleasure. Thanks for coming in. We appreciate your time.

Liu Xiaoming: Thank you for having me.

Jeff Randall Live is one of the most watched evening financial and current affairs programmes in the UK and reaches elite audience from the British political, business and financial circles.

A Live Interview with Robert Peston on BBC *Newsnight*

On 3rd September 2015, I was invited to a live interview with BBC *Newsnight* hosted by Robert Peston. I elaborated on the significance of the Commemoration of the 70th Anniversary of the Victory of the Chinese People's War of Resistance Against Japanese Aggression and the World Anti-Fascist War, and answered questions about China's military expenditure and China's economy. The full text is as follows:

Peston: Joining me now is the Chinese Ambassador to the UK, Liu Xiaoming. Ambassador, I think of China as this fast modernizing country–a fast enriching country. But we've seen this extraordinary military display today, which takes some of us back to the era of Mao. Is this China again sending a sort of message to the world that, you know, you are fierce and dangerous?

Liu Xiaoming: I think the impression you had is not correct. In fact, the message is loud and clear, that is peace. Peace was hard won and peace should be cherished and maintained. And China will make its due contribution to maintaining world peace and regional stability. You know, in his ten minutes speech, President Xi Jinping used the word "peace" 18 times. So, that's the message.

Peston: So these gunboats that sailed off the coast of Alaska when President Obama was there today, was that just a sort of accident?

Liu Xiaoming: I think we are talking about this commemoration first, then I'll come back to this naval fleet. When I say peace was hard won, not many people, especially in the West, realize how much sacrifice China has made during the war against Japanese aggression. In fact the war, the Second World War, started in China, started earliest, lasted longest, and China suffered the largest casualties. We paid the price of 35 million casualties, and that is the most among all the sufferings of the world in Second World War. It's about one third of the casualties of the world. And so Chinese people see this

70th anniversary as a big occasion for us to celebrate the victory, to honor the fallen soldiers who, sacrificed for their motherland.

Peston: But this peace require defense spending to go up this extraordinary way, 12% last year, 10% this year? Enormous money you're spending.

Liu Xiaoming: You have to remember that China is a large country. China, in terms of territory, it's about 40 times the size of the UK. In terms of population, it's about 20 times. Yet in terms of per capita military expenditure, China is only 1/22 of the United States and 1/9 of Britain. And also in terms of proportion of expenditure with regard to GDP, the growth is decreasing. This year, in fact, is the lowest of the past 5 years. And you know China is, as I said, a large country to defend; the Chinese military has a lot of commitments.

Peston: I think it's the share of the GDP that's actually gone up a bit, given the rapid growth of the economy. But you talk about obviously your desire for stability. What do you think when you hear the leading Republican Presidential Candidate Donald Trump talking about how he thinks that Chinese want Americans to starve?

Liu Xiaoming: I don't think it represents the majority view in United States. You always have some voice in the US, but I don't think...

Peston: But if he became President, how serious would that be?

Liu Xiaoming: I think it's a very hypothetical question. I do not know how you would answer that. But I certainly will not answer this hypothetical question. But I can assure you that we want to have good relations with United States. And you mention in your film before this interview, that China wants to challenge the dominance of the United States, and even want to challenge the US leadership. That is not our position, not our intention at all. I think in China, we have a lot of challenges to deal with in our domestic development, and we have no intention to challenge US dominance. And we believe that the US and China should be good partners in the Asia-Pacific region.

Peston: Now is this display of military strength a distraction from the slowdown in the Chinese economy which many economists think is quite serious?

Liu Xiaoming: I think China's economic difficulties have been exaggerated by Western observers. I think we have some difficulties, challenges, that's for sure. But they are the natural outcome...

Peston: 5 trillion dollars lost of the Chinese stock market. Is that trivial?

Liu Xiaoming: No. I think the stock market has its own rule of the game. It has ups and downs, like in the United States. We have to focus on the big picture of China. I think the basics and fundamentals of the Chinese economy are still good and sound. We achieved 7% increase for the first half of this year. That 7% increase is about the same size of the total GDP of the 20th largest economy in the world which is Switzerland.

Peston: And very briefly, your president has said he wants a modernized economy and see markets liberalized. A really important part of free markets is that people should be free to say whatever they like about those markets. Now journalists, hedge firm manager have been arrested for allegedly scaremongering about the stock market. To us in the west, that is very shocking.

Liu Xiaoming: I think Chinese people enjoy, freedom of speech. The cases you have mentioned are those who involve in violation of law. China is a country ruled by law. And...

Peston: But I said much scarier thing about British markets than they said about Chinese market. Do you think the British government should arrest me?

Liu Xiaoming: No. It's not only about the scary comment about the market. It's also about, making and spreading the rumors, causing disturbances in the market. And you know, China and Britain are run by different rules of game. And maybe in some of the cases in Britain, it's not a violation of criminal law. But in China, you know, it constitutes a wrong-doing. So they have to be held accountable for their wrong-doings.

Peston: Ambassador, many thanks!

Liu Xiaoming: Thank you for having me.

An Interview with Lord Jim O'Neill on BBC Radio 4

On 6th January 2017, BBC Radio 4 broadcasted an episode of *The New World: Fixing Globalisation*, in which I was interviewed by the renowned economist Lord Jim O'Neill and shared my views on China's economy and globalisation.

The transcript of the interview is as follows:

O'Neill: As I said, when talking about globalisation, it's kind of impossible to ignore China. I've become well-known for creating the acronym of BRIC which refers to Brazil, Russia, India and China. China is bigger than the other 3 put together. Even growing by just 6.5 percent, slower than India's rate of more than 7 percent, China will be the equivalent to several "brand new" Indias before this decade is over. For further flavor of the staggering impact China has on the world, I've met with Chinese Ambassador to the UK, Liu Xiaoming.

Liu Xiaoming: The achievement China has achieved is really a miracle that has never been seen in the history of humanity. China has pulled 600 million people out of poverty just within 30 years. China has developed into a country which has more than 100 million middle-class population with the life expectancy tremendously increased to about 76 years. It is much higher than the world average and also much higher than any other developing country.

O'Neill: Through this remarkable journey, China has become in many ways the most important country in world trade.

Liu Xiaoming: As a matter of fact, China is the largest trading partner with over 120 countries and regions.

O'Neill: 120, so more than half of the world's population.

Liu Xiaoming: Yes, very much so. China is also the largest export market for more than 70 countries and regions. Every year China imports about 2 trillion US dollars of goods, so it is a huge market for many countries. For the next 5 years, China will import more than 8 trillion US dollars of goods from the rest of world. That shows what kind of contribution China is making and China is going to continue to make.

O'Neill: But the challenges brought up by globalisation is not just about making sure people are trained and ready for new industries. What about those whose skills are no longer needed? The Chinese Ambassador explained how the Chinese government approaches this dilemma.

Liu Xiaoming: We also have people in China who felt left behind in this economic, structural transformation, and you have to do away with over capacities. For instance, there is a lot of talk about the steel industry. In fact, when I read news that 4,000 people have to be laid off in this country, I fully understand their feelings because we also face the same challenge to re-allocate about 2 million steel workers.

O'Neill: What's the best way of doing that?

Liu Xiaoming: You have to train these workers, and you have to create new start-up business. So on the one hand, we have redundant steel workers, on the other, there is still big demand for services, domestic care, logistic services, etc. So we can train these steel workers to work in these sectors.

O'Neill: Maybe western policy makers need to consider doing more to boost the income for workers. This of course is something I think China has been deliberately doing in a significant way in the past decade.

Liu Xiaoming: Very much so. The wages of workers have been increased. Our government has also set the minimum level of basic wages that you have to guarantee. And lots of efforts have been made to improve the livelihood of migrant workers in the city. Every year, around 100 million migrant workers settle in the big cities. So the government made a lot of efforts, such as building affordable houses. The slogan in China is, "do not let a single person be left behind."

O'Neill: "Not a single person left behind. " But one can't just assume that markets will be able to spread the considerable benefits of globalisation on their own. If we could solve this, globalisation has got lots of good to spread it to all, and it's not stopping anytime soon. In fact, the Chinese are planning a new Silk Road that is gonna take it up to another gear.

Liu Xiaoming: I regard this as new globalisation. One of the reasons why there's resentment towards globalisation is that some people feel left behind and some countries feel left behind. So the purpose of the Belt and Road, or the main theme of it, is "inclusiveness", to include all countries.

O'Neill: So we are talking about countries like Kazakhstan.

Liu Xiaoming: Yes. And Russia, Afghanistan, Pakistan and also many European countries along the Silk Road. For instance, in the past three years, the Eurasia Express railway has been very successful. Over 2,000 trains have been in operation, transporting goods from China all the way to European countries.

O'Neill: Going through Vienna, if I am not mistaken.

Liu Xiaoming: Yes. The other road we are talking about is the new maritime Silk Road linking China to Southeast Asia, including the Philippines, Indonesia, etc. Though China's growth slows down a little bit, China is still an engine of the world economy. So China wants other countries to share the benefits of its growth. China believes it can only continue this momentum by linking with other countries.

Lord Jim O'Neill is British but an outstanding global thinker and opinion leader.After a career with Goldman Sachs as its Chief Economist he was Commercial Minister in the UK Treasury with Chancellor George Osborne. Following that he became Chairman of the world famous think tank Chatham House.

A Live Interview on ITV *Peston on Sunday*

On 19th November 2017, I gave a live interview on ITV's *Peston on Sunday*, in which I shared my views on the 19th National Congress of the Communist Party of China. I also answered questions about the DPRK nuclear issue and the latest developments in Zimbabwe.
The transcript of the interview is as follows:

Peston: Very nice to see you, Mr. Ambassador. You are just back from that incredibly important Congress in Beijing. Is it right–it was widely reported as establishing President Xi as perhaps the most powerful leader China has had since Mao–is that right? Is he now the most powerful Chinese leader since Mao?

Liu Xiaoming: I would say, he has been re-elected as the General Secretary of the Party and he will lead the country into a new era of building socialism with Chinese characteristics.

Peston: You use the phrase socialism with Chinese characteristics? One of the things that is very striking about China, as it is in this country, is that there is a big gap between rich and poor in China. Is that acceptable in a socialist country?

Liu Xiaoming: There is a gap. I wouldn't say a big gap, if you compare China today, the gap between rich and poor, with some other developing countries.

Peston: A lot of billionaires?

Liu Xiaoming: That is exactly what the Party Congress is trying to address. We realize there is unbalanced and inadequate development in China. A lot has to be done to address the ever-growing needs of the people for a better life. That includes, as the President said during the Congress, we will do everything possible to address this gap between poor and rich. We will do everything we can to elevate the poor population. In China right now there are still 40 million. In the past 30 years we have elevated 700 million people out of poverty.

Peston: That's a remarkable achievement.

Liu Xiaoming: The target for the Party and the government is to get those 40 million people out of poverty by the year 2020. That means we will wipe out poverty, according to the poverty line in China, when we successfully build a moderately prosperous society in China.

Peston: There's a lot to talk about. You were Ambassador to North Korea for quite some time?

Liu Xiaoming: For three and a half years.

Peston: In the West, there's concern that China isn't putting enough pressure on North Korea to abandon its nuclear tests. What do you say to that?

Liu Xiaoming: That's not true. As a matter of fact, China has done everything we can. We tried to dissuade the DPRK from developing their nuclear weapons programme. When I was Ambassador there, I did my best to convince them that it would not be in their interest to develop nuclear weapons.

Peston: Why have they gone ahead?

Liu Xiaoming: Because they have their legitimate concerns. The DPRK nuclear issue is an issue of trust and an issue of security. Because of the distrust between the DPRK and the United States, it is the root cause of this issue, so that's why from day one we set the goals for the Six-Party Talks to make sure that Korean peninsula will be nuclear free and address this issue with a comprehensive approach. We are also calling for the normalization process...

Peston: Shouldn't there be tougher sanctions? Many say China should impose tougher sanctions.

Liu Xiaoming: We have voted consistenlly in the UN since 2006, when I was the Ambassador. Since then, there have been 11 UN resolutions on the DPRK. China voted along and China abided by the resolutions strictly and implemented our obligation. The important thing you have to realize is you can't impose sanctions for sanctions' sake. Sanction is a means but not the purpose. The purpose is to get the DPRK to Keep committed to denuclearization. So you need to engage them. So the UN resolution is not only about sanctions.

Peston: No, no.

Liu Xiaoming: It is also about negotiations, about diplomatic solutions...

Peston: Are you pessimistic about North Korea at the moment?

Liu Xiaoming: No, I am still cautiously optimistic. I still believe that if all parties could engage each other and we encourage the DPRK to return to the negotiation table, we can still find diplomatic solution to this crisis.

Peston: Can I ask one other question about the international picture? China has big economic interests in Zimbabwe. Is China pleased with seeing the end of Mugabe?

Liu Xiaoming: It has always been China's policy not to interfere into the internal affairs of other countries. Zimbabwe is a friendly country to China and we supported the Zimbabwe people in their days for independence, and later on for their development. We will never interfere into their internal affairs...

Peston: Can I press you on that, because there are widespread reports the army would not have taken the action against Mugabe without the support of China?

Liu Xiaoming: No, that's not true. We never interfere into their internal affairs. This is up to them, the Zimbabwean people, with regard to what to do with the future of their country. We certainly hope that things will be resolved peacefully.

Peston: Very nice to see you again, Mr. Ambassador. As always it is a great pleasure talking to you!

Liu Xiaoming: Thank you for having me.

Peston on Sunday is the flagship political discussion programme on the British television network ITV. The programme is presented by Robert Peston, the Political Editor of ITV News.

A Live Interview with Adam Boulton on Sky News *All Out Politics*

On 21st June, 2019, I gave live interview on Sky News' *All Out Politics* hosted by Adam Boulton. I talked about, among other topics, China-UK relations in the context of the just concluded 10th round of the China-UK Economic and Financial Dialogue. The transcript is as follows:

Boulton: This is *All Out Politics*–news, debate and opinion from the heart of Westminster. A high-level Chinese delegation was in the United Kingdom this week to sign a trade deal worth more than £500 million. But questions remain about the future of the UK-China relationship, given the row over Huawei and the continuing protests in Hong Kong. Joining me now is Chinese Ambassador to the UK, Liu Xiaoming. Welcome to you, indeed!

Let's talk about trade. First of all, Brexit. Does it offer greater opportunities to the UK or China in their trade relationship?

Liu Xiaoming: I hope both. You mentioned this high-level visit by the Chinese Vice Premier. It was very significant. During the visit, 69 outcomes have been signed. This is the tenth Economic and Financial Dialogue, co-chaired by Chinese Vice Premier and the Chancellor of the UK. So, in the past 10 years, each year we had one round of dialogue. The trade between China and the UK in goods and services doubled, and investment from China tripled. What is significant of this round of Dialogue is that there is the launch of the Shanghai-London Stock Connect. That was very significant.

Boulton: This is basically selling each other's stocks.

Liu Xiaoming: Right. For the first time UK listed companies can sell their shares in Shanghai Stock Market. The UK investors can buy directly from Shanghai.

Boulton: Presumably the United Kingdom is going to need a new trade arrangement with China as we leave the European Union.

Liu Xiaoming: We are open to this, but first you have to complete your Brexit. We have been very actively engaged with the UK side in discussing about new arrangement. We want to have partnership with both the EU and the UK.

Boulton: I read in newspapers and magazines that China is bemused by the decision to leave the European Union. Would that be fair?

Liu Xiaoming: I don't think so. China will leave it to the UK and the EU to decide. There are both challenges and opportunities. We want to seize the opportunities and try to handle the challenges in an orderly way. The other thing I should mention about this latest round of the Dialogue is the beef. I do not know if you care much about the beef. There has been a ban on import of UK beef for the past 23 years because of the mad cow disease. Now the restriction is lifted.

Boulton: Something for British farmers there.

Liu Xiaoming: There is a big demand in China for beef. Every year we import one million tonnes of beef. The UK is an exporter of beef. Each time when the Chinese visitors are here–and tourists–they are all looking for Angus beef and Welsh black cattle beef. So, I think there is a big demand for UK beef.

Boulton: Given the relations between Donald Trump's America and China, do you think the UK's gonna have to choose basically?

Liu Xiaoming: We want to have good relations with both the UK and the US. I trust that the UK will make its decision independently, in the UK's national interest and in the interest of UK-China cooperation.

Boulton: There is a sort of ideological divide. China has a one-party state. We have a western tradition of democracy. In the end, it would seem that those may be strained.

Liu Xiaoming: China has been around for 5,000 years. We have had different systems. 70 years ago, the Communist Party led China's revolution and established the People's Republic. I think there have always been differences, but these differences have not prevented our countries from working for the common good. I can not say that we have a one-party system. In China, we have eight democratic parties. Of course the country is led by the Communist Party of China, just like the UK is led by the Conservative Party. We have a Chinese democracy, or democracy of Chinese characteristics. We have a different way to elect our leaders. But we need to respect each other.

Boulton: Yeah, if you take for example tech or communications, China has used tech for surveillance of its citizens. Therefore, should Huawei be allowed to gain a significant foothold in our 5G system here?

Liu Xiaoming: I don't think the Chinese government use tech for surveillance of its citizens. Here in the UK, you have a lot of CCTV cameras. For us, it is for the security of the country to prevent terrorist attacks and so on. Huawei is a good company. They have been here for 18 years, and they have made their contribution to the telecom industries in this country. They are the leader in 5G technology. I do hope that the UK will keep Huawei for the benefit...

Boulton: What would be the consequences if the new prime minister did not admit Huawei?

Liu Xiaoming: I think this would send a bad signal, a negative signal, not only to Huawei but to Chinese businesses. The UK is regarded as the most open, most business-friendly. That's why in the past 5 years, you have seen a soaring of Chinese investment here. In the past 10 years, Chinese investment here tripled. If the door is shut on Huawei, it will send a very negative message.

Boulton: Have you had any representations from the British government about the situation in Hong Kong?

Liu Xiaoming: We do have a talk. They expressed their concerns. We explained to them why the decision is legitimate and necessary. And why we support the Hong Kong government in their decision, both to start the amendments and also to suspend the decision. We also expressed our concern that some foreign countries try to use this to interfere into the internal affairs of Hong Kong. We told the British government that Hong Kong is entirely an internal affair of the Chinese.

Boulton: These are extraordinary scenes of civil disobedience. People are talking about a quarter of the Hong Kong population taking to the streets. How do you think that this situation is going to be resolved? Would, for example, the removal of Carrie Lam be the answer?

Liu Xiaoming: Most British media focus on the people on the street, the demonstrators. They overlooked that there are 800,000 people signing up to support the Hong Kong government to amend the Ordinance. When they sent out the amendment to solicit opinions, they got 4,500 replies, and 3,000 of them support the amendment. Only 1,500 made their observations opposing it. I do hope things will calm down. We have full trust in Hong Kong SAR government in resolving this matter. The SAR government has decided to suspend the amendment and they want more time to listen to the people. I hope the people will respond positively to Carrie Lam and her administration.

Boulton: Lord Patten, the last British Governor of Hong Kong said this is a clear breach of the agreements that were reached at the time of the handover.

Liu Xiaoming: We don't think so. I think it is just the opposite. I think the decision to amend the ordinance is just for the purpose of making Hong Kong a better place and not a safe haven for fugitive criminals.

Boulton: What do you think of Boris Johnson?

Liu Xiaoming: I know him very well. When he was Mayor of London, he did a great job to promote business relations between Chinese cities and London. When he was foreign secretary, he visited China on several occasions. I also know Jeremy Hunt very well. I wish best luck to both candidates.

Boulton: Ambassador, thank you for joining us.

Liu Xiaoming: My pleasure.

Adam Boulton is a British journalist and broadcaster who was formerly editor-at-large of Sky News, and presenter of *All Out Politics*. He has interviewed every British Prime Minister from David Cameron back to Alec Douglas-Home.

An Interview with Annette Weisbach on CNBC

On 14th November, 2019, I gave an interview on CNBC with Annette Weisbach after delivering a keynote speech at the Global Markets Conference 2019 held by BNP Paribas. I shared thoughts on Huawei, China-US relations and trade negotiations, China-UK relations, Brexit and other questions. The interview was broadcast on CNBC "*Squawk Box Europe*" the next morning, and carried on CNBC website and Twitter. The transcript is as follows.

Weisbach: There's a lot of controversy about Huawei's role in 5G network and its equipment. What is your response here? Can you assure European and also the US consumers that there won't be any sort of problems with those equipments?

Liu Xiaoming: I do not foresee a major problem between Huawei and their business partners, because Huawei is really a good company. They contribute a great deal not only in terms of telecom industry in this country, but also in terms of corporate responsibilities. They supported 51,000 jobs in the UK and have invested 3 billion US dollars in this country. And they are the leader in 5G. I think the British business partners still welcome Huawei.

There are some noises. I don't want to name the country. They do not want to see Huawei have a better presence in European countries. They twist arms of, they put pressure on, these countries. But so far, I think some European countries, like Britain, Germany, and France, have not yet made a final decision. In terms of government's decision, I think it is still debated, with divided views.

We understand people might have some concerns. Huawei also understands the so-called security concern, so they try to address this concern. Huawei has set up Cyber Security Evaluation Centre staffed by British people. Huawei paid for this facility to monitor and analyze their own facilities–whether they are secure and safe, whether there's a problem. So they are very transparent. They want to be a good partner. I always say that Huawei will present golden opportunities for China and the UK and for China and European countries to collaborate in 5G. If you kick out Huawei, you really miss opportunities.

So I do hope that, the British government, German government, or French government, they will make decision based on their own national interests, based on their collaboration with China in building a strong partnership with China, but not based on some political witch hunt or, I would call, Cold War mentality. So I do hope Huawei will be here for win-win cooperation. As China will open its door wider, I do hope other countries will also open their doors and will not shut the doors to China.

Weisbach: You have said Cold War. And it feels a bit that these geopolitical tensions between United States and China do have a bit of a feel of the Cold War. And also, it feels that Europe has to make up its mind, at least the pressure is on Europe. How do you see China positioned here?

Liu Xiaoming: We make it very clear. We're not interested in any war, whether it is cold war, or hot war, or trade war with the United States. We want to build a cooperative, coordinated, a non-confrontation relationship with the United States. We believe that there will be no peace or prosperity in the world without sound relations between China and the US, the two largest economies in the world. We always believe that China and the United States will benefit from cooperation and lose from confrontation. So we are not interested in any wars with the United States. I'm very pleased that Chinese and American negotiators are working very hard to address trade issues.

With regard to Europe, we do not ask European countries to take side between China and the US. The UK has a special relationship with the US, but we're also building a "golden era" between China and the UK. So we want to work for win-win, not a zero sum game. Not Europe wins, America wins and China loses. Not China wins, Europe wins and America loses. We want win-win for all. That is our position.

Weisbach: Let's talk about this phase one deal between the US and China, and where the sticking points are, because it seems that the deal is within reach but there seems to be some sticking points. What are they from the Chinese position?

Liu Xiaoming: I think the negotiators are still very much occupied with the details.

I do not have the details. Even if I had, I would have to be cautious. I don't want to interrupt the process. But I think the tariffs might be one of the very important issues, based on my understanding of the negotiations. Because the trade war started with the tariffs, it should be ended with removing all the tariffs imposed by the other side, because it is not in the spirit of free trade. So we do hope that we can clinch the phase one deal sooner, so that we can move on to phase two and phase three.

Weisbach: What one is hearing is that intellectual property rights are also at the center of that debate or the negotiations. Would China be in a position to compromise a bit in that stance?

Liu Xiaoming: China has made great efforts in the past 40 years since the reform and opening up in terms of improving intellectual property rights. First, I would say people should recognize the tremendous progress that China has made in this respect. Number two, we also realize that we need to do more. As I always say, the largest room in the world is the room for improvement. So no country is perfect, but we are serious about addressing the concerns of other countries, including the United States. That is the second point I want to make. Third, I don't think resorting to war of words, accusing each other, is helpful at all. Some politicians criticize China for so-called "stealing technology" from the United States. I think they have a wrong impression. China's miracle is not built on theft of other countries' property. It's built by the hard working people of China in the past 70 years. So I think you really have to address this issue in sincerity and try to tackle this problem with honesty, sincerity, rather than accusing China of so called stealing. That will be helpful for the two sides to work on this important issue.

Weisbach: President Trump once said the trade war is easy to win. What would you respond to that?

Liu Xiaoming: I said on many occasions that there will be no winners in trade wars.

Weisbach: And let's talk about the further evolution of the trade negotiations. What do you think will be the timeline? Because we are clearly, next year, heading into new elections in the United States, so it could be all tied together. Would the Chinese position rather be to wait and see who will be the next president?

Liu Xiaoming: I don't think that is China's position. We are open-minded. We always want to resolve this problem sooner than later because we believe it is in the interest not only of China but also of the United States, and of the world.

The trade war between China and the United States really created a lot of uncertainties and unpredictabilities. And I think the world is watching. I think the negotiators of the two countries really have a big duty on their shoulders. I don't think it is the intention of China to wait and see. That is not our position. We want to clinch the agreement as soon as possible. But you need two to tango.

Hong Kong

A Live Interview with John Humphrys on BBC Radio 4 *Today* Programme

On 29th June 2017, I gave a live interview on the *Today* programme of BBC Radio 4 hosted by John Humphrys, in which I shared my views on the progress and achievement of Hong Kong Special Administrative Region since its establishment 20 years ago and the success of "one country, two systems" policy. I also answered questions about Hong Kong's political reform, China's place in the world and the DPRK nuclear issue.

The transcript of the interview is as follows:

Humphrys: I am joined in the studio by the Chinese Ambassador to this country, Liu Xiaoming. Good morning to you.

Liu Xiaoming: Good morning.

Humphrys: Isn't it the reality that it is "one country" that is increasingly "one system"?

Liu Xiaoming: No. I think "one country, two systems" has been implemented with great success. I can't agree with some of the interviews aired just before me saying that China did not deliver its promises. As a matter of fact, the Central Government of China delivered everything it promises, that is "one country, two systems". I think that basically Hong Kong has maintained its social, economic system, way of life, rule of law, and I think Hong Kong now is much better placed compared with 20 years ago. So this is really an occasion for us to have a grand celebration.

I think in the past 20 years we've seen Hong Kong maintaining prosperity and stability, the GDP doubled, and foreign exchange reserve quadrupled. Hong Kong still remains a global centre of finance, trade and shipping. The life expectancy of its people increased tremendously. They are ahead of many developed countries. So I would say people in Hong Kong are now living longer and living happier.

Humphrys: Nobody I think would argue that there has been economic prosperity in

Hong Kong. That is accepted. But the impression we get is that China is determined to tighten its grip, and there is clear evidence for that, isn't there?

Liu Xiaoming: I don't think so. I don't agree with her. I think if people compare the political governance of Hong Kong today, including democratic governance of Hong Kong today with what was 20 years ago...

Humphrys: A democratic government?

Liu Xiaoming: Democratic governance.

Humphrys: Really?

Liu Xiaoming: Let me say: 20 years ago, did you have election in Hong Kong? Who elected the governor of Hong Kong?

Humphrys: It was a colony. Nobody would argue other than that. It was a colony and there was a governor there and it was fine.

Liu Xiaoming: In the past 20 years there were 5 elections in Hong Kong.

Humphrys: And the last leader was elected with 777 votes, 0.03 percent of the registered electors. That doesn't sound very convincing.

Liu Xiaoming: Number does not tell you everything.

Humphrys: It tells you a lot in a democratic system.

Liu Xiaoming: What about here in the UK? What about UK's national leader? You have 65 million people and your national leaders get elected from their constituency of tens of thousands of voters, by a small majority. People can challenge that it doesn't represent the population of the entire country.

Humphrys: The number of people who voted for the British Prime Minister ultimately was more than 0.03 percent and there we go. All right, let's...

Liu Xiaoming: Hong Kong's chief executive is elected according to the Basic Law, according to the Election Law in Hong Kong...

Humphrys: But it has to be approved...

Liu Xiaoming: You have to achieve this through incremental, gradual process and step-by-step. As we say, Rome or maybe London is not built overnight and Hong Kong is not built overnight.

Humphrys: Why do you think that the foreign office says ... You know there was a report by the foreign office in February 2016 and Boris Johnson, our present Foreign Secretary, has said seriously breached the *Sino-British Joint Declaration* by undermining the "one country, two systems" principle. And that is what the British government fears has happened, that is, the principle has been undermined.

Liu Xiaoming: First of all, we disagree with this so-called report on Hong Kong, which is published twice a year. Hong Kong is an integral part of China, and Hong Kong's affairs are internal affairs of China. It's not for foreign governments to interfere. Having said that, even with this report, the British government commends the Chinese government for implementing "one country, two systems" and they believe "one country, two systems" is a great success. There are some differences between China and the UK but on the whole we all believe that the long-term stability and long-term prosperity in Hong Kong are not only in the interest of China but also in the interest of Britain and the international community.

Humphrys: And many people looking at your country from the outside believe that the facts are the elections are orchestrated, the protesters are locked up and democracy is being weakened rather than strengthened and your response now, in the end, is to say that it's our country.

Liu Xiaoming: When you say "one country, two systems", I think some people forget that this is one framework. You have to remember that Hong Kong is part of China, not part of UK, and not a so-called independent entity.

Humphrys: And therefore it has to be a single system?

Liu Xiaoming: Two systems. You told me your last visit to China was 12 years ago. You need to go to Hong Kong, to go to China, to see the changes. Even in the area where we have a difference, on democracy, you have to compare Hong Kong today with Hong Kong 20 years ago. You have to compare Hong Kong now with Hong Kong one year, two years ago.

Humphrys: Can we talk about China's place in the world at large? Do you see the day, perhaps not very far away, when China will be the world's great superpower instead of the United States, as it is today?

Liu Xiaoming: I do not foresee that China will become a superpower in the foreseeable future. I believe China is still a developing country.

Humphrys: Even when China becomes the largest economy in the world?

Liu Xiaoming: Even when China becomes the largest economy in the world, it will take a long way for China to become so-called superpower. China is a large country, and there are great differences between regions. After serving as Ambassador in Egypt, I was seconded to one of the poorest provinces in China, Gansu. It is very poor, poorer than, the Americans used to call their west "Wild West".

Humphrys: So what will it take, as you've said, you are the second largest economy, you may very well very soon become the largest in the world, so what will it take for you to be the world's superpower?

Liu Xiaoming: We are not interested in becoming a superpower...

Humphrys: Oh you are not...

Liu Xiaoming: We are interested in improving the livelihood of the people, and addressing the disparity between regions. When people look at China, they like to focus on the coastal region, the eastern part of China–Beijing, Shanghai, Guangdong. They are very much developed. For example Guandong is the 15th largest economy in the world. It's about the size of Spain. But if you look at other provinces–Gansu, Ningxia, they are rather backward...

Humphrys: Just a final thought about North Korea and its threat to, potentially, world peace. What would it take for North Korea to so disturb you in Beijing that you will take action against the North Korean regime? What would they have to do for you to say, enough, we are now going to intervene?

Liu Xiaoming: China has done a lot. Before I came here I was Ambassador there–I'd been there for three and a half years. China actively engaged with the DPRK . We tried to persuade them to be committed to denuclearization.

Humphrys: And it's failed?

Liu Xiaoming: No, I can't say it's failed. Sometimes we make two steps forward, one step backward, and one step forward, two steps backward. But the DPRK nuclear programme is a complicated issue. It has to be addressed comprehensively. A comprehensive approach is necessary. That's why China proposed to have this "dual suspension", "double track" approach. That means, on the one hand, we should keep sanctions in place, we should persuade the DPRK to be committed to denuclearization and on the other hand...

Humphrys: And if you fail, the United State will intervene...

Liu Xiaoming: On the other hand, the United States, the ROK and other countries should also take steps. They should suspend their military exercises. Each time I tried to persuade the DPRK to be committed to denuclearization, they would say, we are threatened by big superpower, the States, joined by their allies. The US and its allies have done many military exercises directed at the DPRK .

So we are calling for "dual suspension": the DPRK suspend their nuclear and missile activities; Americans, the ROK, their allies suspend their military exercises. Then we return to the negotiation table and start talks to find solution for a nuclear-free Korean Peninsula and a mechanism for lasting peace. We call it "dual track".

Humphrys: Alright, Ambassador, many thanks for joining us.

Liu Xiaoming: Thank you for having me.

John Humprys was the main presenter for the *Nine O'Clock News*, the flafship BBC News television programme from 1981 to 1987, and from 1987 to 2019 he presented on the BBC Radio 4 *Today* programme.

A Live Interview with Mark Urban on BBC *Newsnight*

On 12th June 2019, I gave a live interview to BBC *Newsnight* hosted by Mark Urban. I talked about China's position on issues relating to Hong Kong, Xinjiang and Huawei, and answered questions. The transcript is as follows:

Urban: We are joined by Ambassador Liu Xiaoming, who's been the Chinese Ambassador to the UK since 2010. Quite a period! Ambassador, let's start with the Joint Declaration. That treaty. Is China still committed to upholding it?

Liu Xiaoming: We are upholding the principle of one country, two systems. This promise has been made not only to the world, but also to the Chinese people, including those in Hong Kong. The Joint Declaration has completed its mission after Hong Kong's handover. And now, I think the "one country, two systems" has been very successful in Hong Kong.

Urban: You say it has completed its mission, I want to put to you something your foreign ministry spokesman said two years ago, that the Declaration no longer has realistic meaning, it is purely a historic document.

Liu Xiaoming: It is a historic document. It completed its mission.

Urban: So it's irrelevant?

Liu Xiaoming: It's relevant in that it sets a good example for the international community to settle a dispute between nations by peaceful means, so it's still a shining, successful example for people to follow. But that Declaration gives British government no sovereignty, no right, no legitimacy to interfere in the internal affairs of Hong Kong.

Urban: No sovereignty that is clear. That ended in 1997, but still an interest and a feeling on the part of hundreds of thousands of people in Hong Kong that Britain has a duty to protect their rights, under the terms of that promise.

Liu Xiaoming: The British government has a duty to protect your own citizens but not the people of Hong Kong. The citizens of Hong Kong are, you know, they are part of China now, and according to the basic law, Hong Kong people will run their own affairs and they are entitled to implementing their social system different from the mainland. But it has nothing to do with the British government.

Urban: I am sure you can see, putting the British government to one side now, just the feeling of the people in Hong Kong, hundreds of thousands, some say 10% of the entire population have come out on the streets, a nerve has been touched that Beijing is not respecting their right to a separate system...

Liu Xiaoming: This is not correct. The whole story has been distorted. This case is about rectifying the deficiencies, plugging the loopholes of the existing legal system.

Urban: Who is distorting this?

Liu Xiaoming: The media, including the BBC, I think. You portrayed the story as the Hong Kong government making this amendment at the instruction of the Central Government. As a matter of fact, the Central Government gave no instruction, no order about making amendment. This amendment was initiated by the Hong Kong government. It is prompted by a murder case happened in Taiwan and this...

Urban: Sorry. Excuse me, would you advise the Hong Kong government then to drop it, given how controversial...

Liu Xiaoming: Why should we ask them to drop it?

Urban: You can see what people, even the legislators, say. One man said "you are beating people out of Hong Kong" to the police. That is the scene we are seeing in the territory now as a result of this...

Liu Xiaoming: But you have to remember that at the very beginning it has been a peaceful demonstration, but it has become ugly afterwards. A policeman was beaten, and the police had to defend themselves. They had to put the order in place, so you can't blame the policemen. I think there are always the forces inside and outside Hong Kong that try to take advantage of things, to stir up trouble. Let me come back to the...

Urban: But this is a domestic, grass roots movement of people in Hong Kong.

Liu Xiaoming: But, you know, it has been exaggerated to one million. As a matter of fact, according to police count, it is about 200,000 people. But you ignore 800,000 people who signed up to support the amendment. This silent majority has not been reported in this country by the BBC.

Urban: Well, you are making the case now.

Liu Xiaoming: And also the Hong Kong government invited the Hong Kong public for suggestion, opinion, and they received 4,500 replies, 3,000 supported the amendment and only 1,500 opposed the amendment.

Urban: I want to move onto one or two of my other issues. What effect do you think it has on people in Hong Kong when they see the treatment of Uighurs in Xinjiang. An estimated one million people, Muslims minorities...

Liu Xiaoming: Again you are exaggerating. I don't know where you get this "one million people".

Urban: It is a UN estimate.

Liu Xiaoming: I don't think the UN has any report on this. There are education and training centres to help people who have been brainwashed by extremists to return to society, to earn their living, to train them on skills, language and the knowledge of the law, so they can protect their own interests.

Urban: Can we have access, can we see what is going on?

Liu Xiaoming: Of course, we invited journalists and diplomats to visit.

Urban: But we are hearing reports that what happens in there is an assault on their Muslim faith...

Liu Xiaoming: That is completely wrong.

Urban: ... that they are prevented from praying, they are told that as a backward religion...

Liu Xiaoming: These are all distortions, it is all made up, fake news, I would say. We respect people's freedom of religion. People are entitled to have their religion. And the important thing is, you are missing the big picture. The reason for these centres is to educate those young people who have been intoxicated by extremist ideas. And ever since these measures, there have been no extremist violent incidents in Xinjiang for the past three years, which means these measures have been successful.

Urban: I think anyone might understand why you want to prevent terrorist acts or have de-radicalisation. I think that is because you might have in common with many other governments and societies around the world. But what we hear are persistent reports of a very large number of people, up to a million, involved in this re-education process which sounds frankly sinister.

Liu Xiaoming: I don't know where you get this number, one million.

Urban: What would your estimate be?

Liu Xiaoming: It is difficult to give a number because there are those going in, going out. The number changes from time to time, but the important thing to focus on here is the purpose of the centre. It is not to round up people. The purpose is to help these young people to have a better life after education and training.

Urban: You are saying the purpose is not to eradicate the religion among these people, it is not the aim of this exercise?

Liu Xiaoming: Not at all.

Urban: Huawei. It's a big subject, I am sure, for you in your post in London. It's something you care a lot about. The British government has been in a position where it seems to make an interim decision or advise to use some elements of Huawei's technology in its 5G network. Now as you know, quite a lot of pressure from the United States not to do so at all. Will there be consequences, do you think, from the Chinese point of view, if Britain decides not to use it at all?

Liu Xiaoming: First of all, I would say Huawei is a good company. It is a leader in 5G. They are here for win-win cooperation with their British counterparts. And they contribute tremendously not only to telecom industry in this country, but also they supported 51,000 jobs. In terms of win-win collaboration, if the UK collaborates with Huawei, there will be promising future for both sides.

Urban: They have got advanced technology, no one doubts about it. But what if the UK chooses not to?

Liu Xiaoming: I think it would send a very bad message not only to Huawei but also to Chinese businesses. Will the UK remain open? Will the UK still be a business friendly environment for Chinese companies? It would send a very bad signal.

Urban: Negative effects on trade?

Liu Xiaoming: Yes, bad. Not just on trade but also on investment. For the past 5 years, the investment from China exceeded the total investment in the previous 30 years. So, Chinese investments are booming in this country. Last year it increased by 14%, but if you shut the door for Huawei, it will send a very bad and negative message to other Chinese businesses.

Urban: On that note, Ambassador, thank you very much for joining us.

Liu Xiaoming: My pleasure.

Mark Urban is a British journalist, historian, and broadcaster, and is currently the Diplomatic Editor and occasional presenter for BBC 2's *Newsnight*.

A Live Interview with Lucy Hockings on BBC World News

On 13th June 2019, I gave a live interview to BBC World News hosted by Lucy Hockings, in which I talked about China's position on issues relating to Hong Kong. The transcript is as follows:

Hockings: Let's talk about the view from Beijing. With us is the Chinese Ambassador to the UK, Liu Xiaoming, who is with me now. Thank you for joining us.

We've seen hundreds of thousands of people out on the streets of Hong Kong, professionals, lawyers as well, all objecting to this bill. Why does China want it?

Liu Xiaoming: Not all are protesting. I think 800,000 people signed up to support the Hong Kong government's move to amend these ordinances through a bill.

Hockings: Does China want this bill?

Liu Xiaoming: Of course, we support this, because this effort by the Hong Kong government will address the discrepancies of the existing system so that Hong Kong will not continue to be a safe haven for fugitive criminals. So this will make Hong Kong a better place. Why should we not support it?

Hockings: The people on the streets are not objecting to that. But can you address these concerns that this is going to put people at risk to extradition to China for political crimes. That suggest no one is going to be safe, activists, human rights lawyers, journalists, and social workers? Is there commitment from Beijing this will not happen?

Liu Xiaoming: This is totally wrong! In fact, there are 37 crimes listed in the ordinance and none of them has to do with any freedom of expression, freedom of assembly, freedom of speech, freedom of publication, and there is special mention that no offence will be related to political issues. And it has to be crimes in the laws of both places– both Hong Kong and the other jurisdiction. The important thing one has to realize is it's not about extradition to China. It's about special arrangements with all judicial parties of those who do not have a mutual assistance agreement...

Hockings: But you can assure us that this bill will not be used as a tool against political opponents?

Liu Xiaoming: Not at all. It's not the purpose of this bill. I think this has been distorted. I think there is someone with ulterior motives to make it...

Hockings: Who has ulterior motives?

Liu Xiaoming: Those forces who are not happy with stability and prosperity in Hong Kong.

Hockings: What forces?

Liu Xiaoming: Hostile forces that do not want to see Hong Kong...

Hockings: Are you talking about foreign powers, or forces inside Hong Kong?

Liu Xiaoming: You heard some foreign powers express support for the demonstrators, express so-called concerns about these amendments. People have a reason to be concerned about the motives behind it.

Hockings: One of the reasons that people are concerned, and foreign countries are concerned, is because China has a deeply flawed judicial system. There are allegations of torture, forced confessions, arbitrary detentions. There is the concern that when someone is extradited to mainland China, they will not get a fair trial.

Liu Xiaoming: No. I totally reject these allegations. China is a country ruled by law. The legal system is improving. The reform is going on.

Hockings: But Ambassador, there is almost a 100% conviction rate in China.

Liu Xiaoming: No, I don't think so. I don't think this is a correct description of the law system in China. I think you really have to look at how China is changing with each passing day. Especially, China has made great progress in terms of protection of human rights, in terms of building a sound legal system. I think that one of the forces behind this, sterring up the trouble, not only trying to demonize the Hong Kong government but also try to demonize the judicial system in China. So that is the ulterior motive I am talking about.

Hockings: So people in China get a fair trial.

Liu Xiaoming: Yes, of course. Definitely.

Hockings: Many people would dispute that, the world over. We've just even seen the judge in New Zealand not wanting to send someone back to China. But if we can move on from that, could you also reassure people perhaps about the commitment to the One Country Two Systems, because so many of those protesters up there say that they are seeing the system eroded? Is that something that China is still committed to?

Liu Xiaoming: We are very committed to One Country Two Systems. The One Country Two Systems has been very successful. That's why you can have prosperity and stability in Hong Kong in the past 20 years. If it were not for this policy, you would not have this demonstration, I would say. So I am calling for a civilized discussion on this amendment, or a civilized debate. Give the legislative council the time to debate. So I don't think this violence, the riots in Hong Kong in the streets, are in the interest of building a civilized society in Hong Kong.

Hockings: Many leaders of business are also concerned this is going to undermine investors' confidence in Hong Kong, that multinationals will be worried about working there.

Liu Xiaoming: I think it's just the opposite. If Hong Kong continues to be a haven for criminals, you think that was safe? And that will ensure prosperity? I heard that some foreign...

Hockings: The genuine worry is that if someone does something that Chinese government doesn't like in Hong Kong, they may find themselves in a court and an unfair system in mainland China.

Liu Xiaoming: That's a complete distortion of the picture. Let me give you a figure. In the past 20 years, there are only 100 criminals being surrendered by Hong Kong government. That means five cases a year. And I will also give you another example. Since 2006, 248 criminals have been handed over from mainland to Hong Kong. Yet, none has been handed over to mainland. Do you think this relationship could be sustainable? You know, we made requests, but because of this arrangement, this discrepancy, the gap, no surrender of any criminals, no fugitive criminals have been handed over to mainland.

Hockings: There is unprecedented pressure on Carrie Lam right now from the people on the streets and from petitions. The protestors said about a million people are out on the street.

Liu Xiaoming: No, no. According to police accounts, it's 200,000 people. And, in the past four months or so, Hong Kong government invited opinions. And they received 4,500 written replies: 3,000 supporting the amendment and only 1,500...

Hockings: I think we will have to agree that some of the figures are in dispute. Well, you see some of the pictures of people on the streets. There are an incredible amount of people, from right across the society... in the UK.

Liu Xiaoming: The problem of your media is you only focus on the people in the street. You forget the silent majority.

Hockings: That is why you are with us to tell us about that side.

Liu Xiaoming: Yes, that's one of my purposes to share with you the other side of the story.

Hockings: Can I show you, I have been having a look at Xinhua today, the state News Agency in China. There is absolutely no mention of what is happening in Hong Kong on state media in China. Why are you not reporting this in China?

Liu Xiaoming: I just did an interview, before I came here, last night on BBC *Newsnight*. The whole interview was published on the website in China. It was broadcasted broadly.

Hockings: But can I draw your attention to the screen here. This is Xinhua right now. There is no mention of Hong Kong on the front page of the website.

Liu Xiaoming: I would not make comment about the news agency's policies. But I would say...

Hockings: What are people in China being told about what is happening in Hong Kong?

Liu Xiaoming: This is a good move, a good action by the Hong Kong government to turn Hong Kong into a "heaven for justice" instead of "haven for fugitives". It will ensure the prosperity of Hong Kong, and Hong Kong government has the full and resolute support of the Central Government.

Hockings: Ambassador Liu Xiaoming, it was good to have you with us. Thank you very much for joining us here on BBC World News.

Liu Xiaoming: My pleasure.

BBC World News claims to be watched by a weekly audience of 74 million in over 200 countries and territories worldwide. Lucy Hockings is a New Zealand news presenter for the BBC, moderator, events host, and media trainer. Her roles include anchoring *Live with Lucy Hockings* on BBC World News.

A Live Interview
on BBC *The Andrew Marr Show*

On 7th July 2019, I gave a live interview on BBC *The Andrew Marr Show* about issues of Hong Kong, Huawei and Xinjiang. The full text is as follows:

Marr: Now, most diplomatic arguments are restrained muttering affairs, not so the row going on between Britain and China over protests in Hong Kong about a new extradition bill which many people there fear will shred their human rights. Jeremy Hunt, the Foreign Secretary, sympathized with the protesters. The Chinese Ambassador then held a rather rare press conference in which he angrily condemned the UK government for interfering in Chinese internal affairs. He is with me now for his first interview since then. Welcome, Mr. Ambassador. You were quite angry, weren't you?

Liu Xiaoming: Yes, very much so. We are strongly opposed to British intervention in Hong Kong's internal affairs. We believe that this amendment of ordinance has a good reasons because the Chief Executive and Hong Kong SAR government want to make Hong Kong a better and safer place, rather than a safe haven for fugitive criminals. But yet, the British government, senior officials, seemed to voice support for the demonstrators. What makes it even worse is that when the violence happened, instead of condemning the storming of the Legislative Council, they criticized the Hong Kong SAR government for the handling of the situation.

Marr: Jeremy Hunt just said that his heart went out to the protesters and he didn't approve of the violence. A lot of people thought there was a 50-year guarantee that not much would change in Hong Kong when handover happened, and that this is being eroded by this new law, because once you can extradite somebody very easily from Hong Kong to the mainland, then lots of people would stop saying what they would have said and free speech would be slowly silenced. And people do feel this is the beginning of the end of "One Country, Two Systems" agreement.

Liu Xiaoming: Andrew, that shows your lack of understanding of what this bill is about. It is not about extraditing people from Hong Kong to the mainland. Hong Kong has mutual assistance agreements with 30 countries, yet they do not have this similar agreement with more than 170 other countries and regions. So that means if some people committed a crime outside Hong Kong and returned to Hong Kong, Hong Kong cannot punish them. This bill will plug the loopholes. I think some people are trying to use it to scare the Hong Kong people.

Marr: These are powers that Beijing wants?

Liu Xiaoming: I don't think so. The whole thing was started by the Hong Kong SAR government. Just as the Chief Executive said, she received no instruction from Beijing. She received no order from Beijing. It is completely the initiative of Hong Kong SAR government to make Hong Kong system more perfect, to improve the legal system.

Marr: We've seen all the scenes in LegCo in Hong Kong recently. There seemed to be the case that the police there couldn't hold back the protesters. If you feel the situation is getting out of control and the Hong Kong authorities can't control things, does China interfere directly in Hong Kong?

Liu Xiaoming: You mentioned "One China, Two Systems" for 50 years. We are fully committed to this promise. There is no question about that. So you can see that from day one till now, the Central Government has not interfered at all. Every step of the way, we let the Hong Kong SAR government handle this. Instead, it is the British government that was trying to interfere, voicing support for the demonstrators. When the rioters stormed the Legislative Council, they then said that you can't use this violence as a pretext for repression. So they tried to obstruct the legal process. To answer your question in a simple way, we have full confidence in Hong Kong SAR government. And it shows that they are capable of handling the situation.

Marr: Nevertheless, this law would make it easier to extradite people to China. Chris Patten, the last governor, said, things have gone from bad to very bad to even worse. People with the wrong views have been banned from political activity. Freedom of speech has been whittled away in the media and in the universities. Beijing has even abducted individuals from Hong Kong and taken them back to the mainland.

Liu Xiaoming: I totally reject the accusation of Chris Patten. As the last governor of Hong Kong, his body is in the 21st century, but his head remains in the old colonial days. This bill won't make it easier for Hong Kong to extradite people to the mainland.

There are many safeguards. You know, first of all, there are 37 clauses as safeguards in this Bill. That means, no people would be extradited to mainland because of their religious or political beliefs. And the crime has to be punishable in both places. That means, to make an extreme case, if murder was not regarded as a crime in Hong Kong, then people who committed murder would not be extradited to the mainland.

Marr: There has been a very, very angry row by diplomatic standards. Jeremy Hunt is still threatening further, possibly, sanctions and so forth against China if it goes on. Is this a moment when British-Chinese relations are in real crisis?

Liu Xiaoming: I don't think so. We are not interested in a diplomatic row with the UK. We are still committed to building a stronger relationship, a partnership, the "Golden Era" started by President Xi. I still remember the last time you interviewed me was before President Xi's visit in 2015.

Marr: I remember that.

Liu Xiaoming: We are still committed to this "Golden Era" between our two countries. But I cannot agree with some British politicians' description of the relationship. They even use this so-called "strategic ambiguity". I think this language does not belong to the vocabulary between China and the UK. It is a Cold War language.

Marr: Another big row between Britain and China potentially is over the role of Huawei in the 5G electronic communications network. Can I put it to you that there is no way at all that the People's Republic of China would allow Western or British or American companies direct access to your security infrastructure?

Liu Xiaoming: You know, China is developing. To answer your question directly, I don't think Huawei would have access to your security infrastructure.

Marr: But it will be able to eavesdrop on lots of aspects of British life. And the law currently says it is obliged to hand over information the Chinese government wants and that's what scares people.

Liu Xiaoming: No. It will not happen at all. First of all, there is no back door, and also there are a lot of safeguards.

Marr: Can you promise people on this programme that if Huawei has complete access to our 5G network, information will not be passed back to the government in Beijing by

Huawei?

Liu Xiaoming: I can promise that, a hundred percent. I think Huawei is a good company. It is the leader of 5G. I think if you reject Huawei, you will miss enormous opportunities. They are here for win-win cooperation. They are not here to spy on people.

Marr: All right. Let's turn to another big element of difficulties between the two countries, which is the treatment of the Uyghur people in northwest China. Now, there are camps all across that part of China. Up to a million people, according to the United Nations, have been interned in these camps, and BBC has reported on the separation of children from their families, going into camps for children. What is going on?

Liu Xiaoming: I think the BBC have made a distorted picture of what is going on in Xinjiang. Xinjiang is a relatively poor area in China. In terms of GDP, it ranks about 26th in the whole country. There are more than 30 provinces in China. In the past, since 1990s, Xinjiang had been severely hit by terrorism, separatism and extremism. Just ten years and two days ago, on the 5th July, there was a very serious terrorist incident.197 people got killed.

Marr: Can I just put it to you that internment camps are not the answer? We tried them in Northern Ireland and it did not go well for Britain in Northern Ireland. These are camps with razor wire around them, people cannot leave them.

Liu Xiaoming: There is no camp. It is a vocational education and training centre. You know that extremist ideas have easy penetration to the poorer areas. The idea is to help the people, to lift them out of poverty.

Marr: If these camps are only about that, if they are so innocent, why did the Chinese government deny for so long that they existed?

Liu Xiaoming: We didn't deny. We invited journalists and diplomats to visit. That is why BBC has access to interview people over there. I think you need to look at this from the positive perspective. It is for the purpose of early prevention of terrorism. And since the measure was introduced, there has been no terrorist incident for three years.

Marr: Nonetheless, these are quite difficult areas, these camps. They are internment camps and people cannot leave them, can they?

Liu Xiaoming: They can go, of course. They can leave freely. They can visit their relatives. It is not a prison. It is not a camp.

Marr: The BBC talked to some of the parents of Uyghur children who are now in Turkey and they are really upset about the fact that they have been separated from their children and they don't know where they are. I can show you a little clip of it so we can hear what they say. So where are these children? (Video is played)

Liu Xiaoming: Let's first talk about these people. They are anti-government people. You cannot expect a good word about the Chinese government. The children, you know, the government takes good care of the children.

Marr: Are they separating forcibly, parents from their children, in Xinjiang?

Liu Xiaoming: No. If they want to visit their children, they can come back to China.

Marr: So these are all just lies?

Liu Xiaoming: Definitely. There is no forcible separation of children from their parents at all.

Marr: The BBC has been to one town in the province where, in just one town, 400 families lost their children.

Liu Xiaoming: You just give me the names of the families who have lost their children. There is a lot of misinformation about people gone missing. We handled many cases like this. Some said a musician got killed and the other day he emerged alive and happy. If you have people whose children are lost, you give me the names and we will try to locate them and let you know who they are and what they are doing.

Marr: Mr. Ambassador, thank you very much indeed for talking to us.

Liu Xiaoming: My pleasure.

A Live Interview with Dermot Murnaghan on *Sky News Tonight*

On 1st October 2019, I gave a live interview on *Sky News Tonight* with Dermot Murnaghan on China's development and issues of Hong Kong, Xinjiang and Huawei. The full text is as follows:

Murnaghan: With me is the Chinese Ambassador to the UK, Liu Xiaoming. Very good to see you, Ambassador. Can I start with those celebrations in Beijing of the 70 years of foundation of the state? We saw the-state-of-the-art military hardware, inter-continental ballistic missiles, thousands of troops and the President say no force can stop China marching forward. Should the world feel a little bit threatened by all that?

Liu Xiaoming: Not at all. In the President's speech, he said that China will continue to follow the path of peaceful development, and we would like to share the opportunities of China's development with the rest of the world. I think people, especially the media here, when they talk about the celebration, they only focus on the military parade. In fact, military parade is only part of the celebration. There are 15,000 military personnel participating in the military parade, but there are 100,000 ordinary citizens participating in the parade. There are about 70 floats describing the great achievements China has made in the past 70 years.

Murnaghan: It is an amazing achievement: from basically a peasant society to a most advanced economy in the world.

Liu Xiaoming: Not just peasant economy! The People's Republic of China was established after 100 years of countless wars...

Murnaghan: Indeed.

Liu Xiaoming: and foreign aggression, bullying...

Murnaghan: I want to ask you, Ambassador, about how that history forms China's attitude to the future, particularly the foreign bullying, foreign occupations and foreign induced wars. What does China want for the next 70 years? Some analysis is that China wants respect but it does want domination over the next 70 years.

Liu Xiaoming: Not at all. China has no intention to dominate the world. China is still a developing country. We have daunting challenges in developing our country. Like President Xi said, we should consolidate our achievements and we should develop our country well. That is the fundamental task before the Chinese leaders and the Chinese people. China was a victim of foreign invasion, aggression, bullying and humiliation, and we certainly will never ever transfer this to other countries.

Murnaghan: When we see these things in Hong Kong today, one of the protesters was shot at very close range in the chest. People are saying, well, this Chinese crackdown isn't showing a respect for civil rights.

Liu Xiaoming: I cannot agree with you describing what happened in Hong Kong as crackdown at all. We strongly condemn the violent rioters. The violence has been going on for several months. It challenged the bottom line of the "One Country Two Systems", it challenged the rule of law in Hong Kong, and it brought damages to the security...

Murnaghan: Why not engage and hold talks to discuss some of the democratic demands of the protesters?

Liu Xiaoming: You have to separate peaceful demonstration from violent rioters. You talk about the police using live ammunition. It is because their life was in serious threat. The rioter who had been shot on his left shoulder was the one who was using an iron club to attack the police. So, I would ask what would happen if the same thing happened in the UK. What will be the response of the British police to such rioters?

Murnaghan: They wouldn't shoot an unarmed protester with a weapon.

Liu Xiaoming: If their lives were in serious danger?

Murnaghan: The British police are not armed.

Liu Xiaoming: I don't think so. How would the British police respond if the Westminster Hall were stormed by the rioters? I think we should condemn this violence. Hong Kong is based on the rule of law. I think rule of law and "One Country Two Systems" can ensure the future of Hong Kong.

Murnaghan: Can you tell me if these protests continue and they continue to escalate in terms of the violence–there is no doubt there is extreme violence on both sides–then more fire arms will be used by the authorities?

Liu Xiaoming: I do hope things will calm down.

Murnaghan: What if not?

Liu Xiaoming: I would not answer hypothetic questions. I think things have been improving somewhat in the past few weeks since the Chief Executive started conversation with various sectors. And she also set up a dialogue office and engaged sincerely with people from all walks of life. I think people should give an opportunity to Hong Kong SAR government to address their concerns. We acknowledge there are some deep-seated problems, like housing and opportunities for the young people. But demonstration or violence offers no solution to these deep-seated problems.

Murnaghan: Can I ask you about the plight of the Uygur people in Xinjiang? Our correspondent, Tom Cheshire, has been there recently. He reported from there recently about hundreds of thousands of or millions of people being held in prison camps there.

Liu Xiaoming: That is not true. You know, Xinjiang is the largest province in China. It enjoys prosperity.

Murnaghan: How many people are held in those camps?

Liu Xiaoming: They are not prison camps. They are vocational education and training centres. The measure being taken is for the prevention of terrorism. Xinjiang has been a victim of terrorism and extremism for the past twenty years.

Murnaghan: If you just look at those pictures, you say they are re-education centres, are these people going there voluntarily? They are bound, blindfolded and being marched by police. Are they going into these re-education camps voluntarily?

Liu Xiaoming: No, that is a different story. This is transfer of inmates. The media pick up some clips, but this has nothing to do with the education training centre. The measures were taken exactly for the safety of the majority of Xinjiang people. They are part of the UN early prevention action to prevent terrorism.

Murnaghan: So when they are re-educated, are they free to leave?

Liu Xiaoming: Of course. The basic purpose is to educate these young people so that they could get rid of the extremist ideas. They will learn some skills and they can earn their living. They can earn a living by commanding a skill. On the whole, they will not be intoxicated by the extremist ideas.

Murnaghan: Lastly, Mr. Ambassador, can I ask you about the issue of Huawei? As you know, many nations, including the United States, believe that Huawei has very close links with the Chinese government, so much so the US is banning Huawei's involvement in developments of many of its networks. In the UK, it's still involved in our 5G network. But we've just done an interview today with the US Secretary of Commerce Wilbur Rose who says that the United Kingdom should be very wary of Huawei. If the UK pulls out, what would Chinese attitude be?

Liu Xiaoming: First, I would reject totally the accusation against Huawei. This is a good company. It is a private company. It has nothing to do with the Chinese government. It is a leader in 5G telecommunications. I think they are here for win-win collaboration with British counterparts. They are contributing to the development of telecommunication industry in the UK. I do hope that the UK government will make a wise decision based on the national interest of the UK.

Murnaghan: But President Trump is putting a lot of pressure on Boris Johnson. We know they talked about it together. If the UK did ban Huawei, what would China's attitude be, for instance, to a trade deal with the UK post Brexit?

Liu Xiaoming: I think if UK got rid of Huawei, it would send a very bad, negative message. UK is regarded as a most open, business friendly country. But if Huawei were shut out of it, this would send a negative message worldwide. It would also send a bad message to Chinese businesses, Chinese investments, here in this country. So I do hope that the UK government will make its decision based on UK national interests and the interests of China-UK collaboration.

Murnaghan: Ambassador, thank you very much indeed.

Liu Xiaoming: My pleasure.

A Live Interview with Kirsty Wark on BBC *Newsnight*

On 4th October 2019, I gave a live interview on BBC *Newsnight* hosted by Kirsty Wark to explain China's position on the situation in Hong Kong and the Prohibition on Face Covering Regulation. The full text is as follows:

Wark: I'm now indeed joined by the Chinese Ambassador, Liu Xiaoming. Thank you very much for coming in, Ambassador. First of all, real escalation tonight. More people wear face masks. Are you shocked at the defiance?

Liu Xiaoming: No, not at all. I think the ban is timely and necessary. The purpose of this face mask ban is to stop the violence, to restore order, and to deter further violence.

Wark: But it hasn't worked tonight.

Liu Xiaoming: It's still too early to tell. You know it's just a few hours. We will see. it's too early to tell the result of this ban. I think the Special Administrative Region government is determined to stop violence and restore order.

Wark: It hasn't been able to restore order so far. And the ban has had, it seems, it has had the impact of saying to people, you know, we're not going to stand for this. We are gonna come out. We're gonna wear a face mask. We are not going to be told what to do.

Liu Xiaoming: I think you really need to separate peaceful demonstrators from die-hard radicals. I think the Special Administrative Region government decided to introduce the ban because the situation has escalated to a dangerous level. So, according to the Chief Executive, it's time to introduce a ban.

Wark: Has Carrie Lam lost control?

Liu Xiaoming: I don't think so. I think the situation is still under control and we have full confidence.

Wark: It doesn't look like under control.

Liu Xiaoming: If she lost control, how could she try to introduce this ban?

Wark: But the problem is that the police are firing live rounds. A young boy had, you know, a shot in the leg. So we've seen shooting before. This is not the look of an authority in control.

Liu Xiaoming: The reason why police shot is because their lives were under a serious threat. Let us see how your British police would have handled the situation. I quote, according to Simon Chesterman, the Chief Constable of the British police, "Armed police officers are highly trained to shoot to neutralise the threat in order to protect the public, their colleagues or themselves. "

Wark: But the public themselves are on the streets. Do you still have full confidence in Carrie Lam?

Liu Xiaoming: Yes, I can say that in a very resolute term.

Wark: You heard Gabriel Gatehouse saying there, and the Reuters reported that the People's Armed Police have already had 3,000 to 5,000 paramilitary police and now it's between 10,000 to 12,000. Is that correct? And will you keep putting more paramilitaries in if you don't think Carrie Lam can deal with this?

Liu Xiaoming: We certainly hope the situation would improve, but we have to prepare for the worst. As I said during my press conference: If the situation in Hong Kong becomes uncontrollable for the Hong Kong SAR government and the Central Government will not sit on their hands and watch. I still stand by my statement.

Wark: But what will you do? The Reuters report says there are 10,000 to 12,000 paramilitaries in just now. That's a doubling of what there was. Can you confirm that, first of all?

Liu Xiaoming: I will say, I can confirm the situation is still under control, and we have full trust in the Hong Kong SAR government and its Chief Executive.

Wark: But you say that there will come a point–you know, if over this weekend, there are more demonstrations in the thousands and thousands in the street–there'll come a point where your government really needs to make a decision.

Liu Xiaoming: I think you need to give time to Chief Executive to implement the ban.

Wark: But will you put more troops if you have to?

Liu Xiaoming: If the situation becomes uncontrollable, we certainly would not sit on our hands and watch. Just as the Chief Executive said, her Administration would not allow the situation to get worse and worse.

Wark: You cannot lock up the whole of Hong Kong.

Liu Xiaoming: I have confidence in the Hong Kong SAR Government. I believe this ban will help to improve the situation, and I hope the majority of Hong Kong people will respond to the efforts made by the Special Administration Region and communicate with them.

Wark: But it's been going on all summer. How long will you give it? If Carrie Lam is still, at Christmas, battling protesters, are you not going to do something about that?

Liu Xiaoming: If you compare the situation now with the situation a few months ago, I think things improved somewhat after Carrie Lam withdrew the bill. I think, the problem with the British media, and Western media as a whole, is that you only focus on the rioters and only focus on the violence.

Wark: We are focusing on what we see on the streets. And I wonder if Carrie Lam will have your backing if she has to withdraw this ban in order to restore peace?

Liu Xiaoming: I think she will be determined to implement the ban. And we certainly respect Carrie Lam and her Administration, and we understand her decision, and we show our support for her decision. And we have full trust in her Administration to handle the situation.

Wark: Ambassador, you hear Hong Kongers say they feel they're fighting for their lives, because when they look at the way that you are dealing with the Uygurs on the mainland, the re-education camps, or whatever, and they think this is what lies ahead for them.

Liu Xiaoming: I think this is a made-up story by your media.

Wark: How is it made up?

Liu Xiaoming: What you are talking about is the vocational training and education centre in Xinjiang. That is for the prevention of terrorism. Since this measure was introduced in Xinjiang, there has been no single terrorist case in the past three years.

And before that, for twenty years, there were thousands of terrorist activities. We haven't seen any coverage by BBC or any Western media. Where are you? Where were you then? Tell me!

Wark: Ambassador, as you said, you put in anti-terrorist forces to deal with Uygurs. These paramilitaries that are in Hong Kong are of the same stripe.

Liu Xiaoming: Not in Hong Kong. You mixed up things. They are inside in China. In Hong Kong, it is the Hong Kong police that's handling the situation.

Wark: But we know that there are paramilitaries in Hong Kong at the moment. And according to Reuters, they are increasing.

Liu Xiaoming: No! Not at all.

Wark: So, my point is that people fear for their lives. They feel this is the only alternative they have. Because what they want is: they want Carrie Lam gone, they want an inquiry into the police brutality, and they also want universal suffrage. Are they ever going to get universal suffrage?

Liu Xiaoming: The Central Government has reaffirmed our commitment to "One Country, Two Systems". President Xi Jinping repeated this commitment on the eve of Chinese National Day that we are committed to "One Country, Two Systems". We will continue to let Hong Kong people administer Hong Kong, and Hong Kong will continue to enjoy a high degree of autonomy. That's a very firm commitment.

Wark: So did you have a commitment that the mainland Chinese government will never step in and take over Hong Kong ever?

Liu Xiaoming: That commitment has been made for fifty years and the policy will remain for fifty years and we are committed to it.

Wark: Thank you very much, Ambassador.

Liu Xiaoming: My pleasure.

Kirsty Wark is *Newsnight's* longest-serving presenter, having joined the programme in 1993. She was named journalist of the year by BAFTA Scotland in 1993 and Best Television Presenter in 1997.

A Live Interview with Stephen Sackur on BBC *HARDtalk*

On 26th November 2019, I gave an interview on BBC's *HARDtalk* hosted by Stephen Sackur to expound China's position on Hong Kong, Xinjiang and China's peaceful development. The full transcript is as follows:

Sackur: Ambassador Liu Xiaoming, welcome to *HARDtalk*.

Liu Xiaoming: Thank you for having me.

Sackur: It's a pleasure to have you here. Let us start with Hong Kong. President Xi Jinping has been in power for 7 years. Would you accept that the prolonged unrest and instability in Hong Kong is the greatest challenge he has faced in his presidency?

Liu Xiaoming: I think our government's policy is clear. Twelve days ago, President Xi made a very authoritative statement when he attended the BRICS summit. He said the top priority for Hong Kong is to end violence and restore order.

Sackur: With respect, he's been saying that for months. The violence began in early summer and violence continues. Not just the violence. We also have the massive political expression represented by the results of last Sunday's Council elections. The people of Hong Kong have squarely, by an overwhelming majority, expressed their grave dissatisfaction with the Hong Kong and Beijing authorities.

Liu Xiaoming: First thing first. I think you have to separate the peaceful demonstrators from the violent rioters. You mentioned the latest Council elections. That exactly shows that President Xi's message, loud and clear, has been well received, that you can only exercise the right for democracy in a peaceful environment.

Sackur: If I may just continue with the story about what the Council elections tell us. They had a choice. They had a lot of pro-Beijing candidates. They had a lot of candidates expressing views of the opposition and the protestors, pro-democracy protesters, on the streets. And the overwhelming majority, almost 400 out of the 452 seats, went to those opposition figures. The figures are actually extraordinary, 70% of turnout, 17 of 18 Councils now controlled by the pro-democracy political movement.

Liu Xiaoming: I don't think you should have an over interpretation of the so-called "landslide" victory of the opposition. Though it's 17 out of 18 Councils, in terms of votes, it's 40% versus 60%. So 40% of the voters voted against the opposition. Secondly, like in any country, even in Western culture, incumbents tend to lose votes, if there is a riot, if there is violence, if there is slowdown of economy. That is caused by the violent law-breakers. They cause the big trouble in Hong Kong.

Sackur: But if I may say so, Ambassador, you and many of the Chinese officials have been saying to people like me for months that the silent majority of people in Hong Kong are not with the pro-democracy protesters and demonstrators. They are with Beijing. That's not true and we now know that.

Liu Xiaoming: I think it's still too early to tell. I said 40%, OK. According to some reports, pro-establishment candidates have been harassed, interrupted, threatened and there was even an attempted assassination of one of them, Mr. Ho Kwan-yiu. These violent radicals created terror. I called it "black terror". So that really prevented people from going to the poll.

Sackur: Ambassador, you watched events in Hong Kong from afar like I do on television and you see just as I do the brutal crackdown that Hong Kong police have been implementing against the protesters for months now. The point is that it hasn't worked. Carrie Lam's strategy–she is of course Chief Executive of Hong Kong, representing the interests of Beijing ultimately–she began with a strategy which was built on withdrawing the extradition bill, hoping that would quell the pro-democracy protesters. That didn't work. She then clearly instructed the police to get tough. We've seen that doesn't work. What's Beijing gonna do now?

Liu Xiaoming: I think you missed the whole picture. The problem is not the Hong Kong police. I think the Hong Kong police is the most disciplined, professional and civilized police force in the world. If you compare what is going on in Hong Kong with what is going on in the United Kingdom, do you think the similar situation will go on and on in the UK?

Sackur: Have you seen the picture of a policeman opening fire on the protesters at point blank range?

Liu Xiaoming: The police opened fire in self-defense. They need to safeguard the rule of law. Even here in the UK, I think in the *Newsnight* program, I quoted Simon Chesterman, Chief Constable of the British police. He said that armed police are trained to shoot to protect themselves and to protect lives of their colleagues and public order. You know the problem with the British media is that you only focus on the police reaction. You did not focus on the violent rioters. And you still call these rioters who tossed flammable liquid onto an onlooker who disagreed with them, disapproved their vandalism, and set fire on him–you still say these are protesters.

Sackur: Ambassador, if I may say so, we've interviewed leaders of the protest movement too, and we've asked them about some of the violent tactics that they've employed including the use of petrol bombs and other missiles. So we have questioned them precisely on that basis. But the point for you is that your government is now in a very big hole. The violence continues. The instability continues. Carrie Lam's strategy has failed. Is the next realistic move you have to make to get rid of the Chief Executive, Carrie Lam?

Liu Xiaoming: First, I would say Chief Executive Carrie Lam did a good job. Her team and her administration enjoy full support.

Sackur: That is fascinating. For six months she has failed.

Liu Xiaoming: No, I wouldn't say that she had failed. There are many reasons. She wouldn't if there were no foreign forces behind it, if there were no radical, violent rioters who blocked and sabotaged the conversation. Carrie Lam and her team made many efforts to communicate, to reach out to the public. Since this happened in the past five months, Carrie Lam and her team have conducted more than 100 events to communicate with the local people, but the radicals do not give them the chance or opportunity.

Sackur: You're a veteran ambassador. You know how diplomacy works. I mean, she's got a choice now. She can either make some concessions–that is, establish a truly independent inquiry into the police actions of recent months and make moves towards universal suffrage for the election of the next chief executive–she can either choose to do that or there's gonna have to be a much more serious crackdown, and that crackdown if I may say so is going to have to come not from the Hong Kong police who clearly are not capable of restoring order, but it's going to have to come from the Chinese military,

12,000 of whom are currently based in barracks in Hong Kong. Is that something that you could contemplate?

Liu Xiaoming: I think Carrie Lam and her team made every effort to address the problem. Firstly, she suspended the extradition bill and then she withdrew it. And she also, made what she called four major actions, including more than 100 engagements with local people. But universal suffrage is not something that will come at just a blink of the eye. You know that you, have to go through a legal process. The Central Government is committed to universal suffrage. If it had not been for the opposition to veto the political reform plan in 2015, there would have already been universal suffrage by 2017.

Sackur: There isn't anything like universal suffrage for the key post of Chief Executive. That is ultimately a choice that is based upon nominees selected from Beijing and ultimately voted upon by about 1,000 people. That is very far from universal suffrage. What seems to me is that in the end, Beijing is scared about what is happening in Hong Kong because you fear that the rest of your population in the rest of your nation is watching very carefully to see what happens to this call for genuine, genuine freedom and democracy in Hong Kong.

Liu Xiaoming: I think you missed another big picture. You know, you raised so many topics, so many issues. Let's go one by one. Firstly, about the universal suffrage, as I said, if it had not been for the veto of the opposition to the political reform programme in 2015, by 2017, two years ago, the chief executive would have been selected by universal suffrage. Yes, it's not a hundred percent universal suffrage, but it has to go step by step.

Sackur: Ambassador, you are still a diplomat. You can't dress up...

Liu Xiaoming: You know, when we talk about universal suffrage, there are two areas. One is chief executive and the other is legislative council. So if it had not been for the blocking by the opposition, next year, legislative election will be universal suffrage– one man one vote in Hong Kong for 7 million people.

Sackur: It's not going to be. There isn't universal suffrage. We've just seen the Communist Party in Beijing declared that a decision taken by the High Court in Hong Kong to disregard Carrie Lam's ban on face mask, according to Beijing, according to your Party, is now null and void. So you are now intruding on the fundamental principle of "One Country, Two Systems".

Liu Xiaoming: No, not at all. I think you gave me no opportunity to answer all your questions. You talked about the fundamental question, about the situation in China. You said that people are concerned about what is going on that might spill over to China. That is not the case. You know, we just celebrated 70th anniversary of the founding of the People's Republic of China. So you have to realize what achievements China has made in the past 70 years. People are living better, happier and longer. So within 70 years, we elevated people's life expectancy from 35 to 77. You tell me which country has this achievement. In the past 40 years since reform and opening up, China's status in terms of the world ranking rose from the 11th to the second largest economy. And we have elevated 700 million people out of poverty. So people love the Communist Party of China, and the Communist Party of China is the backbone of the country. So there will be no such thing as you talk about, that what happened to Hong Kong will spill over or cause some huge demonstration in China.

Sackur: You painted a fascinating picture.

Liu Xiaoming: I didn't paint a fascinating picture. It's the fact.

Sackur: Let us explore what you just said, because you're taking it beyond Hong Kong.

Liu Xiaoming: You are taking me beyond Hong Kong.

Sackur: Nobody would doubt the incredible economic achievements of the Chinese government over decades. If you are so insistent that the people of your country are so very happy, why is your government apparently so frightened of dissent inside your country?

Liu Xiaoming: We're not frightened of any dissent.

Sackur: How many political prisoners are there in China?

Liu Xiaoming: There is no political prisoners in China.

Sackur: Ambassador, that's not true.

Liu Xiaoming: The people will not be put behind the bars because of their thoughts. The people are put behind the bar because they have violated the law in China.

Sackur: But your laws preclude genuine political opposition. If people are dissenting from the party line, they will very quickly find themselves contravening your laws.

Liu Xiaoming: No.

Sackur: Not only that, we have seen in the last two or three years, the creation of a surveillance society in China, where every thought and every move made by your population is surveilled.

Liu Xiaoming: Can I ask you a question? How many surveillance CCTV cameras are there here in the UK?

Sackur: Not as many as in China.

Liu Xiaoming: But in per capita...

Sackur: We are not one of the highest...

Liu Xiaoming: So how would you explain this situation?

Sackur: I would explain the situation by pointing out that in China...

Liu Xiaoming: But I am asking you about the CCTV in the UK.

Sackur: In China, there will be one CCTV camera for every two people. You have 1.4 billion people. That is an unimaginable surveillance society. What's it for?

Liu Xiaoming: Have you been to China?

Sackur: I have been to China.

Liu Xiaoming: When was your last visit to China?

Sackur: It was probably about three years ago.

Liu Xiaoming: I think in China, you will feel that people are very free and very happy. You can't feel it? You feel people are under harassment, people are threatened, and they have a lot of complaints? You can see smiling face on the Chinese people. Yes, people have some complaints. In any society people will have complaints. But people have their channels to make their complaints known. We have the National People's Congress and National Committee of the Chinese People's Political Consultative Conference. You feel China has no street politics, so China has no democracy. But

China's democracy is of Chinese characteristic. You can't use your standard to judge other country, just like we would not judge you based on our standard.

Sackur: Let's then talk about Xinjiang, one of the provinces in western China.

Liu Xiaoming: Have you been to Xinjiang yourself?

Sackur: No, I haven't. I would love to go and if you're prepared to invite me to travel.

Liu Xiaoming: Definitely. We have a saying, if you do not go to Xinjiang, you do not know how vast China is and how beautiful China is. This place used to be very peaceful and very prosperous. But between 1990s and 2016, it was not the scene we'd like to see. It became a battleground. There were thousands of terrorist attacks. Thousands of innocent people got killed or injured. In 2014 alone, there were two terrorist attack cases every three days. People cannot walk safely in the street during those days. So people call for the government to take actions. The government, according to law, set up the vocational education and training centres. The purpose is to de-radicalize some young people especially.

Sackur: But you have a problem here, Ambassador. We talked about Hong Kong. We talked about what you're doing to the Uyghurs in the west of your country. The United States Congress has just passed a new round of targeted sanctions against officials in Hong Kong who are leading the crackdown against the protesters. Your diplomatic position, and you know it well yourself because you've just been hauled over by Dominic Raab, the Foreign Secretary in London. You know that your diplomatic position as the Chinese government defends what is happening is coming under enormous pressure.

Liu Xiaoming: I don't think so. I think the Western countries are under enormous pressure for interfering in China's internal affairs. Let me say this. What if China's National People's Congress passed a law concerning a region in the United Kingdom to express our concern and to impose sanction on your politicians if you do not follow the law, what do you think about that? We are in the 21st Century. We are not in the age of the gunboat diplomacy. China is not a country you can kick around.

Sackur: Do you really think that governments in the West in particular are trying to kick you around? You are a long-serving Ambassador. Not so long ago, you and the British government were talking about the "Golden Era" in relations. Now, you've just come back from the foreign office with the Foreign Secretary describing himself as shocked and appalled by the arrest of a former employee in the UK consulate in Hong Kong who was tortured in China. The British government is furious about it. They're just criticizing and condemning your actions in Hong Kong, and in Xinjiang as well. The United States is now saying, and I'm quoting the head of the FBI, "China's goal, it seems, is to replace the US as the world's leading superpower, and they're prepared to break the law to get there". This "Golden Era" has collapsed into recrimination and rivalry.

Liu Xiaoming: So it's my turn to talk?

Sackur: It is.

Liu Xiaoming: I hope you will not interrupt me. I know your *HARDtalk* is about hard subjects. It is not about you talking all the time. First, about Raab's meeting with me. Yes, he did raise this case of Simon Cheng. He didn't mention Xinjiang. Let me tell you this, it is me who expressed our strong opposition to UK interference into China's internal affair, that is, Hong Kong. With regard to Simon Cheng, you know, he violated the law in China for soliciting prostitution. And he confessed all his wrongdoings.

Sackur: I'm sure he did after the usual Chinese torture tactics.

Liu Xiaoming: Would you give me some time to explain before you can interrupt me? You know, you covered so many subjects. I need to come back to you one by one. His so-called charges against China's police are totally rejected. We already made our response to the Foreign Office. We cannot accept the so-called "torture" claim. There's no torture at all. When he was arrested and when he was released, he had physical examinations. His condition was perfect. No problem at all.

Sackur: Ambassador, you have made your points. The bigger point I want to make is...

Liu Xiaoming: So that shows you had such a bias against China.

Sackur: Forgive me. We are almost out of time, so I just want to go to this big point. The US and the UK appear convinced now that, as I just quoted a senior US official, "China's goal is to replace the US as the world's leading superpower". Is that ultimately the strategy in Beijing?

Liu Xiaoming: No, not at all. We're not interested in replacing anyone or challenging anyone. You know, we are still a developing country though we are the second largest economy. In per capita income, we are way behind. You know, it's just less than ten thousand US dollars. This is my third ambassadorship. After my ambassadorship in Egypt, I was seconded to Gansu, one of the poorest provinces in west China. People there did not even have access to drinkable water, you know. They had to build cellars to catch rainwater and then to purify it. Both human being and livestock have to depend on this purified rain water. So it's an enormous challenge for the Chinese government, for the Chinese leaders: How to feed the Chinese population, how to make the Chinese people even happier, live longer. China follows the foreign policy of peaceful development.

Sackur: But you know, Deng Xiaoping famously said China's strategy was to hide the strength, bide your time, never take the lead. That clearly is not the strategy of Xi Jinping.

Liu Xiaoming: Peaceful development is still our strategy, because we benefit from it. People talk about 40 years of miracle in China. We can achieve this because we are in a peaceful environment. We can only have more success by having, and continuing to build, a peaceful environment. So that's why President Xi Jinping calls for building a shared future for mankind. That is our goal and continues to be our goal.

Sackur: Ambassador Liu Xiaoming, thank you very much for being on *HARDtalk*.

Liu Xiaoming: My pleasure.

HARDtalk is a BBC television and radio programme broadcast on the BBC News Channel, on BBC World News, and on the BBC World Service. *HARDtalk* has interviewed many public figures of historical significance. Stephen Sackur is the main presenter. For fifteen years, he was a BBC foreign correspondent and a regular contributor to BBC 4 and a number of newspapers and magazines. He was the moderator of BBC's worldwide broadcast of a debate on climate change with a panel of world leaders.

A Live Interview
on BBC *The Andrew Marr Show*

On 19th July 2020, I gave a live interview on BBC *The Andrew Marr Show* about Hong Kong, Huawei, and Xinjiang. The full text is as follows:

Marr: Ambassador, welcome. Can I, first of all, ask you about Hong Kong? Are rights of dissent and freedom of speech still valued in Hong Kong?

Liu Xiaoming: Fully respected. I think people talk about this National Security Law. National Security Law is about restoring order and protecting the rights of the majority of people. It's targeted on a very small group of criminals who intend to endanger the national security.

Marr: But let me remind people what the National Security Law actually says. It says that Beijing now decides what breaks the law, not Hong Kong itself. Protesters can be arrested just for using placards. Police can search buildings without warrants and trials can be held in secret without a jury. Surely those laws break that "One Country, Two Systems" promise China originally made.

Liu Xiaoming: That is wrong information. I don't know if you have read the National Security Law yet. First, I would say, the Law begins with the statement that China will continue to implement "One Country, Two Systems" and Hong Kong people will administer their affairs with a high degree of autonomy.

The reason why this National Security Law was enacted is that in the past 23 years, although Hong Kong Special Administration Region government is entitled to enact its own law, according to Article 23 of the Basic Law, to protect the national security, because of the opposition–because of these troublemakers' scaremongering–the SAR government failed to enact it. But it is the Central Government's responsibility to take care of national security.

Marr: You said trouble makers. But Amnesty International, which is an organization much respected by many people watching this program, says there was a rapid deterioration in the rights to freedom of peaceful assembly, expression, and association as the Hong Kong authorities increasingly adopted mainland China's vague and all-encompassing definition of national security.

Liu Xiaoming: The Amnesty International is not respected in China because it has made numerous false accusations against China. Never said a nice word, and has never been objective about China. That's the problem of them. We talked about Hong Kong situation last year, this turbulence and riots. Any responsible government has to take measures to address this situation.

Marr: Why couldn't the existing laws be enough to do that, because there are quite strong existing laws? If they are really causing trouble, really trying to cause disruption in Hong Kong, they could have been dealt with by existing laws.

Liu Xiaoming: That is exactly the reason why there should be a national security law, because the existing laws fail to contain this violence, looting, smashing, and storming the legislative council–just imagine if people stormed the British parliament! But that was possible in Hong Kong because there's no law governing national security in Hong Kong for the past 23 years.

Marr: Isn't the real problem that you don't want people in Hong Kong to talk about democracy in Hong Kong. President Trump said this. He says their freedom has been taken away. Their rights have been taken away. No special privileges, and with it goes Hong Kong, he said, because it will no longer be able to compete with free markets. A lot of people will be leaving Hong Kong. They are leaving Hong Kong for Australia, the United States, and for the UK. Will they be free to leave?

Liu Xiaoming: Certainly, they are free to leave. Hong Kong people enjoy unprecedented freedom after the handover for the past 23 years. Before the handover, what kind of freedom did they have? Did they have the freedom to elect their governor? The last governor was appointed by British government. But for the past 23 years, there were five Chief Executives elected by the Hong Kong people.

Marr: Surely the fundamental truth is that under your new leader, you have a nationalistic, more assertive regime in Beijing. And the real question is whether that regime can have a completely open relationship with free markets around the world. And Hong Kong is the epicenter for that.

Liu Xiaoming: I think you have a very wrong impression about what is going on in China. Let me give you an update. You don't trust our statement. You always regard it as propaganda. But it seems to me you trust Americans more. You don't regard them as propaganda. The Harvard University's Kennedy School of Government just issued a report. They did this report covering last 13 years. They did polling. The conclusion is, the Chinese people's rating of satisfaction for Chinese Communist Party and Chinese government is 93%, much higher than any western government, western leadership. So that's the fact about what is going on in China.

Marr: We are going to get a response from the British government this coming week over Hong Kong, and there are reports that, for instance, the Magnitsky Act might be used to ban individual Chinese people from British territory. And also that the extradition agreement is going to be torn up. What would be China's reaction if that's the case?

Liu Xiaoming: That is totally wrong. We never believe in unilateral sanction. We believe that the UN has the authority to impose sanctions. If the UK government goes as far as to impose sanctions on any individual in China, China will certainly make resolute response to it. You've seen what happened between China and the United States. They sanctioned Chinese officials. We sanctioned their senators and officials. I do not want to see this tit-for-tat between China and the US happen in China-UK relations. I think the UK should have its own independent foreign policy rather than to dance to the tune of Americans, like what happened to Huawei.

Marr: You've talked about the possibility of tit-for-tat or reprisals. Let me ask about Huawei because when the Huawei decision was announced, the Chinese foreign ministry said that it would severely undermine mutual trust and come at a cost. Can I ask you what the cost is?

Liu Xiaoming: We are still evaluating the consequences. This is a very bad decision. When this decision was announced, I said, this is a dark day for Huawei. It's a dark day for China-UK relations. It's an even darker day for the United Kingdom, because you will miss the opportunity to be a leading country. I happen to agree with Martin Jacques who is a British scholar and historian.

Marr: He knows China well.

Liu Xiaoming: He knows China well. He wrote a book entitled *When China Rules the*

World. He has this good line: In 1793, the Chinese emperor Qianlong told the English King "We have not the slightest need of your country's manufactures", and that marked the start of 150-year decline of China. History turns full cycle. 227 years later, in 2020, the UK told China, "We do not have the slightest need of your 5G technology". So I do not know what will happen in the next 150 years.

Marr: Is China–looking at the TikTok's decision as well–is China going to punish British companies like for instance Jaguar Land Rover which is operating in China as part of the response?

Liu Xiaoming: We do not want to politicize the economy. That is wrong. It's wrong for the United Kingdom to discriminate against Chinese companies because of pressure from the United States. Some people are talking about "national security risk". There is no hard, solid evidence to say Huawei is a risk to the UK. They've been here for 20 years. They have made a huge contribution not only to the telecom industry of this country. They have fulfilled their corporate responsibility. They have helped the UK to develop. Prime Minister Boris Johnson has an ambitious plan to have full coverage of 5G by 2025. I think Huawei can deliver that. Huawei can be a big help. But now it seems to me the UK just kicks them out and, to use the media words, to purge them under the pressure from the United States. The US leaders have claimed credit for this.

Marr: Let's turn to vaccine development. Now, Britain has accused Russia of trying to steal vaccine secrets. And when I had Rick Scott, the American senator from Florida, very, very close to Donald Trump on this program, he accused China of much the same thing. He said we have evidence–that's the United States–that China is trying to sabotage or slow down our ability to get this vaccine done. It came through our intelligence community. What's your response?

Liu Xiaoming: Those China bashers have made countless accusations. I don't think I should spend time refuting their accusation against China. China is very open and China is working also with the UK scientists on vaccine. And President Xi made it very clear at the World Health Assembly that we'll make it a public good when it's ready. We want to make it accessible, especially in the poorest countries in Africa.

Marr: Let's turn to the single biggest problem at the moment between China and the West, which is the treatment of the Uighur people in north China. Let's look at some very disturbing drone footage that has been widely shared around the world. This is almost certainly over northern China, over Xinjiang. Can you tell us what is happening here? (Video is played)

Liu Xiaoming: I cannot see this as you do. This is not the first time you showed me a video. I still remember last year, you showed me what you thought was happening in Xinjiang. Let me tell you this about, Xinjiang...Have you been to Xinjiang yourself?

Marr: No, I never have.

Liu Xiaoming: Xinjiang is regarded as the most beautiful place in China? There's a Chinese saying you do not know how big China is until you visited Xinjiang...

Marr: Ambassador, that is not a beautiful coverage however, is it?

Liu Xiaoming: That is exactly what I'm going to tell you. Since 1990, Xinjiang has come under a challenge because of the thousands of terrorist attacks. People cannot...

Marr: That was 10 years ago. Can I ask you why people are kneeling, blindfolded and shaven, and being led to trains in northern China? What is going on there?

Liu Xiaoming: I do not know where you get this video tape. Sometimes you need to transfer prisoners, you know, in any country.

Marr: But just what is happening here, Ambassador?

Liu Xiaoming: I do not know where you got these video clips.

Marr: These have been going around the world. They've been authenticated by western intelligence agencies and by Australian experts who say these are Uyghur people being pushed on the train and then taken off to...

Liu Xiaoming: Let me tell you this. The so-called Western intelligence agencies keep making up false accusations against China. They said one million or more Uyghur have been persecuted. What is the population of Xinjiang? Forty years ago, its population was about 4 to 5 million. Now it's 11 million. And people say we have ethnic cleansing. But the population has been doubled in 40 years.

Marr: I'm so sorry to interrupt. But according to your own local government's statistics, the population growth in Uyghur jurisdictions in that area has fallen by 84 percent between 2015 and 2018.

Liu Xiaoming: That's not right. I give you an official figure. I give you this figure as a Chinese ambassador. This is a very authoritative figure. In the past 40 years, the population in Xinjiang has doubled. So there's no so-called the restriction of population and there is no so-called forced abortion, and so on.

Marr: But there is a program of forced sterilization being imposed on Uyghur women at the moment. It's gone on for a long time. And people, who are finally coming out of China, are talking about it. And I've got the witness statement from a woman who's on *Newsnight*, a brave woman who talked about it openly. You can now watch. Here is somebody who went through the forcible sterilization program in China. (Video is played)

Liu Xiaoming: I can easily refute this accusation. There are some small groups of anti-Chinese people working against the interests of China. But the majority of Xinjiang people are happy with what is going on in Xinjiang.

In the past three years, there's no single terrorist attack in Xinjiang. Uyghur People enjoy harmonious life and peaceful, harmonious coexistence with people of other ethnic groups. Uyghur people are just one small portion of the Chinese population and even the Muslims in China. The majority of them are living happily, peacefully and harmoniously with other ethnic groups. We have a very successful ethnic policy. We treat every ethnic group as equal. (Video is played)

Liu Xiaoming: First of all, there's no so-called pervasive, massive, forced sterilization of Uyghur people in China. This is totally against the truth. Secondly, the government policy is strongly opposed to this kind of practice. I cannot rule out single cases. For any country, single cases exits.

Marr: You cannot rule out at all, but the general view...

Liu Xiaoming: The general view is that it is not a government policy and we treat every ethnic group in China as equal.

Marr: When we see interviews like that and we see people blindfolded and led off to trains to be taken to re-education camps. It reminds people in the West what was going on in Germany in the 1930s and 1940s.

Liu Xiaoming: That's completely wrong. There is no such thing as a "concentration camp" in Xinjiang. I think we discussed that before. With regard to that video clip,

I will get back to you. You know, even if we are in the information age, there are all kinds of fake accusations against China.

Marr: Let me remind you what the UN Convention on the Prevention and Punishment of the Crime of Genocide says. It says the genocide is killing people, causing serious bodily or mental harm, deliberately inflicting conditions of life calculated to bring about a group's physical destruction, imposing measures intended to prevent births, and forcibly transferring children to another group. All of those things, it is alleged to have been happening in China and China is going to face accusations at the United Nations about this.

Liu Xiaoming: This is not true. The fact just shows the opposite. People in Xinjiang enjoy happy life. They call for order to be restored in Xinjiang. China is strongly opposed to any torture, persecution and discrimination of people of any ethnic group. This is not the case in China. The policy of the Chinese government is, as I said, every ethnic group in China is treated equal. That's the success story of Chinese ethnic policy.

Marr: Is it any longer possible for the West to deal with the country which is so nationalistic and so much under the thumb of the Communist Party leadership?

Liu Xiaoming: I do not agree with your description of China. It is not China that becomes "so nationalistic". People say China is becoming very nationalistic. That's totally wrong. China has not changed. It's the Western countries headed by the United States. They started this so-called "new cold war" on China. They have this sanction, they have this smearing and name-calling. Take what happened with this coronavirus. They still keep calling it "China virus" and "Wuhan virus". It's totally wrong, but we have to make a response. We do not provoke. But once we were provoked, we have to make a response.

Marr: Ambassador, thanks very much indeed for coming to talk to us today. Much appreciated.

Liu Xiaoming: My pleasure.

COVID-19

A Live Interview
on BBC *The Andrew Marr Show*

On 9th February 2020, I gave a live interview on BBC *Andrew Marr Show* about China's fight against the novel coronavirus epidemic. The full text is as follows:

Marr: The Chinese Ambassador Liu Xiaoming is joining me now.

Liu Xiaoming: Thanks for having me.

Marr: Ambassador, welcome. Can I ask you first of all to update us on the number of people infected in China so far as you know and sadly, the number of people who have died?

Liu Xiaoming: According to the latest figures by midnight Beijing time, the number of death cases is 811 and cured cases is 2,649. That is very encouraging. That means the number of cured cases is three times the death cases. That shows the effectiveness of the treatment. And also, we have seen that the confirmed cases for the first time exceed the suspected cases. That means the hospitalization rate is coming up. You know, we built two hospitals within ten days. These figures show the improvement of the treatment and hospitalization.

Marr: Is it the impression that the rate of infection, however, is still increasing?

Liu Xiaoming: Yes, the rate is increasing. But I think people should not panic. If you compare the fatality rate–currently, it is 2%, much lower than the Ebola which is 40%, and even lower than SARS which is 10%. So there is no reason to panic. The Chinese government has adopted the most comprehensive and strict, unconventional control measures.

Marr: You've done some extraordinary things as a government. You have effectively quarantined, you put a roadblock as it were around whole cities. And big parts of the transport system and the economy have closed down while this is going on. Can I ask you, how long is this going to have to go on for?

Liu Xiaoming: At this moment, it is very difficult to predict when we are going to have the inflection point. We certainly hope it will come sooner. But the isolation and quarantine measures have been very effective. So far, the most cases are concentrated in Hubei and Wuhan. Hubei is about the size of England plus Scotland, and the population is about England plus Wales. So this is such a large area.

Marr: 65 million people, therefore, around about that?

Liu Xiaoming: It's 59 million. The measure has been effective. Otherwise, it will spread out to the other parts of China. And also, I think the Chinese people are making a contribution not only for the safety of life and health of ourselves but also to that of the world people.

Marr: Indeed. Is the Chinese government ready to take the same kind of measures in other places in China, other cities?

Liu Xiaoming: It depends. I think there are some prevention and control measures taken in other parts of China. But, you know, China itself is different.80% of the cases are concentrated in Hubei province. But people have to be cautious. So there are prevention and control measures taken in other parts of China.

Marr: There was the very difficult case of the young doctor Li Wenliang, who was the first person who alerted people that there was something strange going on, a new virus that was worrying and unknown. And the Chinese authorities arrested him and gave him a notice of admonishment and they were very, very tough with him. They said if you are stubborn, refused to repent and continue to carry out illegal activities, you will be punished by the law. And then sadly, he died. Do you think the Chinese state has made a mistake in that case?

Liu Xiaoming: I would correct you here. It's not Chinese authorities. It is local authorities. Chinese authorities as a matter of fact, we have a supervision committee. It has sent an investigation team down to Wuhan to find out what was really going on. People feel very sad. I tweeted to express my condolences and paid tribute to Dr. Li. He will be remembered as a hero. He will be remembered for his bravery and contribution to the fight of this disease. But he is one of the millions of the Chinese medical doctors and nurses. We have so many of them on the forefront of this battle.

Marr: Many of them are being heroic at the moment. But nonetheless, he was very open about the need for openness. Is this the moment where the Chinese state looks into the situation and says, we need to be more open and move more quickly when it comes to this kind of situation.

Liu Xiaoming: We are open. We shared all the information about the practice, the cases of disease. We welcome international cooperation as well. We believe this virus is the enemy of mankind. So people of all countries should work together to fight against the common enemy. And also, we work very hard with British scientists. So my Embassy tries very hard to facilitate Chinese scientists working with the British scientists to develop medicine and vaccine.

Marr: A very simple question is that if the Chinese state, with all its power and the way it operates, can't stop this from spreading–now it's out of China, it's going to spread everywhere, isn't it?

Liu Xiaoming: We will try our best. But I still want to caution people: don't panic. We believe this virus is controllable, preventable and curable. So we are confident that with the strong leadership of the Central Government of China, with the people of China united behind the government and with the broad support of the international community, we can beat this virus and win the battle.

Marr: You also know of course that China is very, very important in the entire world economy. Lots and lots of companies, from Apple, making iPhones, to car-makers and fashion companies, are already seeing problems in the supply chain and they are asking–I'll put this brutally and simply–when will the factories reopen?

Liu Xiaoming: Certainly, there is an impact on the economy. But I think the impact is temporary and short-term. The government now works very hard to encourage people to restore production. You said at the very beginning that we have waged a people's war. So the whole country has been mobilized. And I think you have to keep the confidence in Chinese economy, because the fundamentals of the economy are still sound. The IMF, the World Bank and many respected economists in the world believe that the long-term Chinese economy is very resilient.

Marr: There is going to be a very, very acute short-term hit to the economy. Lots and lots of companies are worried. I will ask again, do you know when Chinese factories will reopen? When will iPhones be manufactured again?

Liu Xiaoming: I can't answer for iPhone. But I think the big smart phone producer Huawei is working round clock. I know you will ask me about Huawei. But they are doing very well in China. In China, we have a saying. Do you speak Chinese?

Marr: I speak no Chinese, as you may have noticed.

Liu Xiaoming: The Chinese word for "crisis" is the combination of two words, crisis and opportunities. We always believe there are opportunities in crisis. So we will try our best to turn crisis into opportunities.

Marr: Let me ask you about the opportunities here. As I said right at the beginning, there is a sense the Chinese state was hiding things and a lot of people were highly skeptical about the Chinese state when it said this or that. And I ask again, is this a moment when the Chinese Communist Party and the people within China look at the situation and think we need to be a much more open society than we have been? This is a moment of change in turn?

Liu Xiaoming: We didn't hide anything. If you talk to the WHO Director-General Dr. Tedros, he spoke highly of the efforts made by China. We shared information with the WHO, shared information with countries like the UK and other relevant countries and regions. They all spoke highly of China's transparency and openness.

Marr: And if I may just interrupt for a second. In Wuhan, about 20 million people were in and left the province after it was known that this virus was out on 22nd January. In other words, right at the beginning there was not enough speed and the local authority did crack down on Dr. Li. Are they going to be punished for that?

Liu Xiaoming: You know, this is a new virus. People do not know it well. It will take some time for people to understand it. But once people realize the risk and danger, people will be mobilized. You have to adopt a reasonable approach. Dr. Li, as I said just a moment ago, he did a marvelous job. People paid tribute to him. And the central authorities sent an investigation team to find out what was really happening. I will get back to you if you would like to have a conclusion to find out what really happened. Those who had misconduct will be made accountable for their conduct, to be held responsible for the handling of this case.

Marr: Ambassador, you said I was going to raise Huawei and I am, absolutely. Because there are five leading conservative MPs who are competing with other conservative MPs to reverse the decision to ensure Huawei is kept out of the system, because they see Huawei as, first of all, absolutely connected to the Chinese state and being unreliable when it comes to transmissions and secrecy. This is part of our national infrastructure, they say, and there's no way China would allow a British company to be absolutely at the centre of their national infrastructure in the same way.

Liu Xiaoming: I think they are totally wrong. What they are doing is a kind of witch-hunt. Number one, Huawei is a privately owned company having nothing to do with the Chinese government. The only problem they have is that they are a Chinese company, and that's the problem. China is more open, as we get back to your original argument. Since the reform and opening up, China has run a market orientated economy, and one third of Chinese economy is privately owned. The other one third is owned by foreign and joint ventures. So Huawei is an independent company and the leader in this area. I think the reason why the Prime Minister decided to keep Huawei is he has a very ambitious plan for the UK. He wants to have 5G coverage in the UK by 2025. Huawei can be of great help.

Marr: But the price he paid for that was the incandescent anger of Donald Trump. How do you respond when you heard Donald Trump absolutely blasting Boris Johnson? Were you pleased when he jumped to your side of the fence?

Liu Xiaoming: I will leave the Prime Minister to deal with President Trump. I always say, Great Britain can only be great when it has its own independent foreign policy. So I do hope that the Prime Minister will stay with his decision, because I think it is in the interest of the UK. It's also in the interest of China-UK cooperation. The important thing is that it is in the interest of maintaining British image as the most open and free market economy in the world. Although we are not 100% satisfied–the 35% percent cap does not show your principle of free economy and free competition–I think it's a good decision.

Marr: Ambassador, thanks very much indeed for talking to us.

Liu Xiaoming: My pleasure.

An Interview with Deborah Haynes on Sky News

On 18th February 2020, I gave an interview to Deborah Haynes, Foreign Editor of Sky News, on the telephone conversation between President Xi Jinping and Prime Minister Boris Johnson. I also answered questions about China's fight against the COVID-19 epidemic and other issues. The contents of the interview were aired on Sky News "*Nightly News*" and every hour. The transcript is as follows:

Haynes: Ambassador, have you something you want to share?

Liu Xiaoming: Yes, very good news. President Xi Jinping and Prime Minister Boris Johnson just had a telephone conversation. This is the first conversation between the two leaders after Prime Minister Johnson got reelected. They had a very good conversation. They talked about China's battle against COVID-19 and President Xi emphasized that China has taken very comprehensive, strict and thorough prevention and control measures. The whole country has been mobilized and our methods are showing positive effect. We are confident that we have the capability to win the battle against the virus. The Prime Minister spoke highly of China's efforts, China's contribution, and appreciated highly the speed and effectiveness of the measures taken by China. They also talked about how China and UK can collaborate to fight shoulder to shoulder against the virus.

President Xi also said that we are open and transparent in terms of collaboration with the international community, including the UK. We are responsible not only for the health and safety of the Chinese people, which is the top priority of the government work. We are also making contribution to safety and health of all people of the world people by contributing to global public health. We appreciate the support given by the British side. Prime Minister Johnson also expressed readiness to assist further.

They also talked about how the two countries will strengthen China-UK relationship for the next ten years. Prime Minister Johnson also mentioned the "Golden Era" and they've reached broad consensus.

Talking about the relationship, the Prime Minister told President Xi that he loves China, and he and his administration want to work with China to elevate the relationship to a new level. President Xi also expressed our commitment to the relationship. China and UK are both countries of global influence and permanent members of the UN Security Council. There are enormous common interests between our two countries not only on bilateral issues but also on multilateral agenda. The Prime Minister mentioned the COP15 (the 15th Meeting of the Conference of the Parties of the Convention on Biological Diversity) and COP26 (the 26th Meeting of the Conference of the Parties of the UN Convention on Climate Change) . He believed that there are lots of opportunities between China and UK to work on the global agenda and address the global challenges, like climate change. It's a very good conversation, which not only set the tone but also set the new direction for China-UK relations at this critical moment between China and UK. That's basically the good news I want to let you know, first hand.

Haynes: Thank you. And in the conversation, did they talk about a trade deal and the timeline, when that would be achieved?

Liu Xiaoming: They covered broad issues. When it comes to the trade deal, we are open. Once UK leaves EU, you'll have a new free trade agreement with China and we are open to that. Last year, the two countries set up a working team to carry out feasibility studies on the trade deal. But last year the British government was so focused on Brexit. This year after you have Brexit done, I think your top priority is still negotiating with your EU partners. China is open and ready to engage with UK to reach a new agreement on trade.

Haynes: Those working groups paused, as I understand, last year because of the Brexit, in part. Have they restarted?

Liu Xiaoming: We are ready to work with British colleagues at any time. I think UK is still in a process of making adjustments: you just had a new administration, a new reshuffle. We do not know who will be the minister responsible for bilateral trade. We are ready to engage with each other, and the British side has already expressed willingness as well. But because now we are focusing on the battle against the virus, it will probably still take some time for the two sides to get into the details. I think both sides have the willingness to engage with each other more positively.

Haynes: Did the two leaders talk about security, and Huawei and 5G?

Liu Xiaoming: I don't have the specific information. But the President mentioned that we hope that the two countries should show respect for each other and attach importance to the main concerns and core interests. Both sides will work together to build open economic relations and to be committed to free trade and multilateralism. I think the messages are very clear.

Haynes: Do you think that frankly speaking, if Britain hadn't made that decision to choose Huawei to be part of the network, this telephone call wouldn't have happened?

Liu Xiaoming: I would not link the telephone call with one specific case. Because this telephone call is about a much bigger picture. Prime Minister Johnson would like to know first hand from the President how things are going on in China. From the President's remarks, the Prime Minister would feel much more confident that the virus is under control and China's measures are showing positive effects. In fact, I think your audience might be interested in the most recent positive signs in our work. I just received the figures which show "three firsts". As of today, it is the first time that the confirmed cases were brought down to less than 2,000, the death cases were brought down to less than 100, and the confirmed cases outside Hubei were brought down to less than 100. That shows the quarantine efforts and measures are taking very good effect. Also it's about how China and UK can work together, to use the Prime Minister's term, "shoulder to shoulder", to fight against this virus. This virus is not only a challenge to the Chinese government, but also a challenge to the whole world. So the international community has to work together. The UK has offered its assistance and expressed willingness to help China. We highly appreciate that. And also about the big picture of China-UK relations, Huawei is just one of the issues or maybe one part of China-UK relations.

Haynes: How can UK help China deal with the virus? What are the specifics?

Liu Xiaoming: First, we appreciate the sympathy and support expressed by the British people from all walks of life. Her Majesty the Queen passed on the message through the Duke of York to President Xi and the Chinese people. The President highly appreciated that. Prime Minister Johnson also wrote a letter to Premier Li Keqiang to show support and sympathy. We received many donations from British businesses, both in terms of medical supplies badly needed in China and also from students, even ordinary people, average citizens. Here at the Embassy we received letters showing their sympathy, support and donations. We highly appreciate it. The British government sent two shipments of medical supplies to China, which is also highly appreciated.

Haynes: Do you believe the peak has been reached now in China?

Liu Xiaoming: I cannot say for sure that we have reached the peak because there are still new confirmed cases and fatality cases every day, though they have been brought down tremendously. Yesterday the death cases outside Hubei was only 5, and most death cases are happening in Hubei. The cured cases are increasing tremendously. Now they are about seven times the number of death cases. That shows the effectiveness of the medical treatment of the patients. I can't say when we are going to have the inflection point. I do hope that we will get there sooner. But I think, with these effective measures, and if we keep working, we will reach the peak. I hope we will see the absolute reduction of death cases sooner.

Haynes: Do you think the authority reacted too slowly and tried to cover up the obvious in the early days?

Liu Xiaoming: I don't think so. I think the Central Government attached great importance to this. As the President emphasized, the life and safety of the people is the top priority of the government work, and he called 3 meetings of the top leadership, that is, the Standing Committee of the Political Bureau of the CPC, to map out emergency measures. The Central Government set up a task force to lead the efforts of the whole country. The military has been mobilized. But this virus is really something very new. People do not understand it. In recent days, it got a new name from the World Health Organization. So people should understand that it will take time for people to understand and to respond. As I said, Prime Minister Johnson appreciated the speed and effectiveness of the measures taken by the Chinese government. So I can say with certainty that the government has made every effort to address this challenge. The government has also tried every effort to be transparent, to share all the information with the WHO and also with relevant countries including the UK. Chinese scientists and British scientists are working together on the drug and vaccine. I do hope scientists will make early success on this.

Haynes: You said at your press conference that you didn't think the Chinese economy will be too badly affected in areas obviously like tourism and travel. And yet we're hearing that South Korea express concern of the knock-on effect on its economic prospects. And big companies like Apple too are saying that their profits are going to be affected. Can you say now, with a better picture of what's going on, how grave the effect the epidemic is having on the Chinese economy, and potentially the world economy?

Liu Xiaoming: I would say there will be impacts on the economy. Even here–I watched the television the other day–I'm not sure it was Sky News or BBC–people are talking about the reduction of tourism and Chinese shoppers, and at the Bicester Village, many shops are closed, and some tourist attractions do not have any more Chinese tourists. Yes, there will be some impacts. But I think the impacts are short-term and temporary, because the fundamentals of the Chinese economy are still good. The Chinese economy is still very resilient. The reform and opening-up will continue and China will open wider. Starting from this year, on 1st January, the Foreign Investment Law took effect. The Chinese government puts emphasis on two fronts: one is the battle against the virus, and the other is the resumption of production. You can see the country mobilized to fight the two battles. I think in the long term, the Chinese economy is still good and President Xi Jinping also told Prime Minister Johnson that we are confident that we will reach the target of our economic development this year. This year is a very important year for China–we'll achieve our centenary goal, that is, to complete the building of a moderately prosperous society in all aspects and to eliminate extreme poverty in China.

Haynes: Do you have a statement too about the Xinjiang-related leaks?

Liu Xiaoming: That is totally a rumor and made-up story. I said on many occasions that Xinjiang is not about human rights, not about religion. It's about anti-terrorism. And the rights of religious freedom are fully protected in Xinjiang, and people enjoy happy life. Thank you.

Haynes: Thank you, Ambassador.

Liu Xiaoming: My pleasure.

A Live Interview with Stephen Sackur on BBC *HARDtalk*

On 28th April, 2020, I gave an interview on BBC's *HARDtalk* hosted by Stephen Sackur, where I shared the timeline of China's efforts to contain the spread of COVID-19 and gave an update on what China is doing to join the international cooperation in response to the pandemic. The full transcript is as follows:

Sackur: Ambassador Liu Xiaoming, welcome to *HARDtalk*.

Liu Xiaoming: Thank you. Good to be with you again.

Sackur: We are delighted to have you on our program in this difficult time. Let me start actually with a very simple direct question: Do you accept that COVID-19 has its origins in China?

Liu Xiaoming: It was first reported in Wuhan, but I can't say it's originated from Wuhan. According to many reports including BBC reports, it can be anywhere. It is found on aircraft carriers. It is even found in the submarine. It is found in some countries with very little connection with China and also found in groups of people who have never been to China. So we cannot say it's originated from China.

Sackur: I'm a little confused by that answer. Clearly, it is a new virus. It originated somewhere. It seems, according to all of the immunologists and virologists, the virus crossed from animals to humans. And there was a first case and then it spread. There is no doubt that the first case was in China. I'm wondering why you are telling me that it spread all over the world and people who caught it had never been to China. That is clear because it's become a pandemic. But the question that matters so much is: Where did it start?

Liu Xiaoming: I think this question is still up for scientists to decide. I read the report that the first case in China was reported on the 27th December by Dr. Zhang Jixian to Chinese local health authorities. But I also read reports that some of the cases were found to be much earlier than that. We read even the report by your newspapers yesterday that your scientists, medical advisers, even warned your government that there might be a virus unknown to us, much earlier, last year. So all I can say is that the first reported case in China was on 27th December in Wuhan.

Sackur: I think there's no doubt experts believe the origin of the first outbreak, first examples of this COVID-19 virus to be found in human beings, came from Wuhan and the surrounding area in China. I just wonder whether you accept that it is very important that we understand exactly what happened at the beginning of this outbreak, that we understand frankly what mistakes and missteps were made, which allowed the first outbreak to become a global pandemic.

Liu Xiaoming: I think it is still debatable. I think we have to agree to disagree. I think it was first reported in Wuhan, China, but I can't say it originated from Wuhan. Let me tell you the timeline of China's fight against this virus. It was first reported on the 27th December by Dr. Zhang, and then Chinese health authorities and CDC notified the WHO four days later, on 31st December, in the shortest possible time, and then shared this information with other countries. China also shared the discovery of the pathogen with the WHO in the shortest possible time, and also shared the information about the genetic sequence of the virus in the shortest possible time.

Sackur: Ambassador, let me just interrupt you on this question of timeline because you missed out one very important point. On 30th December, a doctor in Wuhan, Li Wenliang, used his chat group online to tell fellow doctors that there was a new and very worrying disease in Wuhan. He advised his colleagues that they must wear protective clothing to avoid this new infection. And just a couple of days later, he was summoned to the public security bureau. He was made to sign a letter in which he confessed to making false statements that had severely disturbed the social order. That was the beginning of an official cover-up, which continued through the month of January.

Liu Xiaoming: As I said earlier, now I understand why there's a so-called call for independent investigation. They try to find excuse for them to criticize China for cover-up. But the fact is that Li Wenliang was not the first one who discovered this virus. As I told you, it was Dr. Zhang Jixian, and she reported 3 days earlier than Li Wenliang to the health authorities. Then, the health authorities in Wuhan reported to the Central

Government, and then four days later, that means one day after Li Wenliang spread the word, the Chinese authorities shared the information with the WHO and other countries. No cover-up at all.

Sackur: With respect, Mr. Ambassador, the information that was shared was actually extremely limited, because on 14th January, we now know this from leaks that have been given to the *Washington Post* and the Associated Press, we know that internally China's national health commission head, Mr. Ma Xiaowei, laid out a very grim assessment of what was happening. He said that the situation was severe. Complex, clustered cases suggest human to human transmission is happening, the memo said. The risk of transmission and spread is high, but in public, that was internal, but in public, the head of China's disease control emergency center, the very next day, said the risk of sustained human-to-human transmission is low, that it was preventable and controllable. So, I put it to you again, there is compelling evidence that China for weeks did not tell the truth.

Liu Xiaoming: You give me not enough time to answer your question. I haven't answered the question with regard to Li Wenliang. You talk about cover-up. That's not true. Dr. Zhang reported through a normal channel to health authorities, but Li spread this word among his friends. In any country when you have something like the virus which is dangerous to people's health, when there is something unknown, there might be a panic. So I think the police authority summoned Li to warn him not to do it. You can't say this is a cover-up, since we reported through the normal channel. But on this, we need to make sure that there should be no panic. Even today, in the UK, I think your government is fighting misinformation. Some people try to use this to create panic for their own gain.

I think Li's case is closed. After it's reported to the central authorities, the government sent investigation team down to Wuhan and find out that Li did the right thing and the police reprimand has been revoked. And Li was made a martyr and given the highest honor for his contribution.

Sackur: Dr. Li was in deed regarded by the Chinese people as a hero when he died.

Liu Xiaoming: Not only by the Chinese people, but also regarded by the Chinese government. You cannot separate...

Sackur: With respect, I think the people of China are very aware, and I come back to it, that the Chinese government wasn't straight with them, nor with the outside world. Just tell me, if you can one more time, why on 14th January the national health commission document–that was an internal document–was labeled not to be spread on the internet, not to be publicly disclosed, in which they said that there was evidence of human-to-human transmission, clustered cases, severe and complex problem?

Liu Xiaoming: I think all your information is coming from *Washington Post*. I think you depend too much on American media. I really hope you will depend on the WHO for information. We share all the information with the WHO. I watched your interview with Mr. David Nabarro, and I think China has been straightforward, transparent, and swift in terms of sharing information with the WHO. Of course, inside China, we have to take cautious measures. We have to take strict measures to fight this virus. The virus was still unknown then. So people did not know what will happen, what this virus was about. But on the one hand, we share our knowledge, our understanding, with the WHO, with the other countries.

Sackur: But Ambassador, with all respect, your problem is–you're a very senior diplomat and you know this is a problem–that many people around the world simply don't believe the Chinese version of events. Donald Trump, only a few hours ago, said that he is not happy at all with China's stance. They could have stopped the virus at the source, he said, we are undertaking a thorough investigation. And the Vice President Mike Pence has listed a whole host of reasons why the United States believes that China was not straight with the world and is therefore culpable for the fact this pandemic is now causing so much death and so much economic damage right around the world. You have, as China, a massive problem now.

Liu Xiaoming: I don't think so. When you say that China has a massive problem, I think you're talking more about the Western world. Since the outbreak, China has had very strong cooperation with the WHO and with many other countries. We sent technical assistance and experts to and provide medical supplies for more than 150 countries. All of them spoke highly of Chinese efforts. So I can't say the United States represents the world. And even in the Western world, we've been receiving appreciation from the countries like United Kingdom, from France, from Germany.

You quote President Trump. Let me also quote his comments about China. On 24th January, that was almost one month after we reported this virus. He said, United States greatly appreciates China's efforts and transparency. Six days later and he said, they are working very hard, and we are working very closely with China. In early February, he said, President Xi is doing a great job, he handles it well.

Sackur: Things have changed a great deal since the end of January. You say, look at what we've done to deliver medical assistance and equipment around the world. What many people see is China running a campaign of disinformation and propaganda around the world in recent weeks. Your colleague in the Foreign Ministry use social media to promote the conspiracy theory that the US military has smuggled coronavirus into China. Why is your country running this disinformation campaign?

Liu Xiaoming: I think you've picked a wrong target. It's not China who started this campaign of disinformation. If you could compare China's statements and comments by Chinese leaders, Chinese diplomats, Chinese Ambassadors, with their American counterparts, you will know who is spreading disinformation.

Sackur: Do you agree with Zhao Lijian, the Foreign Ministry Spokesman who did put up the link suggesting that the US military has smuggled coronavirus into China? Is that something that you also believe?

Liu Xiaoming: I think what you're saying is that Mr. Zhao retweeted some media report. I do not know why you focus on some comments by individuals in China but miss the disinformation by senior officials, even the national leaders, of the United States who started this campaign of disinformation, especially by the top diplomat, the secretary of state? When it comes to China, there's no any good word about China. And China is really regarded as an evil force, not as a country which has been lending a helping hand to America in the fight against this virus. I do not quite understand.

Sackur: In your view, Ambassador, how deep is the crisis with the United States right now, that has been sparked by all of the accusations that have arisen from the coronavirus? How deep is the diplomatic crisis?

Liu Xiaoming: We certainly want to have good relations with the United States. I've been posted twice to Washington, DC. I always believe that China and the United States will gain from cooperation and lose from confrontation. And we have every reason to have a good relationship with the United States. But it has to be based on mutual trust, coordination and non-confrontation. But you need two to tango.

Since the outbreak, President Xi and President Trump have kept very close contact.

They had two telephone conversations and compared notes, just as President Xi had two telephone conversations with Prime Minister Johnson. We want to build international response to this virus.

I just want to let Americans know that China is not an enemy of the United States. It's the virus that is the enemy of the United States. They need to find the right target.

Sackur: It's a very important message you're sending. Maybe China could consider some gestures that would improve relations with not just the United States but many other countries, including Australia and the UK who've made the same point to your government.

One, will you now categorically guarantee to close down the so-called "wet markets", that there will no longer be the sale of these live wild animals in the food markets that are known as the "wet markets"? Is that now something that has been banned, not just short term, but absolutely banned forever in China?

Liu Xiaoming: First, on your first point about "many countries", I cannot agree with you that China has a problem with many countries. I would say we have more friends than opponents or enemies. A few Western countries do not represent the world. I think China enjoys good relationships with many countries, and I think we are building an international response to the virus. As President Xi said, solidarity and cooperation are the most powerful weapons to fight the pandemic. I will come back to the "wet market".

Sackur: Ambassador, we are short of time. I just need a specific answer on the "wet markets". Are they right now closed for good, yes or no?

Liu Xiaoming: There's no such a thing as a "wet market". This is a Western, a foreign, notion to many Chinese. We do have fresh food markets where fresh vegetables, fresh seafood, fish, are sold, and some live poultry. I think you are talking about the so-called illegal market for selling wildlife. That has been totally banned. The law has been passed and it will be banned permanently.

Sackur: That is therefore a recognition–I just want to be clear–a recognition on your government's part that the dangers of those markets, where live wild animals were sold alongside other food stuff, they were dangers that did cause the spread coronavirus from animals to humans.

Liu Xiaoming: I agree with that. Finally, we have a few points to agree on. I'm very pleased with that. That's why this market, we're talking about, illegal wildlife market, is totally banned. It's illegal to hunt, to trade, to eat wild animals.

Sackur: So people watching this will only wish that you had made that ban real before coronavirus spread and cause such terrible damage around the world. Are you in any way prepared to say sorry for what has happened?

Liu Xiaoming: So you come to your first point again. You can't blame China for coronavirus. That's the problem of this argument. It was found in China. It was found in many other places that have no connection with China at all. So you can't point your fingers at China for the outbreak, and we have done our best.

China is a victim of the coronavirus, but China is not a source of this problem. China is not the producer of this epidemic, and that is something we have to come clean about.

Sackur: China is seen, for example, by leading politicians in this country, like the Chairman of the Parliamentary Foreign Affairs Select Committee, as very much the cause. He's talked about a soviet style system, a toxic system, inside your government, inside your regime, which he says has been responsible not just for betraying the Chinese people and their health or wellbeing, but betraying the wider world as well. And there are now calls in the United Kingdom, and also calls in the United States and other countries, for a disengagement from close economic ties with China. In Britain, it's of course centered on Huawei, your telephones giant's activities in the 5G sector. People say that should no longer be tolerated in the United Kingdom. As the Ambassador in the UK, are you worried that there is going to be now an economic disengagement?

Liu Xiaoming: Yes and no. I think you talk about this person as a very senior politician, but I don't think this view represents the official position of the UK government.

I think the UK government under Prime Minister Johnson is still committed to stronger partnership with China. In his two telephone conversations with President Xi, he reaffirmed UK's commitment to building a Golden Era with China. And we do have very good cooperation with the UK side throughout this outbreak, in addition to intensive communication. I've been here for 10 years as a Chinese Ambassador. I have never seen that our top leaders have such an intensive communications between them.

126

And also at the ministerial level, we have our State Counselor and Foreign Minister Wang Yi having telephone conversation with Secretary Raab, and Yang Jiechi, Director of the Office of the Central Commission for Foreign Affairs, having close contact with the Sir Mark Sedwill. Here in London, I have very close contact with the government secretaries, including Secretaries Mat Hancock and Alok Sharma, and Foreign Secretary Raab. We have a very strong, robust relationship.

And you quote those people using Soviet example. I think this is a totally Cold War mentality. We are living in the third decade of the 21st century, but those people still live in the old days when they were fighting cold war. China is not the former Soviet Union. I think China and the UK are united by common interests rather than divided by our differences. So I'm very confident about this relationship.

Sackur: All right, Ambassador, we have to end there. But I do thank you very much indeed for joining me on *HARDtalk* at this difficult time. Liu Xiaoming, thank you very much indeed.

Liu Xiaoming: My pleasure.

A Live Interview with Mark Austin on Sky News *News Hour*

On 14th May 2020, I gave an online live interview via zoom on Sky News *News Hour* with Mark Austin regarding China's fight against the COVID-19 outbreak. The full transcript is as follows:

Austin: For months now, there have been growing calls around the world for China to come clean about just how the spread of the coronavirus began. China says and most scientists accept that it began in the city of Wuhan. But some, including the US president, say it may not have been spread naturally, but escaped from a laboratory. China has so far refused to invite scientists from the World Health Organization to join in its internal investigation into the source of the virus. There remain many questions, and today we have a rare opportunity to put some of them to China's Ambassador to the UK. Liu Xiaoming joins us now from his Embassy in central London. Good evening to you, Mr Ambassador. Thank you for agreeing to answer questions.

Liu Xiaoming: Good evening. Thank you for having me.

Austin: First of all, do you accept that China has a problem with trust? The world, simply at the moment, doesn't seem to trust China.

Liu Xiaoming: I don't think so. I think we have a good record. China was the first country to report the virus, the first to identify the pathogen, and the first to share the genetic sequence with the WHO and many other countries in a record time. When you said the world, I can't agree with you. I think there are only a few countries that challenge and make some accusations with no grounds at all.

Austin: Let's look at why some of the world may not trust China. Let's go to the beginning and according to your own state news agency, Doctor Zhang Jixian reported her suspicions of the virus to the authorities on 27th December. She suspected human to human transmission because she treated a couple in Wuhan and then their son. But it was not until 22nd January, nearly four weeks later that China through the WHO confirmed human to human transmission. Why was there such a delay?

Liu Xiaoming: That's not true. Doctor Zhang Jixian reported to the local health authority on 27th December. Then four days later, Chinese health authorities notified the WHO office in Beijing. That was four days later. Then on 3rd January, that was seven days later, the National Health Commission, the highest Chinese Central Government authority for health, notified the WHO officially. Since this is a new virus–it is unknown not only to the world but also to China–we have to be responsible. We have adopted a cautious approach, tried our very best. So eleven days later, we identified the pathogen and shared the genetic sequence without delay at all. So I think it's unfair.

Austin: But the WHO timeline says clearly that it was on 22nd January that they confirmed human to human transmission. And this doctor told Xinhua, your news agency, and I quote, it is unlikely that all three members of a family caught the same disease at the same time unless it is an infectious disease. On 27th December, she knew and the authorities in Wuhan knew, but it wasn't until the 22nd January that the WHO confirmed it was human to human transmission.

Liu Xiaoming: As I said, it will take some process. Even so, we have lost no time in informing the WHO, once we knew there was a risk of transmission from human to human. Doctor Zhong Nanshan is the most authoritative in this field. He said at the briefing on 20th January, earlier than your timeline, that there is a high risk of transmission from people to people. By that time, there were about less than 200 cases in China. It takes time. For any country, there's a certain procedure in terms of determining the infectious disease. That is the responsible way to handle this case.

Austin: I understand that. Why was Doctor Li Wenliang arrested and silenced when he wrote on social media about his fears about the spread of the disease?

Liu Xiaoming: First, Li was never arrested as some media reported. He was summoned to a police station and got a reprimand. As I said, when you have some infectious disease, in any country including the UK, you have to be careful and responsible. You do not want to create panic. But as I said, three days before Li, Doctor Zhang reported to the health authorities. Then the local health authorities reported to the Central Government. Then the Central Government notified the WHO. That was four days later and one day after Li wrote on social media. So there was no cover-up.

And the government took care and attached importance to this complaint and sent an investigation team down to Wuhan to find out what was really going on. Li was made as a martyr and a hero.

Austin: Let's look at another reason why the world may not trust China. Mike Pompeo, the US Secretary of State, says you failed to share information about the virus. Donald Trump says he has seen a report saying there is enormous evidence that COVID-19 began in the Wuhan laboratory, and he said they made a mistake and they tried to cover it up. So my question is, was it a mistake? And did you try to cover it up?

Liu Xiaoming: As I said, there's no cover-up at all. We shared information with the WHO and the world without delay. We notified the United States at the very beginning, on 3rd January. When we notified the WHO, we also notified the CDC of the United States. Since then, there's communication and daily briefing between the Chinese CDC and American CDC. When you said the world, I don't think what the United States says, either their national leaders or top diplomat, represents the world. That's not true. As for Donald Trump, he had a comment on China. On 27th March, after his telephone conversation with President Xi, he said, "We learned quite a lot and China had a very tough experience. We have a good communication and they sent a lot of data. We are getting all that information. " Now, Donald Trump was really different from then and where you quoted him.

Austin: Then let me look at another reason why the world may not trust China. You're refusing to open up for a full investigation, an international investigation by scientists. If you have nothing to hide, and as you say, there's no cover-up, why not allow an international investigation of the lab and the wet market or other places?

Liu Xiaoming: I think this investigation should not be politically motivated. I think first of all, the top priority for the international community is to focus on fighting the virus. I happen to agree with your Health Secretary when he said a hundred percent of the focus should be on working together to fight against the virus. Secondly, we are open, we are transparent, and we have nothing to hide and nothing to fear. We welcome international independent review, but it has to be organized by the WHO. It should be international.

Austin: Would you agree to the WHO organizing international scientists from across the world to come into China to investigate?

Liu Xiaoming: Yes, of course, at a proper time. Not now. The purpose of this review is to compare notes, to summarize, to learn experience: how we can do better for future pandemic. That's the purpose, not to accuse China.

Austin: With respect, 4.5 million people have been infected by this virus and nearly 300,000 people have died as a result of this virus which you can see probably came from Wuhan in your country. It is a global tragedy that has been caused here. Doesn't it need a global investigation now as soon as possible with the world's renowned scientists?

Liu Xiaoming: I think scientists and experts are working. Even now, the scientists from China, from the US, from the UK are working to find the origin. When you say the outbreak happened in China, China is the first to report the cases. You can't say the virus originated from China. It is still up to the scientists, not up to you, not up to me.

Austin: I am using the word "origin" as the first case was in China. It is not the first time. It happened with SARS. It happened with COVID. It cannot be allowed to happen again.

Liu Xiaoming: Definitely. It cannot be allowed to happen again. But this is still unknown to many scientists, right? So you can't blame China. China is a victim. China is not the culprit of this virus. It's not a man-made virus but natural in origin. So we have to adopt the scientific approach. You can't have this campaign of stigmization, disinformation and smearing against China, as some American politicians are doing.

Austin: Then allow scientists in and they would find out the truth. Most modern, fair-minded, open and responsible countries would let international scientists in very quickly.

Liu Xiaoming: We are working with scientists from the international community. There is no doubt about that. But you have to separate it from the politically motivated so-called "independent investigation". When you say the world, they are just a few countries. The United States. Australia. Can you give me ten countries who call for the so-called independent investigation? I think many countries call for global response, solidarity and constructive cooperation, not criticism. The theme of today is to focus on fighting this virus and saving lives instead of playing the game of blaming and scapegoating.

Austin: Why is China or Chinese backed groups trying to steal coronavirus research according to the intelligence agencies? They say you are hacking British and American scientists working on COVID programmes. Why would you want to do that?

Liu Xiaoming: Where did you get these charges? Do you have a proof?

Austin: The FBI said "the hackings have been observed attempting to obtain illicitly public health data".

Liu Xiaoming: This is not the first time that the United States made such a false accusation against China. This is only their attempt to undermine the international collaboration on working together to find the vaccine. A vaccine will be the final solution to the problem. Chinese scientists are working around the clock, first on their own, then engaging collaboration even with scientists from the US. China and the UK are also working very closely. Both our top leaders, President Xi and Prime Minister Johnson, give their support to the scientists to find the vaccine.

Austin: Ambassador, talking about the vaccine, if China discovers the vaccine before other countries, do you agree to distribute it equitably and fairly along the line of advice by the Vaccine Alliance?

Liu Xiaoming: Yes, we certainly would like to share. We regard it as the joint efforts of the international scientists. We would share this to enhance the global response to the virus. That's why we are engaging with other countries in collaboration on science.

Austin: That policy is that it goes first to those at the heart of the outbreak wherever it is in the world, and then it goes to health workers around the world. China will agree to that, will it?

Liu Xiaoming: I think it's still too early to say something in specific terms on this question, because we haven't made the vaccine yet. So you are asking the question of vaccine use in much advance. But as I said, in principle we would like to share what we have achieved with other countries, either with the most needed countries or with the very front line workers, just as what we have done to provide medical supplies to about 150 countries. I think most of these medical supplies have been used on the front line medical workers, including here in the UK. We are donating the most needed supplies, and helping the UK government procure ventilators. I think they have all been put to good use.

Austin: OK. You talked about openness, and let's just talk about that. Why have you expelled 13 American journalists out of China, many of whom were trying to investigate the origin of the virus? That's point one. And why have two citizen journalists who put out videos at the very beginning of this epidemic, Chen Qiushi and Fang Bin, disappeared? Where are they?

Liu Xiaoming: You should ask why the United States expelled 60 Chinese journalists? And you should ask why we have given more preferential treatment to American journalists? We are forced to take counter-measures. That's nothing to do with COVID-19. As I said, China has been open and transparent...

Austin: Mr Ambassador, as far as I know, America doesn't imprison journalists, but you imprisoned 48 in the last year–more than any other country. How was that? How was that "openness"?

Liu Xiaoming: No journalist has been put behind bars because of what he or she had been doing as a journalist. Some people have been put behind bars because they have violated the law. Nobody is above the law, and everybody is treated equally in front of the law. Nobody can use journalism as a cover to do anything that violates the law. The answer is simple.

Austin: OK. You are a country with more than a billion people, and yet you have fewer than 5,000 official deaths. To many that number seems unbelievable. Is it true?

Liu Xiaoming: That's because we have adopted the most strict, comprehensive and vigorous measures in containing the virus. We want to share this with other countries. Wuhan is a city five times larger than London in area, with a population of 11 million which is bigger than that of London and Northern Ireland put together. The city was locked down for 76 days. The local people made huge sacrifice. But the virus can transmit from people to people, so the lockdown has been a very effective measure. And we also have the effective measures that we call the "four earlies"–early dignosis, early reporting, early quarantine, and early treatment. All these have turned out to be very effective. So you cannot blame China for "cover-up" just because we have a low number of death cases.

Austin: I'm not blaming you, Mr. Ambassador, for anything. I'm just making a point Finally, I've got to ask you, in the UK, we have over 30,000 deaths with an obviously much smaller population. Where do you think Britain went wrong?

Liu Xiaoming: I do not want to be critical of the UK policy. What I want to say is that we would like to share our experience, and compare notes with our British colleagues. I just want to give you first-hand information: Tomorrow Secretary Matt Hancock, together with British scientists and experts, will have an on-line meeting with the Chinese health minister. It'll be more than two hours' discussion to compare notes and exchange experience. I think that is what we need now. We need to enhance collaboration. We have to know the virus is our common enemy. We need to pull together, and we should come to the aid of each other to win the final battle against the virus. As President Xi Jinping said, solidarity and cooperation are the most powerful weapons for the international community to combat COVID-19.

Austin: OK, Mr Ambassador, I appreciate your time. And I look forward to the international investigation whenever it happens. Thank you very much indeed for joining us this evening and answering our questions. Thank you.

Liu Xiaoming: My pleasure.

Mark Austin is an English journalist and television presenter, currently working for Sky News. He has won six BAFTA awards.

Sky News *Live Panel Discussion–After the Pandemic: Our New World* with Dermot Murnaghan

On 1st June 2020, I attended a live panel discussion hosted by Dermot Murnaghan on Sky News' special programme *After the Pandemic: Our New World* with Mary Robinson, former president of Ireland, David Miliband, former British foreign secretary and historian Niall Ferguson. The following is a transcript of my Q&A session:

Murnaghan: Let's get the initial thoughts from our panelists on the opportunities and challenges facing our world today.

Liu Xiaoming: I think there's a lot of debate these days about the consequences of this pandemic–whether the pandemic will unite the world or make the world more divided. I tend to believe it makes the world more united. I think this pandemic really shows us again that we all belong to this global village. Just as President Xi said, we should all try to build this Community with a Shared Future for Mankind. I think this pandemic shows us that the international community should cooperate. It shows that those countries who supported each other, who supported WHO in playing a leading role, who supported multilateralism and who listened to the advice of WHO have been able to put the virus under control. But those countries who rejected international corporation, who rejected WHO advice have paid a high price. I think no country, no matter how strong you are, can be immune. You cannot be insulated from this pandemic. Viruses respect no borders, no races.

Murnaghan: When investigations are underway, the core question to China is: Does China accept its culpability and responsibilities during this crisis? Let me ask you straight up: Will you allow independent investigators onto Chinese soil to work out what happened?

Liu Xiaoming: We certainly welcome international review. But the purpose is not to label any country. All the countries should be covered. Together with 120 member states during the World Health Assembly, we supported the international community to carry out a review of the pandemic at a proper time. The purpose is to sum up experience and get better prepared for future pandemics. And this review, firstly, should be independent, free from politicization. It should be based on science, that is, let the scientists take the lead.

Murnaghan: Who do you accept leading it? Who would you like to oversee it?

Liu Xiaoming: The WHO should lead this independent review. All countries should get involved, especially the major players. I found I have differences with Niall. He blamed China for slow reaction. That is not true. I think Niall got a lot of wrong information. He said during the lockdown, there were still many flights going to other countries. That is not true. That's false information. When Wuhan was locked down, starting from 23rd January, there were no flights at all. No flights, no trains, not at all. With regard to how China reacted to this pandemic, China was the first country to report the virus to the WHO, first to identify the pathogen and first to share the genetic sequence with the WHO and other countries. China wasted no time in sharing information and experience in containing the virus.

Murnaghan: During the pandemic, there were hundreds of flights out of China as a whole, and the virus surely started circulating in the world like that. You've got to admit that, have you, before the world's gonna take you seriously?

Liu Xiaoming: Your information is totally wrong. As I said earlier, when Wuhan went into lockdown, there was no flights at all, no connection with the outside world. I am sorry to hear so much cold-war rhetoric from Niall. We knew each other before, but I do not know why he is so interested in having a cold war with China. I just want to let you know that China is not the former Soviet Union. You, being a historian, should have a serious study about China. I can provide you with more information and facts about that. We have a "Reality Checks" of 24 allegations and I will mail it to you. I just want to say that we should not talk down the role played by the WHO just because the WHO spoke positively about the efforts of China. The WHO is a very important international organization. It has 194 members.

Murnaghan: Let's talk about China's responsibilities. Undoubtedly, China was in denial about COVID-19 for so long, about animal to human transition and about human to human transition. You did not tell the world soon enough.

Liu Xiaoming: As I told you, we lost no time in informing the WHO. This is a new virus, you have to be responsible. It was unknown to all of us. You need the scientists to study in a responsible way and seriously. When we identified the virus 11 days after the first report, we immediately reported to the WHO and shared the information with relevant countries. There was no cover-up. There was no delay. China's record is clean. It can stand the test of time and history. What I am also saying is that China first reported the virus, but it does not mean the virus originated from China. In terms of the origin, I think it's up to the scientists to decide. As the situation unfolds, we hear reports that there were some cases in the United States, in Italy, that were much earlier than China. You know, we need to adopt a scientific approach about this matter.

Murnaghan: What about the question of reform of the World Health Organization? China will accept that?

Liu Xiaoming: Yes. The pandemic really shows the weakness of WHO, both in terms of its capabilities and resources, and how WHO could respond more quickly and more effectively, especially taking care of the poorest and the weak countries. I think it needs reform. We can do this after we claim the final victory over the virus. The top priority now is to pull together and to support WHO to lead this battle. We have not put the virus under control yet.

Murnaghan: As the world's biggest emitter, what's China's commitment to keeping up this temporary fall in emissions during the pandemic?

Liu Xiaoming: China is very much committed to the Paris Agreement. China has fulfilled its obligations three years ahead of plan. In 2018, we had brought down the carbon intensity by 45.8% from 2005. We have also brought down the consumption of carbon per unit GDP by 2.6%. China is now the largest investor in new energy and renewable energy, and China is very much committed to mitigation of climate change. According to the original plan. China will also hold the Conference of the Parties to the Convention on Biological Diversity by the end of the year.

Murnaghan: Is it going to go ahead? You are still planning to do it?

Liu Xiaoming: It has not yet been finalized because of the pandemic. So it's still open. This year is supposed to be the year of collaboration between China and the

UK in environmental protection. Now UK has rescheduled COP26 to November next year. But we are still keeping very close contact on line with my British colleagues to compare notes on how to make the conferences successful.

Murnaghan: I want to ask you specifically about rebuilding trust, about the race to develop a vaccine for COVID-19. We noticed the advances China and some other countries are making. But if China were to develop an effective vaccine, would it be willing–and this is in terms of rebuilding trust I suppose–will it be willing to share that vaccine with the planet as cheap as possible?

Liu Xiaoming: Definitely. President Xi made firm commitment during the World Health Assembly that once the vaccine is available, China wants to make it a public good and make it especially accessible and available to developing countries. China is now among the most advanced countries in terms of vaccine research. Now we are in phase II, we already have five clinical trials and we want to share with the rest of the world. China is working with scientists from the UK and other countries including the United States on the vaccine.

I can't agree with the table you just showed that China's reputation has been damaged. It depends on where you get this information. According to the information I have by an independent PR company in United States, the Edelman Trust Barometer of 2020, Chinese government enjoys the highest support among its people. It's about 82%,that is top of all countries. And also according to a Singapore public opinion company Black Box Research, they did a survey of 23 countries, China again tops the rest 22 countries. The Chinese government enjoys more than 85% of public support.

Murnaghan: We are running short of time, I am going to ask the Ambassador finally on this lack of trust, particularly with the younger generation. Well you are seeing that on the streets of Hong Kong: the Chinese state's repression of those protesters–the seekers after democracy.

Liu Xiaoming: No, it's not "Chinese repression". What is going on in Hong Kong is violence. It's a risk to the national security. Those perpetrators stormed the Legislative Council, and they even set fire to innocent people. If the same thing happens on the streets of London, if the rioters stormed the UK Parliament, what would be the UK's reaction? The UK government and police will sit back and let these things go on? I think any responsible government has to take measures. Some people do not realise that

"One Country, Two Systems" has achieved great success since Hong Kong returned to China 23 years ago.

Murnaghan: We are running out of time. I want to say thank you to our panelists. Thank you, Ambassador Liu.

Liu Xiaoming: My pleasure.

China-Japan
Relations

An Interview with John Ray on ITV *News at Ten*

On 3rd January 2014, I talked to ITV diplomatic correspondent John Ray during ITV *News at Ten* programme. I criticised Japanese Prime Minister Shinzo Abe's attempt to revive militarism in Japan, elaborated on China's solemn stand concerning the issue of the Diaoyu Islands, and called on the international community to stop the rise of Japanese militarism, with a view to safeguarding regional stability and world peace. The full text of the interview is as follows:

Ray: Can I start with Lord Voldemort? This is a very vivid language that you've used. Why compare Japan to a character who is pure evil?

Liu Xiaoming: I think there are some similarities between the two because Lord Voldemort will not be destroyed if you don't destroy all the seven horcruxes. And I made the comparison because militarism has not been completely destroyed, and because the Yakusuni Shrine is always alive in the memory of the Japanese people. Some people think China makes a big fuss about this visit. But I do think the visit is a big deal because it is by Japanese leaders, especially national leaders, to pay respect to a shrine which honours war criminals, especially 14 Class A war criminals who inflicted enormous casualties and damages on the people who suffered from that war, including British people. In fact, Hideki Tojo, the top war criminal among the 14, not only started the war against China, but also declared war on America, on Britain and on the Netherlands. So we believe this is really a matter concerning which way Japan is heading. This is really a choice between peace and war, between right and wrong, between light and darkness. So that's why we made a very strong representation about Japanese leaders visiting this shrine.

Ray: So where from your point of view is the pure evil in Japan? Is it what you perceive as their militarism?

Liu Xiaoming: I think that's very much so. We are very concerned about Japanese leaders' anti-peace rhetoric. As you know, Prime Minster Abe even refuses to recognize that Japan started this war of aggression. He even challenges the definition of aggression. The deputy prime minister even tries to, in his word, learn from Nazi Germany to amend the pacifist constitution. And they also play up the so-called "China Threat" in order to create regional tensions to make excuse for Japanese military expansion. So we are very concerned about the spectre of militarism that Abe is trying to raise again. We found some similarities between today's Japan and Germany before the WWII. So we are very concerned about that.

Ray: From the Japanese perspective, you might look at the buildup of Chinese military forces over the past 20 years and say here is a big power emerging in the region. We need to defend ourselves against this new superpower. You have been increasing defence spending by double digit numbers for the past 25 years.

Liu Xiaoming: That's not right. We did see some increase in China's military spending. But if you compare China's per capita military expenditure with that of America, Britain, Japan, China is still the lowest. China is a large country. We are much bigger than Britain and Japan. We have more than 1.3 billion people. We have 22,000 km of land borders and 32,000 km of coastal lines. China is a large country to defend. And if you look at the military budget-to-GDP ratio, and its percentage in China's total fiscal expenditure, the figures are decreasing year-on-year. In per capita terms, the US is 22 times that of China. Even Britain is 9 times that of China, and Japan's military spending is five times that of China. And what is important is the nature of China's defence policy. Chinese defence policy is defensive in nature. You have never seen China occupy a single inch of other country's territory. As a matter of fact, in the past hundred years or so, China has been a victim of foreign aggression and occupation. But if you look at Japan, it is a completely different story.

Ray: When you look at it from a different perspective, you might see not Japan as the aggressor but China as the aggressor. Take for example the Diaoyu Islands. You've declared a sort of defensive zone over there. They belong, according to the international law, to Japan. Do they not? You're claiming them. So it looks as if it is China that has the territorial ambitions there.

Liu Xiaoming: That is not right. In fact, Diaoyu Dao has been China's territory since ancient times. It was not until China-Japan War about 120 years ago that Japan had seized it illegally. According to the Cairo Declaration reached by the Chinese, British and American leaders, Japan must return all the territories it had seized illegally as a result of that war, including Taiwan and the surrounding islands. But after the Second World War, the Cold War ensued. The Americans tried to support Japan. Instead of returning the Diaoyu Islands to China, they transferred the administrative power of the Diaoyu Islands to Japan. We never recognized that. We launched protests against this. But still, Americans do not recognize Japan's sovereignty over the islands. When it comes to sovereignty, they take a neutral position. Diaoyu Dao has always been a dispute between China and Japan. And we had proposed, before the events in the past few years, to shelve the dispute. When Deng Xiaoping visited Japan, he was asked a question at a news conference about the future of Diaoyu Dao. He said we have a dispute with Japan over the Islands. We may shelve the dispute for the time being. Maybe the future generation would be wiser than us today to find a solution to this disputed territory.

Ray: But at the moment, it looks like that China on the islands is not going to compromise, that it is your territory. And you should have it.

Liu Xiaoming: The problem is it is the Japanese who have provoked all this. First of all, a group of right-wing forces in Japan tried to nationalize these islands. So the Japanese government wanted to take it over. This raised the tension over the disputed territory. We had to make a response. China in fact has been passive in making response to Japanese provocations. According to Chinese philosophy, we will never attack others. We are a very pacifist country. But we will make a counter-attack when we are attacked.

Ray: If you watch this from the outside, it's quite alarming. I want to ask you where you think or where you fear all this is heading? When people talk about potential flashpoints for war, they look at this dispute between China and Japan. Do you share that worry?

Liu Xiaoming: We are concerned, I would say. First of all, I would stress that we want to have good relations with Japan. We want to live peacefully with them. In fact, when we normalized relations with Japan about 42 years ago, the leaders of the two countries all proclaimed that there would be no war for ever between China and Japan. We all know that you can not have a peaceful Asia and Pacific without good relations between China and Japan, such two important countries. But it's not really very much up to

China when you have these right-wing forces and militarist forces working and getting momentum in Japan. So we are very concerned. That's why I made a comparison of Lord Voldemort and militarism in Japan. So the only way to maintain peace and stability, to ensure there will be no war, is to stop the militarism in Japan. That's why we call on Mr. Abe and his government to stop it before it's too late.

Ray: At the end of the movie, Lord Voldemort is destroyed.

Liu Xiaoming: Militarism should be destroyed in order to maintain peace and prosperity of the Asia-Pacific.

Ray: Chinese authorities have said, when they are talking about Japan re-arming, that you will not allow it to happen. What does that mean? Does that mean that you will take defensive military action to stop Japan?

Liu Xiaoming: As I said, China will never provoke. China will only make counter-attack. We want to draw the attention, and the alert of the international community, so that's why I wrote this article. I want to share my concern with the British public. In Britain, we attach great importance not only to our relations, but also to how you see this. Britain has played an important role in the past and still has a role to play today in maintaining peace and stability not only in Europe but also in the world. So that's why I'm calling on China and Britain, not only as the victims of the Second World War, but also as victors of the Second World War, to take on our common responsibility. We should work with the international community to ensure that post-war order will be maintained. Because this post-war order really has ensured peace and stability for the world for the past 70 years. Next year will be the 70th anniversary of the end of the Second World War. I think we really have to celebrate it not only with some joy but also with some concerns about whether the history of the Second World War will be repeated. If the militarism in Japan is not to be stopped, we can not rule out the recurrence of another world war. So that's why we are really concerned about this. We want it to work out in a very peaceful way, but sometimes you have to prepare for the worst. So the best way to do it is to resolve it with the efforts of the international community. So I'm very pleased that not only China has lodged strong protests, but also South Korea and America have expressed deep concern and disappointment. Some other countries have done the same. So we do hope that the international community will join force to stop the development of the militarism in Japan.

Ray: Can I ask you a question that I asked you earlier on. We know that Chinese people suffered terribly from the invasion of the Japanese in the 1930s. Has that wound that was inflicted ever been forgiven? Has it ever healed? Or the Chinese people feel as strongly now, as hurt and as angry now as it did 70 years ago.

Liu Xiaoming: I think you are right. The war really inflicted an enormous wound and casualties on the Chinese people. It caused 35 million casualties, and direct or indirect economic losses of $600 billion. We want to see the wound healed, so that's why when China and Japan normalized relations, the Chinese government and Chinese leaders decided that we were not going to seek war reparations from Japan. We believed it was the war criminals, it was the leaders of Japan who started the war should be held accountable, not the average Japanese people. So we do not want the young people of Japan today to bear the cost, to bear the responsibility of their fathers or grandfathers who committed this crime. So we want to live peacefully with Japan. But it was always the Japanese leaders who always open this wound of hatred between China and Japan. In addition to visiting the war shrine, they tried to rewrite the history, refuse to show remorse of their aggressive past, and even tries to alter the text book. They do not want to teach the children about their aggressive past. So it's quite different if you compare Japan with Germany on how they did with their past. For example, you see German Chancellor Brandt kneeling down in front of the tomb of the Jews, and you see Mrs. Merkel showing respect to those dead in Nazi concentration camps. But you have never seen the same political gesture, not even a word of apology to Chinese people from Japanese leaders. So how could you make sure Chinese people would forget this past? So it's very important that the attitude of Japanese leaders and Japanese government really makes a big difference. We do hope that they will change their course, show remorse and make apology not only to Chinese people, but also to Asian people, to all the peoples they have caused casualties and damages, and to start a new life, a new Japan. So I don't think the issue of Japanese war criminal has been thoroughly settled. Therefore, you see the spectre of militarism rising from time to time. So the international community really should be alert about this dangerous direction where Japan is heading.

146

ITV is the second largest public broadcaster in the UK after the BBC. *News at Ten* is ITV's flagship news programme and one of the most watched evening news programmes in the UK with an audience of 4 million. John Ray is an international, award-winning British television journalist for ITV News, currently based in London.

A Live Interview with Julian Worricker on BBC World Service *Weekend*

On 5th January 2014, I gave a live interview on BBC World Service *Weekend* programme. I elaborated on China's solemn stands on Japan's aggressive past and on the Diaoyu Islands, exposing the Japanese Prime Minister Shinzo Abe's attempt to revive militarism in Japan and calling on the international community to keep on high alert. The full text of the interview is as follows:

Worricker: Mr. Abe's claim has been brushed aside by the Chinese leadership. And now Chinese Ambassador to London Liu Xiaoming has called on Britain and the United Nations to be on high alert against what he describes as Japan's growing militarism. Ambassador Liu is with us in the studio. Good morning.

Liu Xiaoming: Good morning, Julian.

Worricker: What is your specific concern here?

Liu Xiaoming: We are very much concerned about this visit. Because, as you said, Yasukuni Shrine has long been the spiritual symbol and instruments used by Japanese militarists for their war efforts, in their war of aggression and colonial rule. The Japanese national leaders pay respect to this shrine which today still honors 14 class A war criminals including Hideki Tojo, who was responsible not only for launching a war against China but also for attacking the Pearl Harbor, for declaring war on the United States, on Britain and the Netherlands. This is a man whose hands were stained with the blood of millions of Chinese people.

Worricker: I can see why the Chinese would be angry about it, but ultimately, is it not an internal Japanese matter?

Liu Xiaoming: It is not an internal Japanese matter. It's not only that we care about how Japanese leaders treat these war criminals. It's not only about their attitude toward the past. It's also about their attitude toward the future.

Worricker: And what do you say their attitude is?

Liu Xiaoming: By paying respect to war criminals, they show no signs of repentance for the past aggression and colonial rule. And also it shows that they want even to, as their deputy Prime Minister asserted, that Japan would like to learn from Nazi Germany to revise the Japanese Constitution. And Abe himself challenged the definition of "aggression of Japan".

Worricker: Let's explore that for a moment, because you are saying this from the point of view representing a country that spends massively on its military, that has a relatively new President who says he wants to spend more on its military. Therefore for you to criticize the Japanese for even contemplating what you have just alluded to, it's surely double-standard.

Liu Xiaoming: I don't agree with you. Let's talk about China's defense. First of all, China is a large country. China's territory is about 25 times that of Japan and the Chinese population is ten times that of Japan. Yet by per capita military expenditure, Japan is 5 times that of China. Also, in terms of the share of military expenditure in GDP, Japan and China are about the same.

Worricker: But China wants to spend more, let's just be clear on that.

Liu Xiaoming: Yes, because of the growth of the economy and because of enormous mission of China's defense. As I said, China is a large country to defend. We have 14 neighbors on land, 7 neighbors on sea. We have 22,000 km of borderlines and 32,000 km of coastallines.

Worricker: I want to talk as well about the current dispute which I referred to at the top of the hour over a group of islands in the East China Sea, uninhabited islands, both China and Japan claim them. As part of that dispute, China has unilaterally declared air defense identification zone over a large part of that area. Inevitably, the Japanese will view that, will they not, as an act of aggression.

Liu Xiaoming: We call them Diaoyu Islands. It is a long story. The Diaoyu Island and its adjacent islands have long been China's territory since ancient times.

Worricker: You know the Japanese would dispute that.

Liu Xiaoming: They would dispute but I can talk about the fact. The fact is fact. It was not until 1895 when China lost war to Japan that Japan illegally seized it. As a result of Second World War, as a result of the Cairo Declaration agreed to by British, Chinese and American leaders that Japan had to return these territories, including Taiwan and Diaoyu Island to China. But in early 1950s, Americans took it over. It was not delivered because of the Cold War. The US needed Japan. And in the 1970s, they transferred administrative power of Diaoyu Island to Japan. But, America still did not recognize sovereignty claimed by Japan. They still remain neutral.

Worricker: In which case, what does this unilateral declaration of air defense identification zone achieve from your point of view other than make the dispute more acute than it is already?

Liu Xiaoming: Let me finish on the Diaoyu Islands. It was not until the recent past when China and Japan normalized relations in early 1970s, both leaders agreed to shelve the dispute. To use Deng Xiaoping's words when he visited Japan, he was asked about Diaoyu Islands, Deng said, I think our future generations will be wiser to find a solution. So they shelved this dispute. But in the recent past, Japanese took a lot of unilateral measures. It was Japan who took provocative actions. They wanted to purchase the islands. They wanted to nationalize the islands. We've been put into a position where we have to make response to what they are doing.

Worricker: That's what you would use as a justification for declaring this unilateral air identification zone.

Liu Xiaoming: This is a normal procedure.

Worricker: But at some point, either side has got to pull back from the situation.

Liu Xiaoming: You are talking about this air defense identification zone.

Worricker: Well, more broadly.

Liu Xiaoming: I want to point out, Japan has established this kind of zone 45 years ago. They have been keeping expanding this zone over the past 45 years. And their so-called zone even got as close as kilome ters from China's coastal line.

Worricker: I want to bring a guest in because I knew he is very keen to ask you a question. George Parker (political editor of Financial Times), you've been listening with interest.

Parker: Very much so. And I totally understand the painful history between you two countries and the upset you felt about Prime Minister Abe going to Yasukuni Shrine. But now you look at military levels in China versus military might of Japan. And China far out-muscles Japan. Are you saying that you still feel some kind of military threat from Japan?

Liu Xiaoming: You are talking about the figures of military expenditure. You ignored the fact that Japan is also expanding their defense budget. In the next 5 years, Japan's military expenditure will increase by 5%. And their military expenditure now is at a historical high over the past 18 years. America's military budget is much bigger than China. It is four times bigger and also in terms of per capita military expenditure, 22 times of China. Even Britain is 9 times that of China. That's number one. Number two. Military expenditure is an important factor to analyze the defense posture of a country. What is more important is the strategy of a country. China is a pacifist country. If you look at the record of China, if you compare the record of China with Japan, you will see Japan is quite a different country.

Parker: But do you still feel a military threat from Japan?

Liu Xiaoming: Because we've been attacked and we've been invaded in history. In the First World War, Japan imposed a lot of unequal treaties on China. In the Second World War, the Chinese people suffered dearly at the hands of Japanese aggressors.

Worricker: Do you still feel that military threat now is the question?

Liu Xiaoming: Of course. Because of the way they treat history, because they still respect the war criminals, because they want to revise the pacifist parts of the Japanese Constitution. So we are very concerned about that.

Worricker: Let me bring in Jyoti Malhotra from Delhi.

Malhotra: Good morning Ambassador.

Liu Xiaoming: Good morning.

Malhotra: Good to talk to you through the BBC. I am an Indian journalist based in Delhi. And I just wanted to say that in India we look at China as a great country and an ancient civilization. You're well on your way to becoming the world's number one economic power. But having said that, I'm just wondering why is that China has so many disputes with its neighbors, including with India. Our disputes of course go back to independence. And we have different views of our border, which is about 4,000 km long. You just talked about China being a pacifist country and yet only a few months ago, the Chinese PLA crossed the line of actual control and came into India. And China was there for 3 weeks at the Depsang plateau. Why?

Liu Xiaoming: First of all, I would say that we would like to have good relations with all our neighboring countries. We enjoy good relations with most of our neighbors. When it comes to a border dispute, we all have to recognize that China has been a victim of imperial power and suffered dearly from foreign aggression. I think most of these border disputes are legacies left by the colonial rulers. Having said that, we are very sincere in sitting down to have sincere, serious discussions and negotiations with our neighboring countries on these disputes, including with the Indian people. I am very pleased to see there has been progress in the negotiations between China and India in terms of boundary issues.

Malhotra: Mr Ambassador, there was an agreement between India and China in 2005 on the border. The agreement talked about the border disputes. But a couple of years later, China unilaterally withdrew from that understanding. And now there is no understanding at all.

Liu Xiaoming: I don't agree with you. You know, I'm here to talk about China-Japan relations. When it comes to dispute, you can't listen to just one side's story. We also have complaints about the conduct, about the actions from the Indian side. But I do not want to debate with you today on this issue. All I want to say is we are sincere in negotiating solutions acceptable to both sides.

Worricker: Mr Ambassador, we do appreciate your coming in this morning. Thank you very much indeed for your time.

Liu Xiaoming: My pleasure.

The BBC World Service is broadcast to 200 countries and regions around the world with an international audience of about 210 million. Julian Worricker is an English journalist, currently working as one of the main presenters of *Weekend* on the BBC World Service.

A Live Interview with James Coomarasamy on BBC World News

On 5th January, 2014, I gave a live interview on BBC World News to presenter James Coomarasamy. During the interview, I analyzed the Japanese Prime Minister Shinzo Abe's attempt to revive militarism in Japan, and elaborated on China's stance on the Air Defense Identification Zone in the East China Sea and China's military expenditure. The full text of the interview is as follows:

Coomarasamy: China reminds the international community to be vigilant against Japanese militarism. What is your main concern here?

Liu Xiaoming: We are very much concerned about Shinzo Abe's visit to the war-linked Yasukuni Shrine, because the Yasukuni Shrine has long been the spiritual symbol and instrument used by Japanese militarists in their wars of aggression and colonial rule. The Shrine today still honors 14 Class A war criminals including Hideki Tojo, who was responsible not only for launching a war against China but also for attacking the Pearl Harbor and for declaring war on the United States, Britain and the Netherlands. We have to express concern about the Japanese Prime Minister paying homage to war criminals.

Coomarasamy: In your opinion, where will Japan be led to by what Yasukuni Shrine symbolizes?

Liu Xiaoming: That is what we are concerned about. The Japanese leaders' visit to Yasukuni Shrine was not an isolated event, but a part of a series of actions that provoked regional tensions. Since Abe came to power, he has challenged the definition of "Japanese aggression". Instead of admitting that Japan was an aggressor, he regarded Japan as a victim of war. The Deputy Prime Minister Taro Aso asserted that Japan would like to learn from Nazi Germany to revise Japan's pacificist Constitution. Meanwhile, Japan is also increasing its defense budget. In the next 5 years, Japan's military expenditure will increase by 5%. This should put us on alert.

Coomarasamy: China has unilaterally declared an Air Defense Identification Zone over the East China Sea, and this has caused more worries among its neighbors. Is this also an act of "aggression"?

Liu Xiaoming: I totally disagree with you. The establishment of air defense identification zones is a common practice of sovereign states. Britain, the United States and many other countries have their own air defense identification zones. In fact, Japan had established such a kind of zone 45 years ago and has kept expanding it ever since. And this Japanese ADIZ is only 130 kilometers from China's coastal line at the closest point.

Coomarasamy: But China's declaration of its air defense identification zone in the current situation has escalated the tensions. Is this not an act of "aggression"?

Liu Xiaoming: I totally disagree with what you termed as Chinese "aggression". What I would like to stress is that the East China Sea Air Defense Identification Zone has been designed solely for defense. It is not a no-fly zone, and it will not affect other countries' freedom of overflight according to the international law, so long as they inform us. Since its establishment, there has never been a conflict in the area, and peace has been maintained. What China did was in full compliance with the international law and international common practice.

Coomarasamy: What action will China take at the diplomatic level to ease the tensions between the two countries? Relieving tensions is also in the interests of China.

Liu Xiaoming: It was Japan who committed provocation first. It is imperative to stop Japan's attempt to revive militarism. We should mobilize the international community to work together to prevent Japan from going farther down the wrong path. After Abe's visit to Yasukuni Shrine, China and Korea expressed their strong indignation, and the United States also expressed its disappointment. The postwar international order can be maintained only if we form an international united front to prevent Japan from taking the old path of militarism.

Coomarasamy: You just said that the United States also expressed its disappointment over Abe's visit to Yasukuni Shrine, but that was not enough, because it failed to stop Japan from visiting Yasukuni Shrine. Do we need external intervention?

Liu Xiaoming: Japan's war of aggression against China caused more than 35 million casualties in China, and direct and indirect economic losses of more than 600 billion US dollars. Korea also suffered a painful loss from Japan's aggression. In fact, the British people are victims as well.

Coomarasamy: What can be the consequences if the current tensions cannot be alleviated?

Liu Xiaoming: We hope that the Japanese leaders will hear the voice of the international community, change its current course and come back to consensus reached by the leaders of China and Japan and the four political documents on Sino-Japanese relations, and reflect and repent deeply over their historical crimes. In fact, the Japanese war crimes have never been fully and completely acknowledged by the militarist forces in Japan who are always ready to make trouble. We must not let anyone raise the spectre of Japanese militarism again.

Coomarasamy: But China is also increasing military spending and deploying an aircraft carrier in the region. Are you sending a wrong signal?

Liu Xiaoming: China and Japan should not be mentioned in the same breath. China is a large country. China's population is ten times that of Japan, and the land area is about 25 times that of Japan. Yet Japan's military spending per capita is 5 times that of China. And if you look at China's military budget-to-GDP ratio and the percentage of China's defense budget against its total fiscal expenditure, the figures are decreasing year-on-year. More importantly, China is a pacifist country and has never waged wars of aggression. Instead, we have been repeatedly invaded by foreign powers. But Japan is quite a different country. In history, it has launched many wars of aggression against foreign countries, including the war of aggression against China.

Coomarasamy: Thank you very much.

Liu Xiaoming: My pleasure.

BBC World News is broadcasted to more than 100 countries and regions around the world, with an audience of 100 million per week. James Coomarasamy is a British presenter of the BBC Radio 4 evening programme *The World Tonight* and the flagship *Newshour* programme on the BBC World Service.

A Live Interview with Jeremy Paxman on BBC *Newsnight*

On 8th January 2014, I gave a live interview to Jeremy Paxman on BBC 2 *Newsnight* programme. I elaborated on China's solemn stands on Abe's visit to the Yakusuni Shrine and the Diaoyu Islands. The transcript of the interview goes as follows:

Paxman: How are you? Thank you very much for coming in.

Liu Xiaoming: Fine. Jeremy, nice to see you again.

Paxman: Nice to see you. How serious do you think this is?

Liu Xiaoming: Very serious. This is a very serious issue. Japanese prime minister's visit to the Yakusuni Shrine, in our view, is not a small matter. It concerns how Japanese face up to their history of aggression. I would quote Winston Churchill's words, "Those who fail to learn from history are doomed to repeat it". So we are concerned that if they do not face up to their disgraceful record of aggression, what will happen for the future?

Paxman: You raised the question of this visit to the Shrine. There have been over 60 prime ministerial visits to that Shrine since the Second World War, and to 20-something of them the Chinese raised no objection at all?

Liu Xiaoming: That was not right. I know this was the Japanese Ambassador's figure. You know it was not until 1978 that the 14 Class A war criminals had been moved in. And then in 1985, the Japanese prime minister, together with the whole cabinet, visited the shrine. We lodged a strong protest. So since then, we made countless protests against it.

Paxman: But let's look at these islands. Why have you suddenly asserted control of the air, for example, above them. Why have you suddenly done that?

Liu Xiaoming: That was a good question. Why has this matter cropped up so suddenly? It has been very peaceful for the past 40 years. First of all, I would say these islands have been part of the Chinese territory since ancient times. It was in 1895 when China lost the war with Japan that they had been seized illegally. But according to the *Cairo Declaration* and *Potsdam Proclamation*, all the territories seized illegally by Japan should be returned to China. That is an international document agreed by the British, American and Chinese leaders.

Paxman: Sorry, I am not familiar with the Cairo Declaration. When was that?

Liu Xiaoming: 1943.

Paxman: Right. Now it has nothing to do, you say then, with natural resources which may be connected with these islands or may be available from these islands?

Liu Xiaoming: It is about sovereignty. It is about territorial integrity. Let me finish about why it came up. When we normalized relations in 1972, both leaders agreed that there was a dispute over the islands. We should shelve the difference. Deng Xiaoping, in 1978 when he visited Japan, was asked this question about Diaoyu Islands. And he said, "We have a dispute with Japan, but I think we can shelve it for the time being. The future generation will be wiser than us. " So we agreed to shelve it. But the Japanese want to change the status quo. In the past few years, you know, what did they do? They tried to "nationalize" these islands. Their government wanted to "purchase" these islands.

Paxman: How far are you prepared to take this dispute?

Liu Xiaoming: How far? First of all, they have to face up to the fact that we have a dispute over the islands. They even refuse to recognize there is a dispute between the two countries over the islands.

Paxman: Implicitly, the Japanese ambassador over there a second or two ago was talking about the need for dialogue. That is an implicit recognition that there is a disagreement over it.

Liu Xiaoming: In fact, it was Abe, the Japanese prime minister, who shut the door to dialogue between China and Japan because he overturned the political foundation of the two countries. How would you expect China would agree to talk to him when he refuses to repent on the war crimes the Japanese did to the Chinese people? This is not only a case for China.The Korean president also refused to meet Abe because of his behaviour on history issue.

Paxman: Thank you very much indeed. Thank you.

Liu Xiaoming: My pleasure.

About the Author

Liu Xiaoming

Graduated from Dalian University of Foreign Languages with a major in English and undertook further studies in the United States, obtaining a master's degree in international relations from the Fletcher School of Law and Diplomacy at Tufts University in 1983.

Liu Xiaoming started to serve as a Chinese diplomat since 1974, acting as Deputy Director-General of Department of North American and Oceanian Affairs of the Ministry of Foreign Affairs, Minister of Chinese Embassy in the US, Ambassador of China in Egypt, Ambassador of China in the DPRK and Ambassador of China in the UK. And Liu Xiaoming presently serves as the Special Representative of the Chinese Government on Korean Peninsula Affairs and Member of Foreign Policy Advisory Committee.

Liu Xiaoming has been awarded the Fletcher School Dean's Medal of the United States, the First Class Friendship Medal of the DPRK, the Fletcher Class of 1947 Memorial Award, the 48 Group Club Lifetime Achievement Award for Contribution to Sino-British Relations, an Honorary Doctorate of Laws from the University of Nottingham, the Freedom of the City by the City of London Corporation and an Honorary Doctorate from the University of Huddersfield.

2010-05-26

Presenting credentials to Queen Elizabeth II at Buckingham Palace. During her reign, the Queen had accepted credentials from 12 Chinese Ambassadors, and I was the last one of them who presented the credentials to Her Majesty in person.

在白金漢宮向英國女王伊麗莎白二世遞交國書。女王生前曾接受 12 位中國大使遞交國書，我是最後一位當面向她遞交國書的中國大使。

2011-11-10

Starting the Panda Pals website together with Mr. Mark Hendrick, Mr. David Longbottom, Mr. Hugh Roberts and Ms. Gigi Luscombe.

與英國議員等共同啟動大熊貓夥伴關係網站。

2012-01-23

Having a live and one-on-one interview with Jeremy Paxman on BBC 2's *Newsnight*.

接受英國 BBC《新聞之夜》欄目主持人帕克斯曼現場直播採訪。

2012-01-23

Talking with Jeremy Paxman after the live interview.

接受英國 BBC《新聞之夜》欄目主持人帕克斯曼現場直播採訪後與其交談。

2012-03-14

Having a live interview with Evan Davis on BBC Radio 4's *Today* programme.

接受英國 BBC 廣播四台《今日》欄目主持人戴維斯現場直播採訪。

2012-12-21

Giving a live interview to Gavin Esler on BBC's *Newsnight*.

接受英國 BBC《新聞之夜》欄目主持人艾斯勒現場直播採訪。

2014-01-05

Giving a live interview on BBC World News hosted by presenter James Coomarasamy.

接受英國 BBC 世界新聞台主持人庫馬拉薩米現場直播採訪。

2014-01-05

Giving a live interview on BBC World Service *Weekend* programme hosted by Julian Worricker.

接受英國 BBC 國際廣播電台主持人沃里克現場直播採訪。

2014-01-08

Giving a live interview to Jeremy Paxman on BBC 2 *Newsnight* programme.

接受英國 BBC《新聞之夜》欄目主持人帕克斯曼現場直播採訪。

2014-01-14

Giving a live interview on *Jeff Randall Live* on Sky News.

接受英國天空新聞台《傑夫·蘭德直播間》欄目主持人蘭德現場直播採訪。

2015-09-03

Having a live interview on BBC's *Newsnight* hosted by Robert Peston.

接受英國 BBC《新聞之夜》欄目主持人佩斯頓現場直播採訪。

2015-10-14

Having a live interview on *Channel 4 News* hosted by Jon Snow.

接受英國《電視四台新聞》欄目主持人斯諾現場直播採訪。

2015-10-15

Giving an interview to the International Affairs Editor of ITV News Rageh Omaar on *News at Ten*.

接受英國獨立電視台《十點新聞》欄目國際主編奧馬爾採訪。

2015-10-09

Having a colloquium hosted by James Harding, BBC Director of News and Current Affairs, with more than 30 anchors, editors and journalists.

與 BBC 新聞總監哈丁、主持人、編輯、記者 30 餘人座談。

2015-10-16

Having a live interview on BBC *Newsnight* hosted by Evan Davis.

接受英國 BBC《新聞之夜》欄目主持人戴維斯現場直播採訪。

2015-10-18

Giving a live interview on BBC *The Andrew Marr Show*.

接受 BBC《安德魯·馬爾訪談》欄目主持人馬爾現場直播採訪。

2015-10-18

Having a live interview with Dermot Murnaghan on Sky News *Murnaghan* Programme.

接受英國天空新聞台《莫納罕訪談》欄目主持人莫納罕現場直播採訪。

2017-01-06

Having an interview hosted by the renowned economist, Lord Jim O'Neill on BBC Radio 4.

在英國 BBC 廣播四台接受奧尼爾勳爵採訪。

2017-06-26

Delivering a speech at the reception celebrating the 20th Anniversary of Hong Kong's Return to China.

在慶祝香港回歸祖國 20 週年招待會上講話。

2017-06-29

Giving a live interview on the *Today* of BBC Radio 4 hosted by John Humphrys. Having a talk after the interview.

接受英國 BBC 廣播四台主持人漢弗萊斯現場直播採訪。採訪後，與漢弗萊斯交談。

2017-11-19

Giving a live interview on ITV's *Peston on Sunday*.

接受英國獨立電視台《佩斯頓星期日訪談》欄目主持人佩斯頓現場直播採訪。

2019-06-21

Giving a live interview on Sky News' *All Out Politics* hosted by Adam Boulton.

接受英國天空新聞台《政治新聞綜述》欄目主持人博爾頓現場直播採訪。

2019-08-15

Hosting a press conference at the Chinese Embassy in UK on Hong Kong issues.

在中國駐英國大使館就香港問題舉行中外記者會。

2019-10-01

Having a live interview on *Sky News Tonight* with Dermot Murnaghan.

接受英國天空新聞台《今夜天空新聞》欄目主持人莫納罕現場直播採訪。

2019-11-26

Giving an interview on BBC's *HARDtalk* hosted by Stephen Sackur.

接受英國 BBC《尖銳對話》欄目主持人薩克現場直播採訪。

2020-02-09

Giving a live interview on BBC's *The Andrew Marr Show*.

接受英國 BBC《安德魯·馬爾訪談》欄目主持人馬爾現場直播採訪。

2020-04-28

Giving an online interview on BBC's *HARDtalk* hosted by Stephen Sackur.

接受英國 BBC《尖銳對話》欄目主持人薩克在線直播採訪。

2020-05-14

Having an online live interview via Zoom on Sky News' *News Hour* with Mark Austin.

接受英國天空新聞台《新聞時間》欄目主持人奧斯汀在線直播採訪。

序言

我於二〇一〇年至二〇二一年擔任中國駐英國大使。使英十一年使我在中國外交史上至少創造了兩項紀錄：一是中英關係史上任期最長的駐英使節；二是中華人民共和國成立以來連續在一國駐節時間最長的大使。然而，最讓我感到驕傲的是另外三項紀錄：駐外一個任期內發表了七百多場演講；在主流報刊撰寫了一百七十多篇文章；接受主流媒體採訪一百七十多次。

大使是一國的代表，全稱是「特命全權大使」，足以顯示其使命光榮、責任重大。大使的主要職責是執行國家外交方針政策，維護國家主權、安全和發展利益，促進本國與駐在國的關係。國家之間的關係涉及方方面面，大使的工作也可謂千頭萬緒。千頭萬緒

抓什麼？怎麼抓？我們常說，國之交在於民相親，民相親在於心相通。使兩國民眾「心相通」，可以說是大使的重要職責，也是做外交工作的最高境界。因此，我抓住各種機會，利用各種平台介紹中國的內外政策，講中國的故事，促進兩國「民相親」「心相通」。

在國外講中國故事與國內有很大不同。特別是在西方國家，講好中國故事更不容易。首先是西方民眾對中國的了解非常有限，他們獲得中國有關信息的主要渠道是西方媒體，包括電視、電台、報刊、網絡、新媒體等。其次是一些民眾對中國存在固有的「傲慢與偏見」。再次是西方媒體對中國片面、歪曲的報道和惡意炒作。最後是一些反華勢力蓄意抹黑中國的形

象。面對這樣的輿論環境，是知難而退，還是迎難而上？我沒有別的選擇，只有挺身而出。有的朋友問我，對於你的每次演講、撰文、採訪，國內是否都有指示？我回答，有，也沒有。國內的指示既原則又明確，就是積極主動發聲，講好中國故事。但怎麼講、對誰講、什麼時候講，則需要使節本人來把握。在講中國故事、傳播中國聲音方面，我始終提醒自己要敢於擔當、不辱使命，要對得起「特命全權大使」這個稱號。

怎樣讓世界聽到中國聲音？我通過演講、撰文、採訪三位一體模式，積極主動開展公共外交，形成全方位立體效應。演講、撰文、採訪各有優勢和短板。演講的優勢是以我為主，主場效果好，答問環節也可有效控場；短板是受眾少，局限於現場聽眾。撰文的優勢是傳播範圍大，讀者群廣泛，特別是對精英階層有較大影響；短板是篇幅受限，而且主動權在報社，能登不能登、登多少字、登什麼版面，甚至連文章標題都由報社來定，據稱這是西方媒體的「行規」，也是「報社特權」。採訪分報刊採訪和廣播採訪。報刊

採訪的優勢和短板與撰文大同小異。廣播採訪和電台採訪又分電視採訪和電台採訪，細分有直播採訪和錄播採訪，還有各大電視台直播或錄播的記者會。電視和電台採訪的優勢是直觀、生動，覆蓋面大，時效快；短板是時長有限，採訪者或主持人掌握發問權和控場節奏。

三種傳播方式不僅優劣勢不同，而且難易差別很大。我把演講、撰文採訪比作「小考」，把記者會比作「中考」，把電視和電台採訪特別是現場直播採訪比作「大考」。之所以叫「大考」，是因為每次現場直播採訪都如同一場「高難度、高強度、高烈度」的博弈。

所謂「高難度」是因為難以掌控。現場直播採訪的主動權完全掌握在主持人手裏。採訪前，對方一般給一個採訪議題範圍。但談起來，主持人可以問任何問題，許多問題與事先商議主題毫無關係。如二〇一四年初英中貿易協會舉辦中國商業大會，當天英國天空新聞台主持人蘭德邀請我作客該台訪談節目《傑夫·蘭德直播間》談談大會情況。結果，整個訪談沒有問一個關於中國商業大會的問題，而是不斷糾纏

新聞自由和網絡監管。在這類採訪過程中，主持人還有意提各種刁難甚至挑釁性問題，有時還搞「突然襲擊」，當場播放幾段編造的視頻，讓你作答。因而，準備一場現場直播採訪是很難的，你不知道對方會問什麼問題，挖什麼「坑」。

所謂「高強度」，是指直播採訪時間短、節奏快、高度緊張。除了個別節目，直播採訪時長一般為五至十分鐘。這樣短的時間內，要談好幾個問題。主持人不停地問，被採訪者抓緊答。主持人經常打斷對方，以掌控對話。被採訪者只能分秒必爭地闡述自己的觀點。

所謂「高烈度」，是指採訪交鋒激烈。西方電視節目主持人與國內的有很大不同。他們不僅把直播採訪看作是討論問題，還看作是鬥智鬥勇的博弈。他們把被採訪者當作對手，準備了各種刁鑽問題，設計了各種陷阱。他們往往對對手的回答並不感興趣，而是刻意讓對手難堪，以顯示他們的智慧和本事，特別是在鏡頭前，他們更是當仁不讓。這就決定了直播採訪必然是針鋒相對，唇槍舌劍，充滿火藥味。英國廣播

公司（BBC）有一檔旗艦直播訪談欄目，乾脆就叫Hard Talk（可譯為《艱難對話》或《尖銳對話》）。

由此可見現場直播採訪的「高烈度」。

在我接受的一百七十多次主流媒體採訪中，五十三次是電視和電台採訪，其中三十三次是英美媒體採訪，現場直播採訪二十九次。對於這二十九次，我都高度重視、認真準備。每次我都召集專門會議，集思廣益。據說，西方公認的「溝通大師」——美國前總統克林頓和英國前首相布萊爾，每次接受直播採訪前，都召集助手假設各種問題，包括模擬現場問答。他們作為諳熟西方媒體運作的西方政治家，又講母語，尚且如此，我們中國外交官更要為之付出幾倍的努力。

為什麼要上電視？為什麼還要選擇現場直播採訪？二〇二〇年新冠肺炎疫情發生不久，以美國為首的西方勢力編造各種謊言和謠言，對中國進行污名化、妖魔化，企圖把病毒源頭扣在中國頭上。我於當年四月接受BBC《尖銳對話》欄目主持人薩克直播採訪，就中國抗疫闡明立場，澄清事實，激濁揚清。

據 BBC 稱，此次採訪在英國國內播放兩次，向全球二百多個國家播放五次，受眾四億多人。這就是我為什麼選擇現場直播採訪，為什麼明知山有虎，偏向虎山行。為了讓世界上更多的人聽到中國聲音，再難、再苦、再累也在所不惜，「三高」擋不住，「大考」難不倒。

本書收錄我使英期間三十二次接受英美電視和電台採訪實錄，其中二十四次為現場直播採訪。我不敢說每次採訪都圓滿成功，回過頭看，的確有不少可以改進的地方，有的可以說得更好些、更全些、更準些。雖然我的能力和水平有限，但我努力了、盡力了，可謂不辱使命，對得起「中國特命全權大使」的稱號。

二〇二二年立春

習近平主席
對英國國事訪問

二〇一五年十月十九至二十三日，應英國女王伊莉莎白二世邀請，習近平主席對英國進行國事訪問。這是中國國家主席十年來首次對英國進行國事訪問，也是在中英建立全面戰略夥伴關係第二個十年的開局之年，我國新一屆領導人對英國的一次重要訪問，具有承前啟後、繼往開來的重大意義。中英雙方決定通過此訪構建面向二十一世紀的全球全面戰略夥伴關係，共同開啟持久、開放、共贏的中英關係「黃金時代」。英國社會各界對習近平主席此訪翹首以待，期待訪問為中英關係確定新的定位、樹立新的目標，制訂新的規劃。英國媒體從電台到電視台，從報紙到雜誌再到新媒體，高度關注、廣泛報道此訪，在英國掀起一股強勁的「習旋風」。同時，也出現了一些不和諧的聲音。少數反華勢力鼓吹「中國威脅論」，一些媒體跟風炒作，編造與中國經貿合作給英國帶來的「安全風險」，並對中國的人權狀況説三道四。

針對這一形勢，我積極主動開展公共外交，廣泛做各界工作，增信釋疑，擴大共識，增進正能量，抑制負能量。除廣泛接觸英國王室、政府、議會、工商、智庫、高校等各界人士外，我還重點做英國媒體工作。我在使館舉行中外記者會，在英國主流大報和習近平主席將訪問的城市地方報紙上發表文章，為西方著名智庫英國皇家國際事務研究所刊物撰文，推動在英國主流社會有較大影響的《名流》《外交家》等刊物出版專刊，介紹習近平主席訪問的重要意義。我還對英國廣播電視媒體實現了全覆蓋，與英國廣播公司（BBC）新聞總監、主持人、編輯、記者等座談，四天接受英國各大電視台五場採訪，其中一天兩場，都是現場直播。採訪中，我介紹了習近平主席訪問的目的和意義，闡述中方在中英關係、人權、網絡安全等問題上的原則立場，澄清事實，批駁謬論。這一系列公共外交活動為習近平主席國事訪問營造了有利的輿論環境。

接受英國電視四台《電視四台新聞》欄目
主持人斯諾現場直播採訪

二〇一五年十月十四日，在習近平主席對英國國事訪問前夕，我接受英國電視四台現場直播採訪。採訪在該台《電視四台新聞》（Channel 4 News）欄目演播室進行，由該欄目主持人喬·斯諾（Jon Snow）主持。

電視四台是英國第三大公共服務電視機構。《電視四台新聞》是該台旗艦新聞節目，以國際報道和深度訪談著稱，觀眾超過一百萬。斯諾是英國著名媒體人，在電視四台擔任主持人近三十年。

斯諾一上來便單刀直入，問習近平主席遠道而來，希望從英國得到什麼，並用典型的英式幽默自嘲英國為中等歐洲國家。他接着就中國的經濟前景、政治制度、人權、司法，英國工黨領袖對華態度等，提出一連串問題。我向他介紹了習近平主席對英國國事訪問的目的和重要意義，回答他的有關提問，重點引導他正確看待中國，特別是正確認識中國共產黨。

斯諾：習近平主席遠道而來，專程訪問英國這樣一個中等歐洲國家，希望從英國得到什麼？

劉曉明：習主席訪英是為了促進中英兩國關係。你把英國稱為「中等國家」，我們並不這樣看。我們認為英國仍是一個擁有全球影響力的國家，是世界經濟增長的動力源之一。中英之間可以合作的地方很多，英國是中國在歐盟內第二大貿易夥伴，中國是英國在歐盟外第二大貿易夥伴，英國是中國在歐洲最大投資目的國，過去三年間中國在英投資迅速增長。

斯諾：難道你不認為這些情況表明，共產黨國家和自由市場經濟這兩種理念在一定程度上存在矛盾嗎？兩者之間能成功結合嗎？

劉曉明：你把中國稱為「共產黨國家」是不對的，中國的國名是中華人民共和國，是由中國共產黨所領導的，正如英國的執政黨是保守黨一樣。

斯諾：但在中國沒有人能選舉一個非共產黨的政黨來管理中國。

劉曉明：但中國經濟形勢不容樂觀，進口下降了百分之二十，股市災難性下跌。習主席是否能夠說這些情況現在都已經過去了？

斯諾：當你觀察中國經濟時，應當關注全局，應從長遠的角度看待中國經濟。從根本上說，中國經濟仍然基本運行良好。今年上半年，增長速度達到百分之七，中國經濟增長速度仍然在世界上領先。

劉曉明：中國共產黨提供了強有力的領導，得到人民的擁護，人民支持共產黨帶領中國由貧窮走向繁榮。這樣好的領導，為什麼要更換？你只需看看中國過去三十年的發展。中國從一個較為貧困的國家一躍成為世界第二大經濟體，這是一個奇蹟。

斯諾：英國是不是在中國人權問題上說得太多了？你認為英國應該停止討論中國的人權問題嗎？

劉曉明：我認為人權問題是可以探討的。沒有哪個國家是完美的。但你們剛才播放的視頻給我留下一種印象，就是一說到中國的人權問題，你們往往只關注負面。要討論人權問題，就必須有全面的觀察，弄清楚人權到底是什麼。我認為，人們有追求更好的生活、更好的教育、更好的工作機會的權利。我想所有人都會同意，中國人民的生活條件比以往更好，人均壽命比以往更長，人們享受幸福生活。

斯諾：但是令人擔憂的是死刑和拘留問題，有很多人被拘留。

劉曉明：你說有「很多人」，你們剛才放的短片說有上百人被拘，但要知道中國有十三億多人口⋯⋯

斯諾：也許不止上百人。

劉曉明：我不知道英國有多少囚犯⋯⋯

斯諾：但英國的囚犯都是經過法律審判的。

劉曉明：在中國，也是要通過正常法律程序進行審判的。中國是一個法治國家，任何人違法都必須承擔法律責任，所有法治國家都應該尊重法律。我們也許在國家治理方法上有所不同，但在厲行法治方面我想我們看法應是一致的。

斯諾：你看過皇家美術學院舉辦的艾未未藝術展嗎？

劉曉明：說實話，我對他的作品不感興趣。英國有這麼多博物館，我都擠不出時間去欣賞⋯⋯

斯諾：但他是國際上最知名的中國藝術家。

劉曉明：我不這麼認為。我認為他之所以在西方出名是因為他對中國政府的政策持批評態度⋯⋯

斯諾：他到底有什麼問題？中國政府跟他有什麼

過節？

劉曉明：他曾因涉嫌經濟犯罪被警方依法調查，被限制出境。但現在有關限制已經取消，他可以出國搞展覽，這恰恰說明了中國很開放。

斯諾：這麼說關係很好？

融洽。

是否感到失望？

劉曉明：最後一個問題，新任工黨領袖科爾賓最近抨擊中國的自由市場理念，他特別提到了最近天津發生的火災，造成許多消防員和工人死亡。他特別批評中國搞自由市場，導致了這場災難。你對這位左翼領導人是否感到失望？

劉曉明：是的，關係很好。至於你剛才提到的事故，這是一場很不幸的悲劇，中國政府正在調查此事，相關的責任人將受到懲罰，決不姑息。

斯諾：非常感謝劉大使接受採訪。

劉曉明：不客氣。

劉曉明：事實上，我今天下午剛和他見過面……

斯諾：噢，這很有意思。

劉曉明：我們商討了他即將和習主席舉行的會見。我們談了很多，談到了工黨對中英關係所作的貢獻，也討論了中國共產黨與英國工黨的黨際交流，談得很

接受英國獨立電視台《十點新聞》欄目
國際主編奧馬爾採訪

作者手記

二○一五年十月十五日，我接受英國獨立電視台（ITV）《十點新聞》（News at Ten）欄目國際主編拉吉・奧馬爾（Rageh Omaar）採訪。採訪中我着重介紹了習近平主席對英國國事訪問的重大意義和中英關係進展情況，並回答了有關中英經貿合作、全球化、人權、野生動物保護等問題。奧馬爾對中英關係的「黃金時代」特別感興趣，我向他詳細介紹了「黃金時代」的由來。

英國獨立電視台設立於一九五五年，是英國歷史最悠久、規模最大的商業電視台，擁有多個頻道，觀眾達四百萬。《十點新聞》是該台強檔新聞節目。

十月十九日，在習主席抵達倫敦當天，獨立電視台在黃金時段播放對我採訪的主要內容，並在該台網站播放採訪實錄視頻。

奧馬爾：為什麼說中英關係進入了「黃金時期」，你的這一認識和信心從何而來？

劉曉明：我的信心來自同英國各界的接觸，來自英國首相和財政大臣對中國的訪問。英國首相和財政大臣都表示，英國希望成為中國在西方最好的夥伴，希望成為中國在西方最堅定的支持者。事實上，「黃金時代」的表述最初來自於卡梅倫首相本人。考慮到今年將迎來中英關係一系列重要事件，我在年初出席英國議會慶祝中國春節活動時，發表了今年第一場公開演講，我用了「大年」一詞來形容二○一五年。在這一年，習主席將對英進行國事訪問。威廉王子於三月份訪華，此訪是繼女王一九八六年訪華後，英國王室成員近三十年對中國進行的一次重要訪問。卡梅倫首相在春節賀詞中使用了「黃金年」的表述，他將今年視為雙邊關係的「黃金年」。在唐寧街舉行的春節招待會上，我見到了卡梅倫首相。我對他說，你的「黃金年」比我的「大年」好，我們於是就今年是中英關係「黃金年」的表述達成共識。卡梅倫首相在今年五月大選後提議，中英雙方為打造中英關係的「黃金時代」共同努力。這一說法得到中國領導人的認同。所以我們不僅在講「黃金年」，也在講中英關係的「黃金時代」。

奧馬爾：但是不久之前你還公開講，英國在發展對華關係方面落後於其他歐洲國家。你的看法為什麼出現這麼大的變化？

劉曉明：事實上，當我說英國在對華關係方面落後於其他歐洲國家時，主要指的是政治領域，媒體沒有完整報道我說的話。當時，有英國媒體問我如何看待中英關係及中法、中德關係。我表示，每一對雙邊關係都各有優勢。我列舉了中英合作在至少五六個領域的優勢，同時表示雙方政治互信和政治關係還有待加強。政治關係是雙邊關係的基礎。英國媒體沒有報道我講話的積極面，而只關注消極面。

奧馬爾：儘管如此，你還是認為英國在發展對華政治

關係方面落後了，現在你已發生了巨大轉變。

劉曉明：那是一年多以前的事了。你知道，在那以後雙方高層交往頻繁。英國首相實現訪華，財政大臣兩度訪華。英國大選剛剛結束，中國外交部部長旋即到訪，在第一時間同英國新政府建立聯繫。今年六月，兩位中國領導人訪問英國。中英關係有三大支柱或機制作為支撐：中國國務委員和英國外交大臣共同主持的中英戰略財金對話；中國副總理和英國財政大臣共同主持的中英經濟財金對話；中國副總理和英國衛生大臣共同主持的高級別人文交流機制會議。今年九月，三個機制均舉行了新一輪對話，雙方高層交往非常頻繁。這些都為習主席的國事訪問做好了鋪墊。可以說，中英政治關係十分有力，政治互信不斷增強。

奧馬爾：國事訪問期間，人權問題——中國的人權問題將被提出來。據我所知，工黨領袖科爾賓表示，他將向中方提出人權問題。針對英國對中國人權記錄的批評，中國如何回應？

劉曉明：正如我在中國大使館舉行的習主席訪英中外記者會上所說，中國對討論人權問題持開放態度。我們不迴避討論人權問題。我們需要全面看待人權問題。一些西方人、政客和媒體只盯着一些個案，卻忽視中國人權進步。三十年來，中國發生了翻天覆地的變化，中國在人權領域取得了巨大進步，任何不抱偏見的人對此都會認同。什麼是人權？當我們談論人權問題時，我們談論的是人們擁有更好的生活、教育、就業機會，更多的言論、結社和旅行自由。有一些人談起人權卻只知道糾纏個案，認為這就是人權問題的核心。為什麼不看一看中國用短短三十年時間使七億人擺脫貧困？這是一個奇蹟，在世界上前所未有。中國醫療保險現在覆蓋了幾乎全部人口，每年出境的中國遊客數量達到一億，中國人人均壽命不斷延長，生活更加幸福。我認為這才是基本人權。

奧馬爾：但總會有人提出與「異見分子」有關的個案。既要提出個案，又想與中國保持良好的經貿合作，這種關係有沒有可能？

劉曉明：雙方要求同存異。我認為，國際關係準則需要各國共同遵守，其中一條基本準則就是不干涉別國內政。如果我認為你的制度不完美，對一些個案不滿意，於是將整個雙邊關係綁架，試問這符合中英兩國的利益嗎？我們有就人權問題開展對話的渠道。我說過，沒有任何國家是十全十美的。雙方都有各自的關切。英國和美國人權也談不上完美，關於中方對英國和美國人權狀況的關切，我可以給你拉一個單子。但我認為高層交往的主要目的、駐英國使館和我作為大使的主要職責並非單單關注人權領域，人權只是雙邊關係中的一個領域。中英在開展合作方面擁有廣泛利益。我認為，英國民眾更關心自己的就業、生活和教育。中國民眾也是一樣。中英兩國政府需要努力尋求共識，共同增進兩國人民的福祉。我們可以就人權問題展開辯論，但不能一葉障目。即使我們把所有的時間用來辯論，恐怕也不會爭出勝負。

奧馬爾：我想問一下中英關係「黃金時代」非常重要的一部分——雙方不斷發展的經貿關係。中國參與

欣克利角核電站項目協議的簽署意義重大。中國企業是否希望更深入參與英國核電項目？

劉曉明：我認為，中國企業對所有能夠產生良好效益、有利於公司發展的項目都感興趣。相信英國企業在中國也是一樣。

奧馬爾：就是說，中國企業對各個領域都感興趣，包括核能、房地產等？

劉曉明：當然。還有基礎設施、酒店。

奧馬爾：中國企業擁有希思羅機場百分之十股份。

劉曉明：擁有希思羅機場百分之十股份、泰晤士水務百分之八股份，還有維他麥、曼徹斯特空港城等，中國企業在英國有一系列投資。

奧馬爾：會有大型商業代表團隨訪嗎？

劉曉明：商業代表團會單獨抵達英國，不作為習主席代表團的一部分。國事訪問和其他訪問十分不同。各界都希望利用訪問加深各自領域的合作，希望習主席和英國首相見證合作協議的簽署。這對企業來說是一種殊榮。

奧馬爾：你將此訪稱為「超級國事訪問」，似乎中英關係要重新開啟，或說是重振中英關係。這是不是說得過頭了？

劉曉明：我確實說過這將是一次「超級國事訪問」，意思是雙方要在現有基礎上將雙邊關係提升到新的高度，給雙邊關係一個新定位。這也是為什麼我認為訪問是承前啟後、繼往開來的新里程碑。過去幾年雙方沒有談到「黃金時代」，而這次，雙方首次達成開啟中英關係「黃金時代」的共識。

奧馬爾：中國對國事訪問的報道多不多？中國人怎麼看這次訪問？

劉曉明：中英兩國人民對彼此抱有好感。幾個月前我看到一項調查，顯示在對中國的好感度上，英國要高於許多其他歐洲國家。我想這在中國也一樣。當英國政府決定率先加入亞洲基礎設施投資銀行時，我剛好在國內。英國此舉得到廣泛好評和歡迎。中國人民認為英國領導人具有遠見，他們看到了英國視中國崛起為機遇，而非威脅。中英兩國把彼此視為真誠夥伴，看到了雙方合作的機遇。這不僅是隆重的場面，也不是空談的口號，而是實實在在的行動。

奧馬爾：近期英國國內關注的焦點之一是雷德卡鋼鐵廠因來自中國的廉價鋼鐵競爭而被迫關閉的問題。英國曾是一個鋼鐵製造大國。在英國，鋼鐵產區的民眾是否有理由對來自中國的競爭表示擔心呢？

劉曉明：我們生活在全球化的時代，每個國家都需要不斷推進經濟轉型。在中國擁有優勢的一些領域，其他國家需要調整轉型，反之也是一樣。你知道，中國

曾在服裝、鞋和玩具製造方面擁有強大的優勢，一度生產了全世界百分之八十至百分之九十的玩具。但現在一些東南亞國家在這些領域的優勢逐漸凸顯，低廉的勞動力成本使它們具有更強的競爭力。這時就需要我們作出調整。如果還是一味固守缺乏競爭力的產業，就會喪失發展的機會。這就是中國積極推進經濟轉型的原因。一些人擔心中國經濟增速放緩，實際上這種放緩是健康的調整過程。即使增速由之前的兩位數降至百分之八或百分之七，中國經濟增長速度仍居世界前列。中國經濟正在轉型，英國經濟為什麼就不能轉型呢？

奧馬爾：威廉王子錄製的關於野生動物非法貿易的電視短片即將在中國播出。中英是否會在該問題上合作？

劉曉明：沒錯。中國是國際打擊瀕臨滅絕物種非法貿易和保護野生動物的堅定支持者。中國在這一問題上的態度積極主動。我曾陪同威廉王子訪華，習主席會

見他時我也在座。雙方談到中英如何開展合作，保護野生動物，打擊非法貿易。習主席介紹了中國作出的努力，包括銷毀五噸象牙。這顯示出中國政府的決心。中國還是許多動物保護國際會議的積極參與者。威廉王子和查爾斯王儲共同倡議召開了倫敦打擊非法野生動物貿易峰會，中國派出大型代表團參會。中國還舉辦了保護野生動物相關論壇。相信中英在該領域合作潛力巨大。

奧馬爾：謝謝大使先生接受採訪！

劉曉明：不客氣。

接受英國 BBC《新聞之夜》欄目
主持人戴維斯現場直播採訪

作者手記

二〇一五年十月十六日，我在英國 BBC《新聞之夜》(Newsnight) 欄目演播室接受該欄目主持人埃文‧戴維斯 (Evan Davis) 現場直播採訪，介紹習近平主席對英國國事訪問有關情況。

《新聞之夜》是英國 BBC 電視二台旗艦時政訪談欄目，以深度分析和激烈辯論著稱，在英國政界和知識界影響較大，全球受眾廣泛，英國及世界政要、商界領袖、社會名流、知識精英經常接受該欄目採訪。

戴維斯是經濟學家，在 BBC 多個欄目擔任主持人，以提問犀利、刁鑽、咄咄逼人聞名。我們圍繞中英經貿和投資合作、中國「機遇論」和「威脅論」、網絡安全、人權、民主等問題展開了激烈討論。

戴維斯：我們今天邀請到中國駐英國大使劉曉明先生。大使先生，晚上好。感謝你來到我們的演播室。

劉曉明：感謝邀請。

戴維斯：如果中英位置互換一下，你認為中國會允許英國的承包商在中國建設核電站嗎？

劉曉明：我想問一個問題，你們有資金，你們有技術在中國建核電站嗎？

戴維斯：假如有，你認為我們可以得到允許嗎？

劉曉明：假如有？我不太確定。我認為，英國希望中國來英投資建設核電站，是因為英國需要中國的資金和技術，中國擁有先進的核電技術，中國的核電站數量比許多國家都要多。

戴維斯：所以中國建造了許多核電站，而英國可以從

中受益。但我認為中國不會允許英國投資中國的核電站。我從中國的政府網站上找到一份限制或禁止外商投資的產業目錄，比英國限制得更為嚴格。目錄六，包括放射性礦產品勘探開採；目錄九，放射性礦產品冶煉加工和包裝，核燃料生產等。中國禁止外國投資其核電行業，你是不是認為我們允許中國投資英國核電站的做法很愚蠢？

劉曉明：你們一點也不愚蠢。事實上，你們很聰明，懂得用中國的資金來建造你們的核電站，讓英國人民獲益。可以的話，我們也想這麼做。

戴維斯：好吧。這是雙贏的局面。

劉曉明：我同意你的說法，雙贏。

戴維斯：很多其他行業是英國的強項，但中國卻禁止外商投資。比如航空交管。英國一家實力很強的空管公司就不能進入中國。還有郵政、拍賣、古董店、高

爾夫球場建設等等。為什麼中國禁止外商投資高爾夫球場？

劉曉明：事實上，有一些外商在中國投資高爾夫球場。你最近一次去中國是什麼時候？

戴維斯：這份禁止外商投資產業目錄上是這麼規定的，這份規定是不是過時了？

劉曉明：事實上，中國企業和外國企業有很多合作，中國有不少合資企業……

戴維斯：為什麼是合資形式？為什麼外商進入中國不能……

劉曉明：他們可以進入中國，建立合資企業。這樣，中國的合資夥伴就可以幫助他們的外國夥伴了解中國市場。你要知道，中國和英國處於不同發展階段。正如你們剛才的短片所說，英國在很多方面都比中國先

進。中國還是一個發展中國家，我們必須一步一步來。我們要借鑑英國的經驗，避免英國曾經犯過的錯誤。因此我們在一些領域要謹慎小心。

戴維斯：這是雙贏的事情，我們歡迎中國來投資，允許中資進入各個領域。可是有時候看起來不太對等。

劉曉明：我不這麼認為。如果不對等的話，英國怎麼能成為歐盟內僅次於德國的第二大對華投資國？而且，英國對華投資還在不斷增長。所以我認為這是雙贏的。

戴維斯：再問一個問題。英國有很多安全關切，今天《泰晤士報》引述了安全部門對核電站合作的關切。有人擔心中國在核電站計算機系統中植入「後門」，這樣一旦英中兩國發生外交爭端，中國可以繞過英國對核電站進行管控。在核電站的安全清潔方面以及核電站的管控問題上，中國如何讓英國人放心？

劉曉明：中國將嚴格遵循國際標準。你們的情報部門不會笨到不知道這些事情。中國到英國來是為了雙贏的合作，我們不是為了控制英國的核電站。控制英國的核電站對中國有什麼好處呢？如果雙方要成為夥伴，相互之間應有一個基本的信任。如果任由這種負面言論發展，中國企業可能就不敢來英國投資了。如果這樣，那麼就與財政大臣奧斯本所說的「英國是對中國投資最開放的西方國家」背道而馳了。

戴維斯：「基本的信任」，但這種基本的信任存在嗎？據說在上海，有一座中國人民解放軍六萬一千三百九十八部隊的大樓，發出大量的網絡攻擊，這是瞎說嗎？

劉曉明：這不過是謠傳、炒作。首先我要告訴你，中國政府堅決反對這種行為。不久前，習近平主席對美國進行國事訪問的時候，中美兩國就共同打擊網絡犯罪達成共識。中國的任何政府部門都不會參與網絡間諜活動，中國政府也不會支持任何這樣的行為。這是中國政府的承諾。

戴維斯：我們不會相信這一點，這是一種承諾嗎？

劉曉明：如果你們都不相信我們，又怎麼能共同建設夥伴關係？

戴維斯：但一份洩露出來題為《軍事戰略科學》的手冊中承認，中國有網絡攻擊部隊。這個網絡攻擊部隊是怎麼回事？

劉曉明：我不相信有這樣的事情。我不認為中國有網絡攻擊部隊。中國是開放合作的國家。事實上，中國本身就是網絡攻擊的受害者。

戴維斯：是的。

劉曉明：孔子有一句名言。很抱歉，我要把你帶回到兩千多年前。孔子曰：「己所不欲，勿施於人。」這

就是中國人的哲學，中國人信奉這一哲學。我們不會去攻擊任何人，因為我們自己是黑客攻擊的受害者。

戴維斯：簡要問一個關於人權的問題。假如下週英國大張旗鼓地談論人權問題，比如進行抗議，假如反對黨領袖或首相大談人權問題以及英國的人權觀，英國會在對華經貿和投資合作方面付出代價嗎？

劉曉明：首先，我想問你兩個問題：第一，你認為英國的人權狀況完美嗎？第二，你認為英國的模式在全世界看來是完美的嗎？我認為每個國家在如何改善人權、如何保護人權的問題上都有自己不同的國情。你同意我的看法嗎？

戴維斯：我同意。

劉曉明：你怎麼定義人權？

戴維斯：我不是在批評中國的人權。我的問題不是關

於中國的人權狀況。我的問題是，如果英國批評中國的人權狀況，當然中國也可以批評英國的人權，我們將為此付出代價嗎？

劉曉明：難道這是習主席對英國進行國事訪問的目的嗎？大家相互批評對方的人權狀況？

戴維斯：不是，當然不是！但如果英方提出人權問題，英國是否會為此付出代價而失去中國投資？我想，如果習主席訪問英國的時候批評英國的人權⋯⋯

劉曉明：這不是中國人做事的方式。

戴維斯：我知道習主席不會這樣做。

劉曉明：我們尊重他國國情。中國憲法保障人權，而且人權說到底是一國的內政問題。我希望你們以全面的眼光看待中國的人權事業。你知道⋯⋯

戴維斯：我不是要爭論人權問題。我的問題是關於貿易。中國是否會用貿易手段阻止我們談論人權問題？

劉曉明：當然不會。

戴維斯：那麼就是說，如果英國談論中國人權問題，不會付出代價，貿易和投資……

劉曉明：你認為我們會把貿易當成武器去爭取我們要得到的東西嗎？這種想法絕對是錯誤的。貿易是雙贏的。我們出口你們需要的東西，進口我們需要的東西，這是雙贏的。

戴維斯：那就是說如果有時我們在人權問題上有不同看法，雙方還可以繼續進行經貿合作？

劉曉明：中英兩國的社會制度，包括政治制度和經濟制度，以及歷史、文化有很大差異，雙方處於不同的發展階段，我們之間有不同，這很正常。但我們仍然

可以合作，我們可以求同存異。你同意我的觀點嗎？

戴維斯：我同意。我很高興我們看法一致。最後一個簡短的問題，我們的衛生大臣談到他的華裔妻子以及亞洲人的工作觀念。他說，希望英國人民能像亞洲國家人民那樣勤奮工作。你認為英國人勤勞嗎？還是享受了太多福利？

劉曉明：中英兩國可以相互學習。中國人民很勤勞，英國人民富有創造性，兩國人民可以相互學習。

戴維斯：你的意思是說英國人不夠勤勞？（笑聲）

劉曉明：應該說中國人民更勤勞。中國之所以能創造奇蹟，在三十年的時間裏，把一個相對落後的國家發展成為世界第二大經濟體，我想這應該歸功於勤勞苦幹的中國人民。

戴維斯：你認為再過四十年，中國會像英國一樣嗎？

可以民主選舉國家主席嗎？

劉曉明：這又回到了我們之間的根本差異問題。你們認為英國的制度是民主的，而我們認為中國的制度是民主的，我們稱之為中國特色的民主。英國的領導人並不是直接選舉產生的。中國的領導人也是通過間接選舉產生的。我們選舉產生縣級人大代表，之後逐級選舉產生市級、省級和全國人大代表，再由全國人民代表大會選舉產生國家主席。

戴維斯：這是一個很大的議題。我們還要請你回來，再討論這個議題。

劉曉明：我們可以花整個晚上的時間來討論民主問題。

戴維斯：大使先生，非常感謝。

劉曉明：不客氣。

接受英國 BBC《安德魯·馬爾訪談》欄目主持人馬爾現場直播採訪

作者手記

二〇一五年十月十八日，我接受英國 BBC《安德魯·馬爾訪談》（The Andrew Marr Show）欄目主持人安德魯·馬爾（Andrew Marr）現場直播採訪。

《安德魯·馬爾訪談》是 BBC 旗艦直播欄目，也是英國最有影響力的時政訪談節目之一，每週日現場直播一小時，收視人群約有五百萬。該欄目每次邀請四至五位嘉賓，就不同的議題與主持人一對一交談。英國首相、內閣大臣、各政黨領袖、社會名流、學術精英等經常接受該欄目採訪。

欄目主持人馬爾是英國知名媒體人、專欄作家、政治評論員、歷史學家，寫過十多部歷史專著，多數被評為暢銷書；獲多項新聞大獎，包括兩次被評為「年度專欄作家」。曾多次採訪英國政要和外國領導人，包括俄羅斯總統普京、美國總統奧巴馬等。他創辦《安德魯·馬爾訪談》欄目，並擔任該欄目主持人達十六年，直至二〇二一年底離開 BBC。

我使英十一年，曾先後四次接受馬爾現場直播採訪，這是第一次。我們圍繞習近平主席對英國國事訪問、中英經貿關係、人權等問題展開了討論。採訪結束時，馬爾預祝習主席對英國國事訪問取得圓滿成功。

馬爾：中國國家主席習近平即將對英國進行國事訪問。在訪問前夕，我們邀請到中國駐英國大使劉曉明。歡迎你，大使先生，很高興你能作客我們的欄目。

劉曉明：謝謝。

馬爾：首先提一個關於英中關係的問題。你是否認為，就中國而言，英國就像一個經濟「乞丐」，沒資格向中國提人權問題？

劉曉明：首先，中國和英國是夥伴關係，我們稱之為全面戰略夥伴關係。兩國都是具有全球影響力的大國，有廣泛領域可以進行合作，實現雙贏。你談到人權，這當然也是我們可以討論的領域，關鍵在於以什麼方式討論。談論人權問題時，人們應以全面的眼光看待中國的人權事業，應該看到中國人權事業所取得的巨大進步。

馬爾：也就是說，情況已經發生變化。英國工黨領袖科爾賓表示要提人權問題。如果他在女王為習主席舉辦的國宴上提出人權問題，這不會冒犯習主席吧？

劉曉明：你覺得科爾賓會在女王舉辦的國宴上提出人權問題嗎？我不這麼認為。習主席對英國進行國事訪問是為合作和夥伴關係而來，不是來爭論人權問題的。我們都知道，中英兩國存在很多差異。兩國歷史、文化不同，處於不同發展階段，雙方有不同看法是很正常的，在人權問題上也是如此。在中國，我們更關心的是人民有權享有更好的生活、更好的工作、更好的住房。我認為中國人民現在過着幸福的生活。另一方面，中國人民也享有……

馬爾：但在中國，有很多「異見人士」因為表達自己的觀點而被投入監獄。

劉曉明：這種說法不對。在中國，所有違法者都要通過正常的司法程序進行審判。

馬爾：但他們因為批評中國政府而入獄，在英國，我們不認為這是犯罪。

劉曉明：沒有人因為批評政府而入獄。服法入獄的人是因為他們從事犯罪活動，包括煽動、從事或組織推翻合法政府。在英國，如果有人從事危害英國國家利益、危害英國人民安全的行動，我想他們也會受到法律的懲罰。也許我們雙方看法不同，我們可以進行討論。

馬爾：大使，我給你舉一個具體的例子。英國皇家美術學院正在舉辦一個非常重要、令人興奮的藝術展，倫敦很多年都未舉行這樣的藝術展，這就是艾未未藝術展。艾未未是一個國際化的中國人，他是個愛國者，為自己是中國人感到自豪。他的父親和毛主席等老一輩關係密切，而他卻曾被短暫地關在監獄裏。你認為艾未未是「異見人士」，或是危險分子，還是愛國公民？

劉曉明：我不知道你對這個所謂「藝術家」了解多少。我曾接受 BBC 另一個節目採訪，我告訴主持人，我對艾未未的「藝術」不感興趣。中國有很多才華出眾的藝術家，比艾未未更有才華。艾未未之所以出名，是因為他批評中國政府。事實上，艾未未從未被關入監獄。他因為涉嫌經濟犯罪，包括做假賬、故意銷毀會計憑證等，而依法受到調查。如果是在英國，一個藝術家也同樣涉嫌經濟犯罪，你們不會對他進行調查嗎？

馬爾：我只能說，我們倆在這個問題上的看法不同，我認為艾未未是一個偉大的藝術家，他的展覽非常精彩。我們意見可以不同，但還是可以繼續談論下一個話題。查爾斯王儲決定不出席女王舉行的國宴，這是否會冒犯中國政府？

劉曉明：查爾斯王儲將在多個場合與習主席會面。如果他不能出席女王舉行的歡迎晚宴，一定有自己的原因。據我所知，查爾斯王儲為接待習主席作了很

026

劉曉明：我曾被問到同樣的問題，而我反問了幾個問題：你們有資金嗎？你們有技術嗎？你們有管理經驗嗎？如果你們都有，我們當然希望與你們合作。比如法國，中國和法國在核電領域有一些合作，因為法國在核電方面擁有先進的技術。我認為英國在其他領域更有優勢，為什麼眼睛總盯著在中國建核電站呢？

馬爾：人們期待下週英中將簽署一個關於核電的大合同，你認為會簽嗎？

劉曉明：我當然希望如此，因為這是兩國的重大合作項目。

馬爾：最後一個問題，你剛才說不認為科爾賓會在女王舉辦的歡迎晚宴上向習主席提出人權問題，但科爾賓的助手說他要提。如果科爾賓真的提出人權問題怎麼辦？

劉曉明：我想，這個歡迎晚宴是女王舉辦的，女王是

多努力。他為了與習主席會面，甚至調整了原先的日程安排。據我所知，查爾斯王儲至少將與習主席會面三次......

馬爾：抱歉打斷一下，我能不能再問一個問題。英國的安全和情報專家警告英國政府，中國正通過核電站建設合同來接近英國國家安全的核心。換句話說，英國正在打開大門，讓中國接觸到一些包括中國在內的其他國家絕不會對外開放的領域。

劉曉明：我不知道那些人從哪兒搞到這些信息。我可以告訴你，中國到英國投資是為了雙贏合作，這符合英國的利益，也有利於中英合作夥伴關係。英國需要中國的投資，英國人民希望過上更好的生活，希望擁有清潔能源。據我所知，今後十多年裏，英國將淘汰不少舊的核電站，因此需要找到新的能源供應。

馬爾：英國當然需要資金和技術。但中國政府肯定不允許外國在中國投資建設核電站吧？

主人。不管是科爾賓還是其他人，都是女王的客人。英國是禮儀之邦，英國人很聰明，他們知道在這樣的場合應該如何做。我們並不迴避討論人權問題。上週，我見到了科爾賓，我們談得很好。我希望⋯⋯

馬爾：那你的建議是，不要在這種公開的場合提人權問題？

劉曉明：我們對「麥克風式外交」不感興趣，對「鏡頭外交」也不感興趣，我們更願意坦誠地交換意見。如果他有關切的問題，我們可以討論。

馬爾：大使先生，非常感謝你接受採訪。預祝習主席對英國的國事訪問取得圓滿成功。

劉曉明：謝謝。

接受英國天空新聞台《莫納罕訪談》欄目
主持人莫納罕現場直播採訪

作者手記

二○一五年十月十八日，我就習近平主席對英國國事訪問，接受英國天空新聞台（Sky News）《莫納罕訪談》(Murnaghan Programme) 欄目主持人德莫特·莫納罕 (Dermot Murnaghan) 現場直播採訪。

英國天空新聞台是除 BBC 新聞台之外英國唯一一個二十四小時滾動播放新聞的有線電視頻道，擁有七百五十多萬觀眾。該台在海外對一百三十八個國家和地區播放新聞節目，約有一點一五億用戶。《莫納罕訪談》是該台旗艦時事訪談節目，以深度辯論著稱。莫納罕是該台資深主持人，曾擔任 BBC 和英國獨立電視台主持人。

我向他介紹了習主席訪問英國的重要意義，回答了他有關網絡安全、中英經貿合作、人權等問題的提問。

莫納罕：中國國家主席習近平下週將對英國進行國事訪問，卡梅倫首相形容兩國關係將進入「黃金時代」。兩國可能將簽署一系列重要協議，包括核能合作。今天，我們有幸邀請了中國駐英國大使劉曉明參與我們的節目。早上好，劉大使。首先，請問英國是否應該對中國感到擔心？

劉曉明：沒有什麼好擔心的。中國是個愛好和平的國家，習主席訪問旨在促進合作，鞏固兩國夥伴關係。兩國有很多領域可以開展合作。作為具有全球影響力的國家，中英兩國攜手合作可以共同建設一個更美好的世界，促進世界繁榮，維護世界和平。

莫納罕：我問這個問題，是因為英國軍情五處網站上開設了一個公眾互動欄目，並進行了一次關於國家安全最大威脅的問卷調查，來自中國的網絡恐怖主義被列為第二大威脅。我想，你也可能看到了這個問卷，軍情五處對中國感到擔憂。

劉曉明：中國堅決反對網絡犯罪，中國自己就是黑客攻擊的受害者。

莫納罕：這些攻擊來自何處？

劉曉明：來自各個方面，網絡空間不是一個安全的地方，各國應共同合作，而不是相互指責。習主席對美國國事訪問期間，他與奧巴馬總統達成共識，中美兩國政府均反對任何網絡犯罪活動，也不支持任何組織參與網絡犯罪活動。

莫納罕：這一共識說得十分清楚明了，但為什麼軍情五處分析認為中國在網絡犯罪問題上是全球最大威脅之一？

劉曉明：聽到這樣的分析，我感到很遺憾。我聽到不少關於對核電站安全的擔心。中國企業是應英國政府和企業的要求前來建設核電站的，他們來不是為了所謂控制核電站，而是為了開展雙贏的合作。他們的活

動將嚴格遵循國際標準和規則，是透明的。英國的安全監管部門不會笨到讓中國企業控制英國的核設施。我認為這些擔心是一些媒體炒作的結果，有些人不想看到……

莫納罕：媒體和安全部門會說，這是軍情五處網站問卷調查得出的結論。

劉曉明：你應該去問軍情五處。中國企業來英國不是當間諜的，不是來刺探英國的核設施的，他們有重要的事情要做，他們來英國是為了合作，為了雙贏的合作，這是中國企業投資的唯一目的。

莫納罕：聽說習主席來訪期間將與英方深入討論「北部振興計劃」，聽說這個詞很難翻譯成中文。

劉曉明：沒那麼難，中文詞彙十分豐富。你會說中文嗎？

莫納罕：對不起，不會。

劉曉明：是有幾個不同的譯法，最終我們選定了一個比較貼切的。

莫納罕：很高興聽到這一點。但是，人們對英格蘭北部地區的發展有不少憂慮，特別是鋼鐵產業。中國是個鋼鐵大國，人們對此很擔心。有人批評中國將自己過剩的鋼鐵傾銷到世界各地，你能接受這種批評嗎？今早英國有家媒體稱，與其說你打造一個「北部振興計劃」，不如說製造一個「北方貧困帶」，你對此有何評論？

劉曉明：在全球化時代，每個國家均需進行相應的產業調整，中國也是一樣。中國過去一直是個加工業大國，生產大量玩具、服裝等，英國和美國百分之八十至百分之九十的玩具來自中國。現在，我們面臨來自東南亞國家的競爭，它們的勞動力成本遠低於中國，競爭力強，許多工廠都轉移到那些國家去了。所以，

中國也在努力從加工業大國向製造業大國轉型，每個國家都需要進行調整。中國企業到英國來了，要努力適應，尋找中英兩國的共同點。我們肯定會考慮到英方的關切，考慮當地民眾的關切。

莫納罕：作為中國大使，你一定聽說不少關於中國人權記錄的關切，尤其是對中國大量死刑人數的關切。卡梅倫首相曾表示，英國反對死刑，哪裏有死刑，英國就會抓住一切機會提出這一問題。假如英國首相向中國主席提出這一問題，你是否覺得很無禮呢？

劉曉明：我在英已任職五年，我經常聽到人們談及人權問題。然而，人們往往看不到中國人權的整體情況。什麼是人權？

莫納罕：就是公正司法的權力，不被輕易判處死刑。

劉曉明：基本的人權就是讓人們生活得更好。在我看來，有些人談論人權時，往往看不到中國在僅僅

三十年的時間裏就使七億人脫貧，沒有哪個國家能在這麼短的時間裏取得這樣的成績。中國人現在生活得更好，壽命更長，享受着幸福生活。在政治生活中，中國人民享有前所未有的尊嚴和自由。你談到死刑問題，中國是個大國，治理一個十三億多人口的國家與治理一個六千四百萬人口的國家自然是不一樣的。中國在死刑問題上十分慎重，死刑數量在逐年下降，而且要經過最高人民法院的嚴格覆核程序。

莫納罕：最後問一個有關工黨領袖科爾賓的問題。前一段時間你一定在密切關注工黨領袖選舉。關於習主席將與英國的在野黨即工黨領袖科爾賓談什麼，你們是否進行過實質性探討？

劉曉明：國事訪問期間，習主席將在白金漢宮會見工黨領袖科爾賓，我們期待習主席與科爾賓進行一次富有成果、有意義的會見。

莫納罕：中國與科爾賓能搞好關係嗎？科爾賓是個社

會主義者，而你們是共產主義者。

劉曉明：社會主義者之間可以辯論，社會主義者和共產主義者之間也可以進行辯論，但我們來英國是為了尋求共同點。事實上，我上星期會見了科爾賓，為習主席與科爾賓的會見作準備。我們的會見很有意義，工黨曾為發展中英關係作出了重要貢獻。現在，我們與保守黨及工黨均保持良好的黨際關係。我真誠地希望，在科爾賓的領導下，工黨繼續為發展這一重要雙邊關係作出積極貢獻。

莫納罕：大使閣下，我們採訪時間到了，非常高興見到你，也非常感謝你。預祝習主席訪問取得圓滿成功。

劉曉明：謝謝。

如何認識中國

英國是最早承認中華人民共和國的西方大國，也是最早同中華人民共和國開展經貿往來的西方大國之一。時至今日，兩國交流覆蓋各個方面，涉及各個領域，廣度和深度均今非昔比。但令人遺憾的是，中英之間仍然存在「了解赤字」和「認知赤字」。英國電視台、電台、報紙、網絡關於中國的報道，仍有不少偏見、誤導，甚至假消息。在這樣的輿論環境裏，英國民眾難以了解真實的中國，他們對中國的認知有很多誤區，特別是對中國共產黨存在很大誤解。一些人聽到「共產黨」和「共產主義」就產生心理障礙，因而也就難以客觀地看待共產黨領導下的中國。針對這種現象，我在英國講中國故事時，重點講中國共產黨的故事，講中國共產黨帶領中國人民實現中華民族偉大復興的故事，使英國民眾了解中國共產黨是什麼，要幹什麼；從哪裏來，到哪裏去。我多次在英國電視台、電台接受現場直播採訪，介紹中共十八大、十九大、人大、政協「兩會」。針對BBC主持人對中國共產黨的誤解，我指出，中國共產黨將馬克思主義理論與中國國情相結合，建立了中國特色社會主義制度。這一制度符合中國實際，給中國帶來了發展與進步，取得了巨大成功，造福了廣大人民，得到了廣大人民的擁護。在英國獨立電視台的現場直播採訪中談到中共十九大，我指出，習近平總書記將帶領中國人民開啟中國特色社會主義的新時代，到二〇二〇年中國將徹底消除絕對貧困，全面建成小康社會。

接受英國 BBC 廣播四台
主持人多德採訪

作者手記

二〇一一年十二月二十日，我在英國 BBC 廣播四台（BBC Radio 4）演播室接受知名主持人菲利普·多德（Philip Dodd）的採訪。

多德是英國著名學者、作家、記者、編輯、企業家、節目主持人，著有多本專著，創辦多種雜誌，擔任 BBC 顧問兼主持人，曾擔任倫敦現代藝術學會會長。他也是國際知名策展人，推動舉辦國際民間博物館峰會，創辦創意產業公司「中國製造」，促成英國維多利亞與艾爾伯特博物館落戶廣東深圳。

此次採訪正值大熊貓「陽光」和「甜甜」剛剛抵達蘇格蘭愛丁堡，這也是我第一次接受英國廣播電台採訪。採訪主要圍繞大熊貓來英國的意義及中英關係。

多德：為什麼大熊貓對中國非常重要？大熊貓是否是中國送給英國的「厚禮」？

劉曉明：大熊貓是中國的「國寶」，也是世界瀕危物種。由於大熊貓發情難、受孕難、育幼難，所以野生大熊貓數量很少。為了拯救和保護大熊貓，中國政府在政策制定、法制建設、資金投入等方面採取多項措施，大熊貓保護狀況呈現不斷向好趨勢。但即使如此，大熊貓野生種群數量也只有約一千六百隻。

我想強調，大熊貓來英國不能簡單被定性為「贈禮」，而是中英雙方一個重要科研合作項目，涵蓋野外生態學、大熊貓人工繁殖和育幼、大熊貓認知演化和行為研究等多個領域。雖然歷史上來英國的熊貓不少，但是從未在中英兩國科學家攜手合作下，大熊貓「甜甜」和「陽光」能盡快產下熊貓寶寶，為中英大熊貓聯合研究帶來新成果，為人工培育的大熊貓重返大自然提供更多幫助。

多德：大熊貓作為中國派出的「形象大使」，將向外界傳達什麼信息？中國是否認為大熊貓來英國有助於提升中國軟實力？據估算，二〇二〇年，中國中產階層將達到六億人，中國是否認為西方國家喜愛大熊貓源自對開拓中國市場的興趣？

劉曉明：大熊貓體態黑白分明，憨態可掬，備受中國人民和世界人民的喜愛。大熊貓來英國傳達的信息可以用三個 P 概括，即 Panda Conservation（熊貓保護）、Public Awareness（普及知識）、Peoples Friendship（民間友好）。在國外開展大熊貓合作首要目的和任務是促進在人工和自然環境下的熊貓繁衍和生存研究；其次是普及熊貓的知識，讓國外民眾近距離、直觀地了解熊貓，更加喜愛熊貓，支持熊貓保護工作；再者是以熊貓為使者，增進人民之間的友誼。

「甜甜」和「陽光」落戶愛丁堡將成為中英增進了解、深化友誼、擴大合作的紐帶，為兩國人民友好交往譜寫新的佳話。

038

了解大熊貓，必然離不開了解它們的故鄉——中國，了解中國的風土人情、經濟社會；了解今天的中國走和平發展道路，願與世界互利共贏；了解中國人民熱情善良，願與各國人民友好相處。

為推動兩國青少年友好交往，中國駐英國使館與英國的一些大學合作，正在全英百所中小學開展大熊貓主題演講和繪畫比賽，特等獎得主將有機會訪問大熊貓的故鄉——中國四川。

中國對加強對外經濟合作持開放和歡迎態度。中國過去三十多年來取得了舉世矚目的發展成就，但中國的中產階層將於今後十年達到六億人的說法似乎有些誇大。中國人均 GDP 仍排在世界一百位以後，一億多人還生活在聯合國界定的貧困線以下。中國在相當長的時間內仍將是發展中國家，中國的發展還有很長的路要走。中國改革開放已經三十多年，中國入世也已滿十年，中國的市場越來越開放，今後中國願與包括英國在內的世界各國擴大互利合作，實現共同發展。

多德：你是否認為西方對中國不夠了解？

劉曉明：坦率地說，西方確實存在對中國不了解，甚至誤解的情況。中西方文化不同，處事風格迥異。比如，西方人送禮物時會說：「我的禮物有多好，希望你喜歡。」但中國人即使送很昂貴的禮物，也只說：「這點薄禮不成敬意，請笑納。」

我還想指出，增加了解是雙向道。中國人應更多地向外界講中國故事，與世界分享成功經驗。同時，西方媒體應該全面客觀報道中國，向西方公眾展示一個真實的中國。讓西方公眾看到，中國取得的成就不僅限於經濟，而是包括政治、社會、文化等全方位的發展進步。希望中西方能共同努力，增進西方公眾對當代中國的全面認識。期待 BBC 為此作出積極努力。

多德：我完全贊同。

接受英國BBC《新聞之夜》欄目
主持人帕克斯曼現場直播採訪

作者手記

二○一二年一月二十三日是農曆大年初一，我來到英國BBC《新聞之夜》（Newsnight）欄目演播室，接受該欄目主持人傑里米·帕克斯曼（Jeremy Paxman）現場直播採訪。

主持人帕克斯曼是英國著名記者、作家、評論家，在BBC旗艦時政欄目《新聞之夜》擔任主持人二十五年。他採訪風格直率、犀利、咄咄逼人，英國輿論界對其褒貶不一。褒者稱讚他知識淵博、頭腦清晰、提問尖銳，特別是對政客毫不留情，常把對方逼到牆角。貶者認為他居高臨下、傲慢偏激、目中無人、言辭尖刻，甚至使被採訪者感到恐懼，因此引起不少爭議。

這是我出任駐英國大使以來，第一次接受電視直播採訪。當時國際上沒有突發事件，中英關係也沒有突出問題。BBC稱，帕克斯曼想跟中國大使結識一下，隨便聊聊，談什麼都行。這的確是一個介紹中國的機會，但也存在很大風險。一是沒有主題，無從準備；二是帕克斯曼的採訪風格令許多英國政客，包括內閣大臣，望而

生畏。我第一次上來就面對一個「狠主」，多少感到有些緊張，但責任感呼喚我必須迎戰。

果不出所料，帕克斯曼一上來就咄咄逼人，問：「你是共產黨嗎？」我知道來者不善，他並不是要搞清楚我的身份，而是要給中國貼標籤。在西方，特別是在冷戰時期，「共產黨」是個貶義詞，「共產黨國家」便成了專制的代名詞。美國有位參議員至死不叫中國的全名「中華人民共和國」，張口閉口「紅色中國」「共產黨中國」。

二十世紀五〇年代，周恩來總理在會見美國青年代表團時，曾糾正美國記者的提問，告訴他中國的國名是「中華人民共和國」，不是「共產黨中國」；就像美國叫「美利堅合眾國」，不叫「共和黨美國」。周總理說，國家是人民的，人民選舉代表來領導這個國家。時至今日，冷戰殘餘未消，「共產黨中國」「共產黨國家」仍不時掛在西方政客嘴邊，出現在西方各種媒體上。我抓住帕克斯曼這個提問機會，批駁冷戰思維，為我們的黨和國家正名。

接著，我們圍繞中國的對外政策和國際作用、中國經濟實力、伊朗核問題、人權問題等進行了討論。他給我留下的印象既是一個善辯者，也是一個傾聽者。我給他留下的印象，用他的話說是能言善辯、有說服力。他希望我今後有機會再次作客《新聞之夜》。我的第一次現場直播採訪，即第一次「大考」算是通過了。

帕克斯曼：大使先生，新年好！

劉曉明：謝謝。

帕克斯曼：讓我們先搞清楚一個名詞。你是共產黨嗎？

劉曉明：中國共產黨在中國是執政黨，擁有超過八千萬名黨員。但是中國有十三億人口，因此不能說中國是「共產黨國家」，就像不能說英國是「保守黨國家」一樣。

帕克斯曼：但可以說英國是資本主義國家。

劉曉明：中國是社會主義國家，實行的是中國特色社會主義。

帕克斯曼：我不久前去北京採訪，與不少年輕人交談。給我留下深刻印象的是，他們對中國在國際上發揮的作用很有信心，認為中國將成為二十一世紀一支不斷崛起的重要力量。你也這麼認為嗎？

劉曉明：中國一定會為世界和平和繁榮作出越來越大的貢獻，但我們不認為中國是一個超級大國。應該說，中國是一個國際影響力和國際責任都在不斷擴大的最大的發展中國家。

帕克斯曼：但人們不理解中國在聯合國安理會的所作所為，如中國反對制裁伊朗和敘利亞。人們在問，中國的目的是什麼？

劉曉明：這種看法不對。事實上，中國四次投票支持聯合國安理會涉伊核問題決議。我們明確反對伊朗擁有核武器。但另一方面，中方認為，通過外交手段和平解決伊核問題才是最佳途徑。和平解決的代價最低，而且有利於維護地區的和平穩定。

帕克斯曼：中方是否認為一個擁有核武器的伊朗會對

世界和平構成潛在威脅？

劉曉明：是的，一個擁有核武器的伊朗不利於地區和平與穩定。所以中方從一開始就明確反對伊朗發展核武器。中國總理不久前訪問海灣國家時再次重申了這一立場。

帕克斯曼：那麼為什麼不能制裁伊朗？

劉曉明：現在已有制裁措施在實施之中。我們不贊成為了制裁而制裁，這樣做徒勞無益。我們鼓勵各方與伊朗通過外交談判以和平方式解決有關問題。

帕克斯曼：你認為中國在世界上能夠發揮道義作用嗎？

劉曉明：我認為，中國在維護世界和平、構建和諧世界方面能夠發揮自己應有的作用。

帕克斯曼：中國在國際上想推動實現什麼？為了推行民主不惜發動戰爭。中國想推行什麼？比如美國

劉曉明：中國致力於構建和諧世界。我們主張國與國相互尊重、相互包容，而不是把自己的價值觀和社會制度強加給別人，這樣的世界才更加和平，更加繁榮。我們主張世界各國攜手努力，保障各國共同安全與福祉，維護世界和平與穩定。我們堅決反對在國際事務中訴諸武力。

帕克斯曼：現在我們來談談中國的經濟實力。中國現在擁有數萬億美元的外匯儲備，這麼多錢幹什麼用？

劉曉明：中國仍然是一個相對不富裕的國家。雖然中國的經濟總量僅次於美國，居世界第二，但中國人均GDP在全球仍排在一百位以後。中國仍有近七億人生活在農村。按照聯合國每天一美元的貧困線標準，中國仍有一點五億人生活在貧困線之下。脫貧致富、改善民生仍是中國政府的重要職責。

帕克斯曼：現在談談人權這個棘手問題。知名藝術家艾未未曾說，缺乏言論自由的世界是蠻荒之地。你是否能理解他在說什麼？

劉曉明：艾未未並不缺乏言論自由，否則，你怎麼知道他講了什麼？

帕克斯曼：不幸的是，他的言論使他遭受牢獄之災。

劉曉明：你的說法不對。事實是，他曾因涉嫌逃避繳納稅款、故意銷毀會計憑證等犯罪行為而受到調查。在任何法治國家，公民都需要尊重、遵守法律，沒有人可以凌駕於法律之上，即使所謂的「知名」藝術家也不例外，觸犯了法律，就要受到法律的制裁。這在中國如此，在英國恐怕也是一樣。

帕克斯曼：但艾未未應該有自由表達言論的權利。

劉曉明：如果艾未未沒有自由表達言論的權利，你怎

麼會知道他的言論？

帕克斯曼：好的，大使先生，非常感謝你接受採訪。

劉曉明：感謝你的邀請。

044

接受英國BBC廣播四台《今日》欄目
主持人戴維斯現場直播採訪

二〇一二年三月十四日，我在英國BBC廣播四台《今日》（Today）欄目演播室，接受主持人埃文・戴維斯（Evan Davis）現場直播採訪。當天，十一屆全國人大五次會議閉幕，BBC邀請我談談中國「兩會」。

《今日》欄目是BBC廣播四台旗艦節目，每天早上六至九點播放時政要聞、訪談、座談，以深度新聞分析和激烈辯論著稱，在英國被譽為對設置政治議題最具影響力的節目，是英國首相、大臣、議員、政黨領袖、社會精英必聽的節目，每週聽眾達一千一百萬人次。前文已介紹過主持人戴維斯，這是我們第一次見面。採訪主要圍繞「兩會」、民主、選舉、中國政治體制改革以及朝鮮等問題展開。

採訪實錄如下：

戴維斯：中國「兩會」剛剛閉幕。中國的全國人大是世界上最大的議會，有近三千名代表，每年會期兩週左右。在今年人大會議閉幕記者招待會上，溫家寶總理發表了一些有意思的講話。他說中國將推進經濟和政治體制改革，促進財富共享，同時將允許人民幣匯率更大幅度自由波動。

今天我們很高興邀請到中國駐英國大使劉曉明來到我們的演播室。早上好！

劉曉明：早上好！

戴維斯：感謝你接受採訪。我們能談談民主嗎？你認為中國正在走向擁有更加公開、自由選舉的西方式民主嗎？現在中國的全國人大並不是選舉產生的吧？

劉曉明：中國的全國人大代表是選舉產生的，我認為這樣的選舉體現了中國式的民主，即有中國特色的民主體制。西方輿論很關注溫總理關於政治改革的講話，我認為溫總理的講話是重申中國政府在這一問題

戴維斯：但是中國有這麼一群人，他們已躋身中產階級，比上一輩人富裕很多。你認為他們是否希望在國家事務中多一點發言權、能夠擁有對領導者不好的做

戴維斯：你認為中國的政治體制改革能走多遠呢？

劉曉明：我想如果拿現在的中國和三十年前相對比，你會發現中國取得了長足進步。中國改革開放的總設計師鄧小平先生在開啟改革開放之初，就將政治改革作為一項重要任務。中國過去實行了幾千年的封建統治，直到中華人民共和國成立後才建立了社會主義民主制度。這個制度並不盡善盡美，我們在持續不斷地探索如何加強中國政府的問責制，使其運作體制更為高效和民主。但是看看今天中國的變化，恐怕只能用「天翻地覆」來形容。

上的基本立場。對中國過去三十多年來的改革開放，西方一些人只看到經濟改革，而看不到中國的改革是全方位的，不僅有經濟改革，也有政治體制改革。

法進行反抗的權利？他們可能會說：「我們不想處處聽人指揮，我們要發言權。」你認為你剛剛所描述的漸進式改革能否滿足公眾的需求而不帶來嚴重危機或社會動盪？

劉曉明：我認為，中國的政治改革正處於進行時。任何制度都不是完美的。我們取得的進步是巨大的，但仍有改進空間。中國政府作了很多努力確保中央和地方政府更好地對人民負責，打擊腐敗，使人們享有公平獲得信息的渠道。舉個例子來說，最近中國全國人大改革了代表選舉辦法。過去城鎮代表要多於農村代表，現在城鎮和農村可按同一比例選舉人大代表，這就是要賦予所有人平等發聲的權利。

戴維斯：你是《今日》欄目的聽眾嗎？

劉曉明：是的。

戴維斯：當你聽到我的同事們在訪談節目中痛斥政客或對他們態度強硬時，你會怎麼想？這是好事還是壞事？

劉曉明：這也許不是壞事。我發現一個很有趣的現象，它也許反映了東西方文化的不同。中國和不少亞洲國家的民眾比西方民眾更尊重他們的領導人。究其原因，不知是你們的政治家幹得不好，還是中國和亞洲國家領導人工作更出色。總而言之，亞洲領導人更受到他們國家人民的尊重。

戴維斯：要談的東西太多了，比如敘利亞、朝鮮。你曾經在朝鮮工作，對嗎？

劉曉明：是的，我在那裏常駐了三年半。

戴維斯：雖然我應該談敘利亞，但我還是想問朝鮮問題。中國什麼時候採取行動？因為那裏的形勢最終取決於中國。朝鮮的情況很糟糕，二千五百萬人被一個「瘋狂的」家族劫持着。中國想什麼時候結束這種情

況，說「夠了，我們需要朝鮮也進行改革」？

劉曉明：朝鮮是我們的近鄰，我們希望他們經濟發展、繁榮。在我們看來，當務之急是保持朝鮮半島的和平穩定。因此，我們希望與朝鮮保持良好關係。朝鮮人民應當有美好的未來。我們認為，確保朝鮮半島穩定的最佳辦法是與朝鮮接觸，而不是孤立他們。中國一直與朝鮮保持積極接觸。現在朝鮮有了新的領導人，應當為他執政提供良好的外部環境。朝鮮新領導人上台以來，已經有了一些積極的變化，朝鮮和美國在核問題和援助方面達成了一些協議。如果有關國家都能相向而行，共同努力，朝鮮半島的未來必將更加美好。

戴維斯：但重要的是要幫助朝鮮人民。據我們所知，二十世紀九〇年代一場饑荒就餓死了數百萬人。我們要讓朝鮮，或者說鼓勵、強迫朝鮮領導層進行中國式的改革。

劉曉明：中國一貫奉行不干涉內政的原則。我們認為，應當由一國的人民自己決定國家的未來。

戴維斯：我真希望我們的採訪能一直談下去。大使先生，我現在知道你也是我們節目的聽眾了，以後可以邀請你再次接受採訪，談更多的問題。謝謝你。

劉曉明：不客氣。

接受英國 BBC《新聞之夜》欄目
主持人艾斯勒現場直播採訪

二〇一二年十二月二十一日，我在英國 BBC 旗艦欄目《新聞之夜》（Newsnight）演播室，接受該欄目主持人加文·艾斯勒（Gavin Esler）現場直播採訪。

艾斯勒是英國知名作家、記者、評論員，擔任《新聞之夜》欄目主持人長達十一年，並兼任 BBC 多個欄目主持人，曾採訪多國政要。從二〇一四起，擔任英國肯特大學名譽校長。其採訪風格以穩健、專注、深邃著稱。

當時正值中共十八大閉幕不久，採訪圍繞十八大展開。我向他介紹了十八大選出的新一屆領導集體和十八大為中國未來五年乃至更長時間繪製的新藍圖。我們還談了反腐敗、互聯網、新聞自由、民主、人權、中國的大國作用、中日關係、敘利亞等問題。

在他要宣佈採訪結束前，我指出演播室背景中國地圖的錯誤，説它缺少中國領土十分重要的一部分，那就是台灣。中國人民十分珍視領土完整。艾斯勒説，他確信這一點，並表示希望我回來接着討論這個話題。

艾斯勒：大使先生，談到高層換屆，我們首先想到的是選舉——大規模人事調整和新領導人當選。外界對中共十八大領導人換屆並不太明白。你認為這次換屆重要嗎？

劉曉明：我認為中共十八大對中國未來發展至關重要。十八大選出了新一屆領導集體，他們將在今後五年乃至更長的時間領導中國。他們年富力強、作風務實，基層經驗豐富。他們中有的人有農村工作經歷，有的在廠礦工作過。十八大還為中國未來五年甚至更長時間描繪了新的藍圖，那就是全面建成小康社會。我們的目標是到二○二○年實現 GDP 在二○一○年的基礎上翻一番。

艾斯勒：十年內 GDP 翻一番？

劉曉明：對。不僅 GDP 翻一番，而且人均收入也翻一番。

艾斯勒：中國共產黨的新領導人習近平談到打擊腐敗問題，他很清楚腐敗引發了民眾的不滿。中國必須整治腐敗，否則老百姓會更加不滿。但中國將如何打擊腐敗？

劉曉明：我認為腐敗不是中國獨有的問題。中國現在處在社會轉型時期，總會出現這樣那樣的問題。鄧小平先生在中國改革開放初期曾說，窗戶打開了，清新的空氣會進來，同時蒼蠅和蚊子也會進來。關鍵是看黨如何面對問題，如何採取措施解決問題。我認為，中國領導人對打擊腐敗問題，決心是堅定的，態度是堅決的。

艾斯勒：你認為互聯網是蒼蠅、蚊子嗎？互聯網是否讓中國感到棘手？我們不理解中國為什麼要控制公眾交流信息，中國在擔心什麼？

劉曉明：我認為這是對中國互聯網發展的誤解。事實上，中國在互聯網問題上是很開放的。我們擁有世界

050

上最多的網民。

艾斯勒：但我們的記者在中國就用不了臉書、推特等西方社交網站。情況和你所描述的不完全一致。

劉曉明：每天，在中國，博客們在網上發表成千上萬條評論，百分之六十的中國網民在網上經常發表評論。政府的職能是管理規範互聯網使用，使網民獲得有益的信息，對不健康及有害的內容予以清除，以確保互聯網健康有序運行。

艾斯勒：但這應該由普通民眾決定。中國有數千年的發明創造史。我們認為信息自由是創造力的源泉。西方人認為中國因為不喜歡某些觀點而採取嚴屬壓制措施，這影響了信息流動，是非常不利的。

劉曉明：如果你在中國上網，你會接觸到各種觀點，非常開放。包括政治、經濟、文化的各種議題都可以討論。你應該對中國互聯網有更加全面的認識。

艾斯勒：大使先生，有一個重要觀點能否幫我們解釋一下？這就是中國希望在二〇二〇年 GDP 翻一番，成為世界上最大的經濟體，中國希望在世界上發揮什麼樣的作用？

劉曉明：中國當然希望發揮一個負責任大國的作用。我們稱自己為負有全球責任的最大發展中國家。我們希望為世界和平與穩定作出貢獻，因為我們需要一個和平的國際環境發展自己。

艾斯勒：因為沒有和平，經濟發展就無從談起。

劉曉明：確實如此。另一方面，中國的和平發展也將對世界和平與繁榮作出貢獻。同時，中國的經濟發展也會推動世界經濟的增長。

艾斯勒：但與此同時，如何理解一些看似小問題但可能會演變成大問題的事態？比如中日圍繞海上一些礁石的爭端就可能引發衝突。

劉曉明：我們當然願與日本保持良好的關係。我知道你是在說釣魚島，事實上，釣魚島自古以來就是中國的領土。

艾斯勒：但日本好像並不這樣認為。我們對此感到擔心。

劉曉明：日本藉一八九五年中國在甲午戰爭中戰敗之機，非法竊取了釣魚島。一九四三年，英美中三國領導人丘吉爾、羅斯福、蔣介石在開羅開會，發表了《開羅宣言》，明確要求日本無條件將所有竊取的領土歸還中國。

艾斯勒：中國是否能夠和平解決這一問題？

劉曉明：中國當然致力於通過和平方式解決釣魚島問題。

艾斯勒：中國可以發揮作用同時也很具有爭議的另一個問題是敘利亞。俄羅斯總統普京表示並不關心阿薩德政權的命運。中國政府關心阿薩德政權的命運嗎？

劉曉明：我們關心的是敘利亞人民的命運。我認為，應當由敘利亞人民來決定誰是他們的領導人。中國之所以反對西方國家在聯合國安理會提出的一些涉敘決議，就是因為這些決議主張政權更迭。

艾斯勒：你認為阿薩德倒台是件壞事嗎？

劉曉明：我想這要由敘利亞人民來決定。敘利亞人民認為符合自身利益的選擇，中國都會贊同。由誰來擔任敘利亞的領導人，敘利亞應建立什麼樣的政權，不應由中國來決定，而應由敘利亞人民自己來決定。

艾斯勒：但很明顯，大多數敘利亞人民希望阿薩德下台，期待獲得外國幫助，這才是問題所在。

劉曉明：這要看你同敘利亞哪一方說話。當前敘利亞

正陷於內戰狀態，國內既有反對派，也有政府的支持者。現在重要的是立即停火止暴，早日啟動政治過渡進程。

艾斯勒：我們西方人需要明白的一點也許可以用英國作家魯德亞德‧吉卜林的一句話來概括，就是「東方與西方永遠無法完全理解對方」。你是否認同這一說法？

劉曉明：在我看來，西方未能很好地理解中國。在西方一直存在着嚴重的對華偏見。一談到中國，一些人總是擺脫不掉冷戰思維，所以往往以觀察蘇聯的視角來看中國，從而無法了解真實的中國。我希望人們能多一些「理智與情感」，少一些「傲慢與偏見」。

艾斯勒：這的確又是另一位英國作家的名言。可以說，自鄧小平時代以來，中國發生了翻天覆地的變化。「中國共產黨」這一稱謂已經很難幫助外界理解

中國的發展道路。現在聽起來，中國共產黨已經不是一個真正意義上的共產黨了。

劉曉明：我認為，這是對中國共產黨的誤解。在中國，中國共產黨堅持走中國特色社會主義道路。中國共產黨將馬克思主義理論與中國國情相結合，建立了中國特色社會主義制度。這一制度符合中國實際，給中國帶來了發展與進步，並取得了巨大成功。對於這樣一種行之有效、造福廣大人民、得到廣大人民擁護的制度，為什麼要改旗易幟呢？

艾斯勒：你非常明確地指出西方對中國存在誤解。但中國是不是對西方也有誤解？當我們談論人權、互聯網等西方十分看重的問題時，並不是要試圖佔上風，而是相信指出這些問題有助於提升中國的創新能力。

劉曉明：我們歡迎善意的批評。同任何一個國家一樣，中國並不完美，還有很多需要改進的地方。但我們堅決反對別國干涉中國的內政，反對以人權為工具

企圖改變中國的政治制度，企圖抹黑中國，這是我們不能接受的。

艾斯勒：大使先生……

劉曉明：在我們結束之前，我還想指出一點來說明中西方之間的不同。在你們演播室，我身後這張背景中的中國地圖就有錯誤。它缺少中國領土十分重要的一部分，那就是台灣，它比這張地圖上海南省的面積還要大。我們中國人民十分珍視領土完整。

艾斯勒：我確信這一點。看來我們還要請你回來，下次我們再接着討論這個話題。感謝你，大使先生。

劉曉明：不客氣。

接受英國天空新聞台《傑夫·蘭德直播間》欄目

主持人蘭德現場直播採訪

作者手記

二〇一四年一月十四日，我在英國天空新聞台（Sky News）演播室，接受該台訪談欄目《傑夫·蘭德直播間》（Jeff Randall Live）主持人傑夫·蘭德（Jeff Randall）現場直播採訪。

《傑夫·蘭德直播間》是天空新聞台財經和時事旗艦訪談欄目，主持人邀請英國和外國政要、商界領袖、知識精英等，就國內外熱點問題進行一對一對話。每週一至週四晚七至八點黃金時段播出，觀眾一百多萬人次。

蘭德是英國著名專欄作家、記者，曾在BBC擔任商業主編。二〇〇七年創辦《傑夫·蘭德直播間》欄目，直至二〇一四年三月。也就是說，我是作客《傑夫·蘭德直播間》的最後幾位嘉賓之一。

採訪當天，英中貿易協會在倫敦舉行「中國商業大會」，卡梅倫首相發來賀信，我在會上發表主旨演講。天空新聞台提出，蘭德希望邀請我談談「中國商業大會」。

但整個採訪過程，蘭德沒有提一個關於「中國商業大會」的問題。針對他對中國的一些誤解，我介紹了中共十八屆三中全會和中國特色社會主義。我們還談了中國的網絡管理、中英經貿合作、東西方交流、中日關係等問題。

蘭德：下面接受採訪的是中國駐英國大使劉曉明。見到你很高興，感謝你接受採訪。

劉曉明：感謝你的邀請。

蘭德：在我看來，今年對中國領導人來說是決定成敗的關鍵一年。二○一三年，中國領導人推出了財政、土地和商業等一系列改革計劃。而今年，落實計劃的時候到了。

劉曉明：沒錯。去年對中國來說是十分重要的一年。中國共產黨召開十八屆三中全會，中國新一屆領導集體推出了全面深化改革的總體計劃。這一計劃涵蓋五大領域，不僅包括經濟改革，也包括政治、社會、文化和生態環境改革，這些改革將給中國帶來翻天覆地的變化。

蘭德：在我看來，為了保持人們的信心，中國必須對私營資本競爭開放更多領域。用不了多久，中國將成

為一個由共產黨領導的資本主義國家。

劉曉明：這種看法是不對的。我們現在建設的是中國特色社會主義。正如鄧小平所說，市場和計劃都是經濟手段。計劃經濟不等於社會主義，資本主義也有計劃；市場經濟不等於資本主義，社會主義也有市場。中國取市場和計劃兩者之長，最大限度發揮制度優勢。

蘭德：顯而易見，中國希望進入高端產業並成為全球商業領軍者。當今世界，發展最為強勁的產業之一當數媒體。我們今天都看到了時代華納有線電視公司招標的消息。然而，《紐約時報》、彭博社、臉書、推特在華均被屏蔽。中國想要掩飾什麼？

劉曉明：中國依法管理媒體。重要的是，無論是中國媒體還是外國媒體都必須遵守中國法律，服務於人民的利益。我們關注的是信息健康以及是否有利於增進中外相互了解。

蘭德：你的意思是說，中國要的是「宣傳」，而非「事實」？

劉曉明：這種說法是錯誤的，我們一直講的就是事實。

蘭德：但是彭博社、臉書和推特究竟會發表什麼損害中國利益的信息？

劉曉明：這個問題你應該去問他們。我們希望他們在中國依法從業，遵守職業道德，而不是散佈詆毀中國的謠言和偏見。這不利於促進中外相互了解。

蘭德：隨着中國日益成為全球經濟的重要力量，這種秘密封鎖總有一天會被打破。隨着中國人日益走出國門，人們最終會發現真相。

劉曉明：中國的開放程度遠遠超出西方人的想象。如今，中國人足跡遍佈世界各地，中國人十分了解國外

的情況。遺憾的是西方卻缺乏對中國的足夠了解。兩者之間存在巨大不平衡。西方總有一些人抱着冷戰思維，戴着有色眼鏡和陳舊的思維定式看中國。我認為，西方媒體和記者尤應以更加廣闊的視野全面看待中國。

蘭德：關於雙邊貿易，中國公司在英國表現強勁。他們收購了許多英國著名企業，包括維他麥、地產公司、時裝品牌、羅孚汽車等。但英國公司卻不能赴華收購中國公司。這種情況是不是應該結束了？這方面應該是雙向的才行。

劉曉明：的確應當如此。貿易是雙向的。事實上，英國在對華貿易方面做得很好。

蘭德：可英國還是不能收購中國公司。

劉曉明：為什麼不能？本週初，我出席了中英首隻在倫敦發行的 RQFII 投資基金發起儀式。任何個人投

資者都可以對其進行投資。說到貿易，英國去年在對華出口方面表現出色。英國對華出口增長百分之一十三點八，遠遠超出中國其他歐盟貿易夥伴。

蘭德：最後一個問題是關於你們「家門口」的外交問題。中國與日本之間在一些無人居住的小島問題上存在爭端。許多人認為中國正在展示軍事實力、清算舊賬。不是這樣嗎？

劉曉明：不是這樣。事實是，日本首相悍然參拜供奉有甲級戰犯的靖國神社，甲級戰犯就是日本的納粹。試想如果德國領導人參拜希特勒或其他納粹戰犯，英國人民將作何感想？將心比心，就能更好地理解中國人民的感受。

蘭德：大使，很高興與你交談，感謝你撥冗接受採訪。

劉曉明：謝謝邀請。

接受英國BBC《新聞之夜》欄目主持人佩斯頓現場直播採訪

二〇一五年九月三日，我在英國BBC總部演播室，接受BBC旗艦訪談欄目《新聞之夜》(Newsnight)主持人羅伯特‧佩斯頓 (Robert Peston) 現場直播採訪。

佩斯頓是英國著名政治評論員、記者、編輯、作家，在多家電視台擔任過主持人，曾獲多項新聞大獎，包括皇家電視學會年度人物獎。

採訪當天正值北京舉行紀念中國人民抗日戰爭暨世界反法西斯戰爭勝利七十週年大會，採訪就從紀念大會開始。我向他介紹了習近平主席在十多分鐘的講話中，十八次提到「和平」，強調這就是中國發出的信息。

我們討論了中國的軍費開支、中國經濟、言論自由等問題。

佩斯頓：我們今天邀請到中國駐英國大使劉曉明先生。大使先生，當我想到中國時，我想到的是一個國土遼闊、正邁向現代化、逐漸富裕的國家。但我們今天看到的令人震撼的閱兵場面，會使有些人覺得中國又回到了「毛澤東時代」。中國是否再次向世界發出這樣一個信息，即中國是一個危險且令人生畏的國家？

劉曉明：我認為你得出的印象是錯誤的。事實上，中國發出的信息響亮而明確，這就是和平。和平來之不易，和平應當珍愛，和平應當維護。中國為維護世界和平和地區穩定作出自己的貢獻。習近平主席在十多分鐘的講話中，十八次提到「和平」。這就是中國發出的信息。

佩斯頓：今天，美國總統奧巴馬訪問阿拉斯加時，幾艘中國軍艦正好出現在靠近阿拉斯加的公海上。這是巧合嗎？

劉曉明：我想，我們還是先談談今天的紀念大會，之後我再回答你的問題。我說和平來之不易，在西方很少有人了解中國人民為抗日戰爭作出了多大犧牲。事實上，第二次世界大戰發端於中國。中國人民抗日戰爭開始時間最早、持續時間最長、傷亡人數最多。中國軍民傷亡三千五百萬人，佔世界各國傷亡總人數約三分之一，是二戰中傷亡人數最多的國家。因此中國人民把抗日戰爭和世界反法西斯戰爭勝利七十週年視為一個慶祝勝利、緬懷為國捐軀英烈們的重要時刻。

佩斯頓：但和平需要中國軍費保持如此之快的速度增長嗎？去年百分之十二，今年百分之十。這是一筆巨大的開支。

劉曉明：請不要忘記，中國是一個大國。中國的面積是英國的四十倍，人口是英國的二十倍。而中國的人均軍費僅是美國的二十二分之一，是英國的九分之一。而且中國軍費佔 GDP 的比例逐年下降，今年是過去五年來最低的。正如你所知，中國有遼闊的國土

需要保衛，此外，中國軍隊承擔着多重任務。

佩斯頓：考慮到當前中國經濟的增長速度，我認為中國軍費佔 GDP 的比例事實上略有上升。你談到中國要維護穩定，美國共和黨總統參選人特朗普說中國人想要餓死美國人，你對此有何評論？

劉曉明：我不認為他此番言論代表美國主流民意。在美國，你總會聽到某種聲音，但……

佩斯頓：但如果特朗普當選美國總統呢？你認為問題會有多嚴重？

劉曉明：這是一個假設性的問題，我不知道你會怎麼回答假設性的問題，我是不會回答假設性問題的。但我可以肯定地告訴你，中國願意和美國建立良好關係。在訪談開始前播出的節目中，你說中國想挑戰美國的主導地位，甚至挑戰美國的世界領導地位。這不是中國的立場，我們無意這麼做。中國在實現自身發展方面已經面臨足夠多的挑戰，我們無意去挑戰美國的主導地位。我認為中美在亞太地區應該成為好夥伴。

佩斯頓：中國舉行閱兵式是為了展示軍力，轉移人們對中國經濟下滑的注意力嗎？很多經濟學家認為中國經濟面臨嚴重問題。

劉曉明：我認為西方觀察家們誇大了中國經濟面臨的困難。中國經濟確實面臨一些困難和挑戰，這在中國發展過程中是正常的。

佩斯頓：中國股市市值蒸發了五萬億美元，這是小數目嗎？

劉曉明：我認為股市有其自身的運行規律。股市有起有伏，美國股市也是如此。我們要看中國經濟的全貌。中國經濟的基本面是好的。今年上半年中國GDP 增長了百分之七，增量相當於世界第二十大經

濟體瑞士的GDP總量。

佩斯頓：習近平主席表示希望中國經濟更加現代化，市場更加自由化。自由市場的一個重要組成部分就是，人民應該能自由地表達對市場的意見。而在中國，一些記者和基金經理因為涉嫌製造股市恐慌而被逮捕。這對西方人來說是十分令人震驚的。

劉曉明：中國人民享有言論自由。在你所說的案件中，那些人違反了法律。中國是法治國家。

佩斯頓：我說過關於英國市場很可怕的話，比那些人說中國市場的話要可怕得多。你覺得英國政府應該逮捕我嗎？

劉曉明：那些人不僅僅是發表「可怕」的評論。他們製造謠言，引起市場恐慌。中英兩國國情不同，法律制度也不盡相同。一些行為在英國可能不違法，而在中國則不同，如果違法，就要受到法律的懲罰。

佩斯頓：非常感謝，大使先生。

劉曉明：感謝邀請。

接受英國 BBC 廣播四台
奧尼爾勳爵採訪

作者手記

二〇一七年一月六日，英國 BBC 廣播四台（BBC Radio 4）播出專題節目《全新世界：改變全球化》（*The New World: Fixing Globalisation*）。我在該節目中接受了英國議會上院議員、著名經濟學家吉姆‧奧尼爾（Jim O'Neil）勳爵的採訪，就中國經濟發展成就、中國對全球貿易的貢獻、中國經濟結構改革及社會收入平等、「一帶一路」建設等與全球化密切相關的議題闡述了看法。奧尼爾因首創「金磚國家」的概念，被譽為「金磚之父」，他曾擔任美國高盛集團負責資產管理事務的主席、英國財政部商務大臣、英國皇家國際事務研究所主席，長期研究全球化議題。奧尼爾在專題節目中還採訪了時任世界銀行行長金墉、英國前首席大臣兼財政大臣奧斯本、哈佛大學全球化問題專家羅德里克等世界政治、經濟、金融、學術界知名人士。

BBC 廣播四台是英國最有影響力及最受歡迎的廣播電台，是 BBC 最重要和投入資源最多的金牌旗艦電台，以新聞、時政、科教、歷史類節目為主。聽眾人數超過一千一百萬人次，主要在英國國內，同時覆蓋愛爾蘭、法國和北歐地區。

奧尼爾：談論全球化不可能忽略中國。我本人因創造了「金磚四國」（BRIC，巴西、俄羅斯、印度和中國）概念而為世人所知。在「金磚四國」中，中國的經濟總量超過其他三國總和。即使中國經濟僅以百分之六點五的速度增長，略低於印度百分之七以上的增長率，到二○二○年中國經濟總量將相當於數個「新印度」加起來的總和。為更好地理解中國對世界的巨大影響，我採訪了中國駐英國大使劉曉明。

劉曉明：中國取得的發展成就堪稱奇蹟，在人類歷史上沒有先例。在三十年時間裏，中國七億人口擺脫貧困，超過一億人進入中產階級，人均預期壽命大幅提高，達到七十六歲，遠高於世界平均水平，也遠高於其他任何一個發展中國家。

奧尼爾：經歷了這一非凡歷程，從很多方面來看，中國已成為世界貿易最重要的國家。

劉曉明：中國已成為世界上一百二十多個國家和地區的第一大貿易夥伴。

奧尼爾：一百二十多個，覆蓋了全球一半以上人口。

劉曉明：是的。中國也是七十多個國家和地區的最大出口市場。每年，中國進口商品總額近兩萬億美元，這為許多國家提供了巨大市場。預計未來五年，中國商品進口總額將達到八萬億美元。這些都表明中國對世界經濟已經作出並將繼續作出重要貢獻。

奧尼爾：全球化帶來的挑戰不光是如何培訓新興產業的工人，更重要的問題是如何幫助那些技能已經被淘汰的產業工人。劉大使曾對中國政府如何應對這一困境進行過說明。

劉曉明：在中國也有同樣的問題。由於經濟結構調整和轉型，一部分人感到被落在了後面。但是我們必須解決產能過剩問題。例如，許多人都在談論鋼鐵產業。事實上，當我看到英國媒體報道一些英國鋼鐵廠

關閉導致四千人失業的消息，我完全理解這些鋼鐵工人的處境和感受，因為我們也面臨同樣的挑戰，需要重新安置大約二百萬鋼鐵工人。

奧尼爾：什麼才是最好的解決辦法呢？

劉曉明：我們需要對這些工人進行培訓，同時要鼓勵他們自主創業。一方面，我們有大量下崗鋼鐵工人；另一方面，服務業又存在巨大的需求，包括家政、物流等。因此我們可以培訓這些鋼鐵工人從事此類工作。

奧尼爾：也許西方國家的政策制定者需要考慮在增加工人收入方面做得更多。我認為，過去十年中國在這方面下了很大功夫，並且一直是這麼做的。

劉曉明：確實如此。工人的工資水平提高了，中國政府還設定了最低工資標準，以確保工人收入。在改善城市農民工生活方面，政府也作了巨大努力。每年約

有一億農民工進城務工，所以政府要採取大量措施，包括為農民工建造廉租房等。中國的口號是：「不讓一個人掉隊。」

奧尼爾：「不讓一個人掉隊」，但我們不能想當然地認為市場會自動均攤全球化的巨大好處。如果我們能解決這一問題，全球化將繼續帶來好處，也不會很快止步。實際上，中國計劃建設的「一帶一路」將進一步提升全球化水平。

劉曉明：我把這看作是「新全球化」。有人反對全球化，是因為一部分人、一部分國家感到被甩在了後面。所以中國「一帶一路」倡議的主旨是包容性，讓盡可能多的國家受益。

奧尼爾：比如像哈薩克斯坦？

劉曉明：對，還有俄羅斯、阿富汗、巴基斯坦以及絲綢之路經濟帶沿線的許多歐洲國家。例如，過去三年

來，中歐班列取得了很大成功，運行了兩千多趟，將中國商品一路輸送到歐洲國家。

奧尼爾：途經維也納，如果我沒記錯的話。

劉曉明：對。新海上絲綢之路則將中國同菲律賓、印度尼西亞及其他東南亞國家連接起來。雖然中國經濟增長有所放緩，但仍然是世界經濟的引擎。中國希望同其他國家分享中國經濟增長的好處。同樣，只有同其他國家加強互聯互通，中國的發展勢頭才能得以延續。

接受英國獨立電視台《佩斯頓星期日訪談》欄目
主持人佩斯頓現場直播採訪

作者手記

二〇一七年十一月十九日，我在英國獨立電視台《佩斯頓星期日訪談》（Peston on Sunday）欄目演播室，接受該欄目主持人羅伯特·佩斯頓現場直播採訪。

英國獨立電視台《佩斯頓星期日訪談》是該台政治主編佩斯頓主持的旗艦時政類欄目，主要就英國政治、經濟、社會、外交和重大國際問題，進行一對一的現場直播採訪。被採訪者包括英國和外國政要、議員、企業家、作家、社會名流、知識精英等。該欄目於二〇一六年五月開播，很快在英國社會受到廣泛關注，產生較大影響。

當天，在我前後參加該欄目訪談的還有英國財政大臣哈蒙德、前外交大臣米利班德等。

二〇一五年他在BBC《新聞之夜》欄目擔任主持人時，曾採訪過我，給我留下較深刻的印象。他的採訪風格直率、專注、興趣廣泛、歷史縱深感強，熟悉國際事務，提問跨度大，可以從亞洲一下跳到非洲，從朝鮮核問題一下轉向中國與津巴布韋的關係。

這次採訪正值中共十九大召開不久，我們圍繞中共十九大、中國特色社會主義、貧富差距、脫貧攻堅、朝鮮核問題、中國與津巴布韋的關係等問題進行了討論。

佩斯頓：劉大使，很高興見到你。你剛從北京回來，出席了極為重要的中國共產黨第十九次全國代表大會。外界普遍認為，中共十九大習近平主席成為自毛澤東之後最有權威的中國國家領導人，是這樣嗎？

劉曉明：習近平主席在中共十九大再次當選中共中央總書記，他將帶領中國人民開啟中國特色社會主義新時代。

佩斯頓：說到中國特色社會主義，我注意到，和英國一樣，中國社會也有着巨大的貧富差距。中國是一個社會主義國家，能夠接受這樣的貧富差距嗎？

劉曉明：中國是有貧差距問題。但其他發展中國家相比，不能說今日之中國貧富差距是「巨大的」。

佩斯頓：有許多億萬富豪，不是嗎？

劉曉明：事實上，減少貧困、縮小貧富差距正是中

共十九大的重要議題。我們已經意識到，中國存在發展不平衡、不充分的問題。習近平主席在十九大上指出，我們將盡一切努力消除貧富差距，滿足人民對日益增長的美好生活的需要。我們將盡一切努力打贏脫貧攻堅戰。中國現在仍有四千多萬貧困人口。過去三十年，我們已經使七億貧困人口脫貧。

佩斯頓：真是了不起的成就！

劉曉明：中國共產黨和中國政府的目標是，到二〇二〇年中國全面建成小康社會之時，使這四千多萬人口全部脫貧。這意味着按照中國的貧困線標準，全面消除貧困，在中國全面建成小康社會。

佩斯頓：今天要談的內容很多。你曾擔任中國駐朝鮮大使相當長的時間……

劉曉明：三年半。

佩斯頓：西方關切的是，中國沒有對朝鮮施加足夠壓力，迫使其放棄核試驗。你怎麼看？

劉曉明：這不是事實。事實是，中國已經盡一切努力勸說朝鮮放棄核試驗。我擔任中國駐朝鮮大使時，一直努力勸說朝鮮，發展核武器不符合朝鮮的國家利益。

佩斯頓：那它為什麼還是要發展核武器？

劉曉明：因為它也有自己的合理訴求。朝核問題事關信任與安全。朝鮮與美國之間缺乏互信，這是問題的根源。因此六方會談積極致力於推動實現朝鮮半島無核化，尋求全面綜合解決這一問題的辦法。我們還推動實現關係正常化⋯⋯

佩斯頓：難道不應該加大制裁力度嗎？許多人認為中國應該對朝鮮實施更嚴厲的制裁。

劉曉明：從二〇〇六年開始，那時我還擔任中國駐朝鮮大使，中國就一直參與聯合國的相關決議。聯合國前後通過了十一項決議。中國不僅投了贊成票，而且一直嚴格遵守這些決議，履行自己的義務。重要的是，國際社會應該認識到不能為了制裁而制裁。制裁只是一種手段，而非最終目的。我們的目的是要促使朝鮮堅持半島無核化方向，因而應該與朝鮮進行接觸。聯合國決議不是只有制裁（佩斯頓插話：「當然不是。」），而且還包括談判和外交解決⋯⋯

佩斯頓：當前，你對朝核問題的前景感到悲觀嗎？

劉曉明：不，我仍持謹慎樂觀的態度。我始終相信，只要各方保持接觸，鼓勵朝鮮重返談判，我們就能夠找到解決危機的外交方案。

佩斯頓：我想再問一個國際問題。中國在津巴布韋有着巨大的經濟利益。如果穆加貝下台，中國會感到高興嗎？

劉曉明：中國始終奉行不干涉別國內政的外交政策。津巴布韋是中國的友好國家，中國曾支持津巴布韋人民爭取國家獨立，後來一直支持津巴布韋發展經濟。中國絕不會干涉津巴布韋的內政……

佩斯頓：我想追問一下，有許多報道稱，如果沒有得到中國的支持，津巴布韋軍方不會對穆加貝採取這樣的行動。

劉曉明：這不是事實。我們從未干預津巴布韋的內政。津巴布韋的前途和命運應當由津巴布韋人民決定。我們當然希望局勢能夠得到和平解決。

佩斯頓：很高興再次見到你，大使先生，與你交談總是令人十分愉快。

劉曉明：感謝邀請。

接受英國天空新聞台《政治新聞綜述》欄目
主持人博爾頓現場直播採訪

作者手記

二〇一九年六月二十一日，我在英國天空新聞台演播室，接受該台時政欄目《政治新聞綜述》（All Out Politics）主持人亞當·博爾頓（Adam Boulton）現場直播採訪。

《政治新聞綜述》是天空新聞台旗艦時政欄目，聚焦英國政治和國際上的重大事件，邀請英國和外國政要、議員、政治評論員、國際問題專家與主持人舉行一對一的對話，英國首相、內閣大臣和各政黨領袖是該欄目常客。

博爾頓是英國著名的政治評論員、專欄作家、主持人，擔任天空新聞台政治主編和新聞總編長達三十二年，採訪過九位英國在任首相，主持過英國大選主要政黨候選人電視辯論。

這次採訪正值中英第十次經濟財金對話舉行，我們圍繞英國脫歐、中英關係、中英美關係、中國政治制度、華為、香港、英國保守黨領袖候選人等問題進行了討論。

博爾頓：這裏是天空新聞台《政治新聞綜述》欄目，我們從威斯敏斯特——英國政治的中心發佈消息，開展辯論，提出見解。本週，中國高級別代表團到訪英國，雙方簽署了價值超過五億英鎊的貿易協議。但由於圍繞華為和香港遊行示威等問題引起的爭論，英中關係未來發展仍然存疑。我們邀請了中國駐英國大使劉曉明先生，非常歡迎你！

首先談談貿易問題，就雙邊貿易關係而言，你認為脫歐會給英國還是中國帶來更大機遇？

劉曉明：我希望對雙方都是如此。你剛才提到的來訪十分重要。近日，中國國務院副總理率領高級別代表團訪問英國，與英國政府舉行第十次經濟財金對話。訪問期間，雙方達成了六十九項合作成果。過去十年來，中英每年舉行一輪經濟財金對話，兩國商品和服務貿易額翻了一番，中國對英投資額增長了三倍。「滬倫通」的啟動是本次對話的亮點之一，意義重大。

博爾頓：這意味着兩國股票可以相互交易嗎？

劉曉明：是的。英國的上市公司首次可以在上海股市出售股票，英國投資者也能購買在上海股市上市公司的股票。

博爾頓：英國脫歐之後，估計需要同中國談判達成新的貿易安排吧？

劉曉明：我們對此持開放態度。當然，英國必須首先完成脫歐。中英雙方就新的貿易安排一直保持密切溝通。中方願意同歐盟和英國都保持良好夥伴關係。

博爾頓：我從報紙和雜誌上了解到，中國對英國脫歐的決定感到困惑，是這樣嗎？

劉曉明：我不這麼認為。首先，這是英國與歐盟之間的事情。對中國來說，挑戰和機遇並存，我們希望能夠抓住機遇，妥善應對挑戰。

第十次中英經濟財金對話的另一個亮點就是中國對英國牛肉開放市場。我不知道你是否喜歡吃牛肉。

過去二十三年，因為「瘋牛病」，中國禁止從英國進口牛肉。現在限制解除了。

博爾頓：這對英國農民來說是個好消息。

劉曉明：中國國內對牛肉的需求很大，每年進口超過一百萬噸牛肉。英國是牛肉出口國，中國訪客與遊客來英都想品嚐一下安格斯牛肉和威爾士黑牛肉。因此，我認為中國對英國牛肉需求量很大。

博爾頓：鑑於特朗普的美國與中國之間的關係，你認為英國需要在美國和中國之間作選擇嗎？

劉曉明：我們希望與英國、美國都發展良好關係。我相信，英國將獨立作出符合英國自身利益並有利於中英合作的決定。

博爾頓：中英之間存在意識形態差異。中國是一黨制國家，而我們實行西方傳統民主制度，兩者必將

衝突。

劉曉明：中國存在了五千多年，中英兩國有不同的制度。七十年前，中國共產黨領導中國革命，成立了中華人民共和國。中英之間一直存在一些差異，但這些差異並未阻止兩國攜手合作，實現共贏。我不同意你所說的中國是一黨制國家，中國有八個參政的民主黨派，準確地說，中國是共產黨領導的國家，如同英國是保守黨領導的國家。我們實行中國特色社會主義民主制度，通過自己的方式選舉國家領導人。中英兩國應該彼此尊重。

博爾頓：中國政府利用先進技術和通信設備對公民進行嚴密監控。在這樣的情況下，英國還能允許華為深度參與5G網絡建設嗎？

劉曉明：中國政府從未利用科技監控老百姓。而在英國，你們在很多地方安裝了監控設備。中國在一些地方安裝監控設備是為了國家安全和防範恐怖主義。華

為是一家優秀的企業，在英國經營十八年，為英國電信產業發展作出了貢獻。華為是 5G 技術的領軍者，我希望英國能夠繼續與華為合作。

博爾頓： 如果新任英國首相決定拒絕華為，會有什麼後果？

劉曉明： 這將不僅對華為而且對中國企業發出十分錯誤和負面的信號。英國被認為是最開放、最具良好營商環境的國家。過去五年，中國在英國投資迅猛發展。過去十年間，中國在英國的投資額增長了三倍。如果英國拒絕華為，肯定將對外發出十分負面的信號。

博爾頓： 英國政府是否已就香港形勢向中方交涉？

劉曉明： 雙方有接觸。英方表達了自己的關切，中方向英方闡明香港特區政府修例決定的合法性和必要性，表明中央政府支持特區政府的決定，包括修例和

暫緩修例的決定。中方同時也就一些外部勢力企圖利用此事干涉中國內部事務表達了關切，我們告訴英國政府，香港問題純屬中國內政。

博爾頓： 市民反抗的場面很大，據說有四分之一的香港人上街遊行。你認為怎樣解決這個問題？比如說，林鄭月娥辭職？

劉曉明： 大多數英國媒體只關注上街的示威者。它們忘記了有八十萬香港民眾簽名支持特區政府修例。特區政府就修例徵求了民眾的意見和建議，收到的四千五百份反饋中，三千份支持修例，只有一千五百份反對。我希望事態平息下來。我們對特區政府有信心。香港特區政府已經決定暫停修例，願花更多時間傾聽民眾的聲音。我希望民眾對林鄭月娥特首和特區政府作出積極回應。

博爾頓： 英國末任港督彭定康認為修例破壞了香港回歸之時英中達成的協議。

劉曉明：這種說法不對。我認為恰恰相反，修例正是為了把香港建設成為一個更加美好的地方，而不是「避罪天堂」。

博爾頓：談談你對保守黨領袖候選人約翰遜的看法。

劉曉明：我們很熟。他在擔任倫敦市長期間有力促進了倫敦與中國城市之間的經貿關係。他擔任外交大臣期間曾多次訪問中國。我與另一位保守黨領袖候選人——外交大臣亨特也很熟。我祝他們兩人好運。

博爾頓：謝謝劉大使接受採訪。

劉曉明：不客氣。

接受美國全國廣播公司商業頻道
記者威斯巴赫採訪

作者手記

二〇一九年十一月十四日，我在出席「法國巴黎銀行全球市場大會」並發表主旨演講後，接受了美國全國廣播公司商業頻道（Consumer News and Business Channel，CNBC）資深記者安奈特·威斯巴赫（Annette Weisbach）的採訪。

CNBC 是全球三大財經電視媒體之一，每天二十四小時通過有線電視、衛星電視和互聯網向全球九十多個國家播放財經新聞，在美國擁有九千三百六十多萬收費家庭用戶，佔全美收視家庭總數的百分之八十以上。

威斯巴赫是該台資深記者、經濟學家，曾採訪多國政要和商界領袖。我們的採訪圍繞華為、中歐關係、中美關係、知識產權保護等問題進行。

CNBC 將這次採訪在該頻道《歐洲財經論壇》（Squawk Box Europe）等欄目播出，並在其網站和推特同時刊登。

威斯巴赫： 關於華為及其設備在 5G 網絡中的作用，有許多不同的看法。對此你怎麼看？你能否向歐洲和美國的消費者保證，華為設備不存在任何問題？

劉曉明： 我認為，華為的確是一家很好的企業，它不僅為英國的電信業發展作出巨大貢獻，而且很好地履行了企業責任，在英國創造了五點一萬個就業機會，投資三十億美元。華為是 5G 技術的領軍者，英國電信企業都歡迎華為。

當然也有一些雜音，有些國家不願看到華為在歐洲的發展，向歐洲國家施加巨大壓力，我就不點這個國家的名了。截至目前，英國、德國、法國等歐洲國家對此仍存在不同意見，仍在進行討論，政府尚未作出最後決定。

我們理解一些國家的安全關切，華為對此也理解，而且正在努力解決這些安全關切。華為成立了完全由英國人組成的網絡安全評估中心，出資請專家來監測、分析華為的設備是否存在安全隱患和問題。

因此，華為是非常公開透明的，它希望能成為很好的合作夥伴。正如我常說的，華為將為中英、中歐 5G 領域合作帶來「黃金」機遇，禁止華為意味着錯失良機。

我衷心希望英國、德國、法國政府從自身國家利益，從發展強有力的對華夥伴關係出發，作出正確選擇，而不是受冷戰思維影響，更不能搞政治打壓。我希望華為能在英國實現互利雙贏合作。正如我剛才在演講中所說，中國開放的大門只會越開越大，我們也希望其他國家同樣保持開放，而不是對中國關上大門。

威斯巴赫： 你提到了冷戰，中美之間地緣政治的緊張狀態讓人感受到了一絲冷戰氣息。歐洲因此承受壓力，尚未作出決定，對此中國怎麼看？

劉曉明： 我們已經說得很明確，中國無意與美國打仗，無論是冷戰、熱戰，還是貿易戰。我們希望與美國建立合作、協調、不對抗的關係。中美是世界上最

大的兩個經濟體，中美關係是世界和平與繁榮的決定性因素。中美合則兩利，鬥則俱傷。因此我們對與美國開戰不感興趣。我高興地看到，中美談判官員正在加緊努力工作，解決貿易問題。

我們不要求歐洲國家在中美之間選邊站隊。英美有特殊關係，但中英也在致力於打造「黃金時代」。

我們追求互利共贏，而非「零和」遊戲，既不是歐洲贏、美國贏而中國輸，也不是中國贏、歐洲贏而美國輸。我們希望大家實現共贏，這就是我們的立場。

威斯巴赫：我們談談中美貿易談判第一階段協議吧，協議似乎已經達成，但仍存在一些難點。中方認為癥結在哪裏？

劉曉明：我認為雙方正在就細節進行密集磋商。我並不了解細節，即便我了解，我也必須謹慎表態，以免干擾談判進程。但根據我的理解，關稅應該是重要議題之一。加徵關稅不符合自由貿易原則，「貿易戰」起於加徵關稅，也應該以取消所有加徵的關稅而告

終。我希望第一階段協議能盡快順利達成，以便能夠進入第二、第三階段。

威斯巴赫：有人認為知識產權保護也是中美貿易談判的一個焦點，中方在此問題上是否會有所妥協？

劉曉明：改革開放四十年來，中國在加強知識產權保護方面作出了切實的努力，取得了超乎尋常的進步，這一點毋庸置疑。首先，應該肯定中國所取得的巨大進步。其次，中國認真對待美國等國家在知識產權問題上的關切，也承認各國均需要不斷改進。正如我常講的，沒有哪個國家是完美的，世界上最大的空間就是不斷改進的空間。再次，我認為動輒指責、聲討毫無益處。一些西方政客指責中國「竊取」美國技術，這種說法是完全錯誤的。中國的發展奇蹟靠的是中國人民過去七十年的艱苦奮鬥，不是靠「偷竊」他國知識產權。西方應該公正客觀地看待這個問題，而不是指責中國「偷竊」。這樣才有益於雙方就這一重要議題開展合作。

威斯巴赫： 特朗普總統說過，打贏貿易戰很容易。對此你怎麼看？

劉曉明： 我在許多場合都講過，貿易戰沒有贏家。

威斯巴赫： 關於貿易談判進程，你認為有時間表嗎？很明顯，明年美國將舉行大選，貿易戰與選戰交織在一起，中國是否持觀望立場，等着與下一屆美國總統再談？

劉曉明： 這不是中方的立場。中國持開放態度，我們希望問題解決得越早越好，因為這不僅符合中美兩國的利益，也符合全世界的利益。中美貿易衝突已給世界帶來許多不確定性、不可預測性，全世界都很關注，中美雙方談判官員責任重大。我認為中方不會觀望，這不是我們的立場。我們希望盡快達成協議，但是「一個巴掌拍不響」，需要雙方共同作出努力。

香港問題

英國對中國香港特別關注。歷史上，英國對香港殖民統治一百五十六年。回歸前，香港問題始終是中英關係的障礙；回歸後，它成為中英關係的積極因素。但是，英國總有一些人殖民心態揮之不去，他們的身體進了二十一世紀，腦袋還停留在殖民時期，一有風吹草動，就跳出來，對香港事務指手畫腳、說三道四。我使英十一年，趕上香港三件大事：慶祝香港回歸祖國二十週年、「修例風波」、頒佈實施香港國安法。圍繞這三件大事，我率領中國駐英國使館外交官，在英國這個國際輿論中心、西方輿論高地，積極開展公共外交，講中國香港故事，講「一國兩制」故事，講香港國安法故事。

「修例風波」以後，西方媒體，包括英國媒體，扮演了十分不光彩的角色，它們不僅沒有公正客觀地報道，而且混淆是非、顛倒黑白、誤導公眾：連篇累牘地渲染所謂「和平示威權利」，卻對極端暴力分子破壞社會秩序、襲警傷人的違法犯罪行為熟視無睹，支持特區政府、守護香港法治的正義聲音更是鮮有見報；將破壞香港法治、為非作歹的暴徒美化為「支持民主的人士」，卻將特區政府和警隊維護香港法治、保護市民生命財產安全的正當合法舉措惡意污衊為「鎮壓」。正是這些媒體的「選擇性失聲」和「歪曲性報道」，使錯誤輿論大行其道，誤導了西方廣大民眾。針對這種情況，我多次發表演講，接受媒體採訪，在各主流大報上發表文章，先後舉行四場中外記者會，一百多家中外媒體、兩百多名記者出席。後來，英國報紙拒絕刊登我的涉港文章，稱它們只能登支持所謂「民運」分子（即反中亂港分子）的文章，我就把主要精力投向廣播電視媒體。僅二〇一九年六月—二〇二〇年七月一年多的時間，我就香港問題七次接受英國各大電視台現場直播採訪，分別兩次上 BBC 旗艦欄目《安德魯‧馬爾訪談》和《新聞之夜》，一次上《尖銳對話》。我利用這些上電視的機會，澄清事實，批駁謬論，揭穿謊言，為「一國兩制」正名，為國安法助陣，讓世界聽到中國聲音。

接受英國 BBC 廣播四台《今日》欄目

主持人漢弗萊斯現場直播採訪

二○一七年六月二十九日，我在 BBC 總部演播室接受 BBC 廣播四台早間旗艦時政欄目《今日》（Today）主持人約翰・漢弗萊斯（John Humphrys）現場直播採訪。

BBC 廣播四台是英國最具影響力、最受歡迎的廣播電台，是 BBC 投入資源最多的旗艦電台。前文已介紹了《今日》欄目。

漢弗萊斯是英國著名記者、作家、評論員，擔任《今日》欄目主持人長達二十二年，是 BBC 資歷最深的主持人之一，獲多項新聞大獎，曾於一九七二年赴華參加報道美國總統尼克松訪華。他的採訪風格以直率、犀利、咄咄逼人著稱，一些政治人物抱怨他的採訪過於尖酸、刻薄、不留情面。

這次採訪正值香港回歸二十週年，漢弗萊斯在採訪我之前放了一段短片，包括採訪香港所謂「民主人士」。他上來第一個問題就是，有人說香港的制度日益成為「一國一制」，這是不是事實？我向他介紹了「一國兩制」在香港的成功實施，同時指出，「一國兩制」是一個有機整體。有的人講「一國兩制」，只談「兩制」而忽視了「一國」，忘記了香港是中國的一部分，不是英國的一部分，更不是一個獨立實體。

我們還討論了中國的國際地位和朝鮮核問題。

漢弗萊斯：劉大使，早上好。有人說香港的制度日益成為「一國一制」，這是不是事實？

劉曉明：這不是事實。「一國兩制」在香港得到了成功實施。在我之前你們採訪的人說，中國中央政府沒有兌現承諾。我不同意這種觀點。事實是，中國中央政府完全兌現了「一國兩制」的承諾。我認為，按照《基本法》和「一國兩制」原則，香港的社會制度、經濟制度、生活方式、法律制度保持穩定。與二十年前相比，香港變得更好了，此時此刻的確值得我們隆重慶祝。

二十年來，我們看到香港經濟繁榮，社會穩定，GDP 翻番，外匯儲備增長了三倍多。香港繼續保持國際金融、貿易、航運中心地位，香港人均壽命大幅增加，超過許多發達國家，民眾生活幸福。

漢弗萊斯：沒有人懷疑香港的經濟繁榮，這是公認的，但給人的印象是，中央政府很顯然決心收緊對香港的管控。對此你怎麼看？

劉曉明：我不這麼認為，我也不同意這種說法。我認為，人們只需要把香港二十年前和現在的政治管理、民主政治作一番比較，就可以得出結論。

漢弗萊斯：民主政治？

劉曉明：對，民主政治。

漢弗萊斯：真是這樣嗎？

劉曉明：二十年前，香港有選舉嗎？港督是選出來的嗎？

漢弗萊斯：沒有人質疑這個，因為那時候香港還是殖民地，有港督很正常。

劉曉明：但在過去的二十年，香港舉行了五次特區行政長官選舉。

漢弗萊斯：但香港新任特首僅得到了選舉委員會的七百七十七票，這一數字僅代表了百分之零點零三的香港民眾，聽起來不太令人信服。

劉曉明：數字並不能說明一切。

漢弗萊斯：但數字在民主體制中很說明問題。

劉曉明：如果拿數字說事，那麼英國國家領導人選舉又是如何呢？六千五百萬人口的國家領導人只是在其幾萬人的選區內以微弱多數取勝，人們可以提出異議，這是不是就不能代表整個國家人民的意志？！

漢弗萊斯：英國首相得到的選票最終還是超過了百分之零點零三。這件事就不說了。

劉曉明：我想強調的是，香港特首的選舉是嚴格按照《基本法》和香港特區有關選舉法律進行的。

漢弗萊斯：但需要得到批准……

劉曉明：民主選舉進程是一個不斷發展、漸進的過程。俗話說「羅馬不是一天建成的」，我也可以說倫敦不是一天建成的，香港也不是一天建成的。

漢弗萊斯：二〇一六年二月，英國外交部發表了《香港問題半年報告》，外交大臣約翰遜發表了一個講話，說中國嚴重違背了《中英聯合聲明》，破壞了「一國兩制」的原則，也就是說，英國政府不願看到的事情卻發生了。

劉曉明：關於這個報告，首先，我們反對英國政府每年發表兩次所謂香港問題報告的做法。香港是中國不可分割的一部分，香港事務純屬中國內部事務，不容任何外部勢力干涉。然而，即使在這樣的報告中，英國政府也讚賞中國政府執行「一國兩制」政策，承認香港「一國兩制」實踐取得巨大成功。雖然中英之間存在一些分歧，但是雙方都認為，香港長期繁榮和穩

定不僅符合中國的利益，而且符合英國的利益，同時也符合國際社會的利益。

認為中國取代美國成為世界第一「超級大國」指日可待？

漢弗萊斯：在外人看來，香港的選舉受到操縱，示威者被關押，民主被削弱而不是加強。現在你告訴我，香港是「我們國家」的。

劉曉明：我不認為中國在可預見的將來會成為「超級大國」，我認為中國仍然是一個發展中國家。

劉曉明：有些人講「一國兩制」，忘記了這是一個有機整體，忘記了香港是中國的一部分，而不是英國的一部分，更不是一個獨立實體。

漢弗萊斯：中國如果成為最大的經濟體，還是發展中國家嗎？

漢弗萊斯：那就是「一種制度」了？

劉曉明：即使有一天中國經濟總量達到世界第一，中國要成為所謂「超級大國」的路還很長，中國地域遼闊，地區發展差異很大。我在擔任駐埃及大使後，曾經在中國西部最貧困的省份之一甘肅省工作過，比當年美國「不發達的西部」還落後。

劉曉明：是兩種制度。採訪前你告訴我，你是十二年前去過的中國。你應該再去中國看看，去香港看看，看看發生的變化。即便我們之間在諸如「民主」等概念上看法有差異，我們也應該把今天的香港和二十年前的香港，和兩年前甚至一年前的香港對比着來看。

漢弗萊斯：中國現在是第二大經濟體，很可能很快發展成為第一大經濟體，中國要怎樣做才能成為「超級大國」？

漢弗萊斯：我們來談談中國在世界的地位，你是否

劉曉明：我們對成為「超級大國」不感興趣。我們感

興趣的是改善中國人民的生活，解決地區發展不平衡等問題。許多外國人只看到北京、上海、廣東和東部沿海地區，這些地區的確比較發達。比如廣東省經濟規模相當於西班牙，在世界上可以排第十五位，但是中國西部的甘肅、寧夏等省區經濟還是很落後的。

漢弗萊斯：最後談談朝鮮對世界和平的潛在威脅。朝鮮給中國造成的干擾要達到什麼樣的程度，中國才會說：夠了，我們要採取行動了，要介入了。

劉曉明：我認為中國為緩和朝鮮半島局勢已經做了大量工作。你知道，我來英國之前曾在中國駐朝鮮大使的崗位上工作了三年半。實際上，中國一直在積極做朝鮮工作，竭力說服朝鮮堅持半島無核化方向。

漢弗萊斯：但這些努力都失敗了？

劉曉明：不能說失敗了，有時候「進一步退兩步」，有時候「進兩步退一步」。朝核問題十分複雜，需要綜合施策，採取綜合全面的措施是必要的，所以我們

提出了「雙暫停」倡議和「雙軌」並進思路。也就是說：一方面採取制裁措施，說服朝鮮堅持半島無核化方向；另一方面……

漢弗萊斯：如果你們失敗，美國就介入……

劉曉明：另一方面，美國和韓國也應該採取措施，暫停軍事演習。記得當年，我每次勸說朝鮮堅持半島無核化方向，朝鮮方面就會說，他們受到了美國這個「超級大國」及其盟友的威脅，他們的軍事演習直接針對朝鮮。所以我們呼籲「雙暫停」，即朝鮮停止核導活動，美國及其盟友停止軍事演習。然後大家回到談判桌上來，通過對話解決問題，並行推進實現半島無核化和建立半島和平機制，這就是我們所說的「雙軌」並進思路。

漢弗萊斯：好的，大使先生，非常感謝你今天接受採訪。

劉曉明：感謝邀請。

接受英國 BBC《新聞之夜》欄目
主持人厄本現場直播採訪

二〇一九年六月十二日，我接受英國 BBC 旗艦訪談欄目《新聞之夜》（Newsnight）主持人馬克·厄本（Mark Urban）現場直播採訪。

厄本是作家、記者，擔任 BBC 外交編輯，兼任《新聞之夜》欄目主持人。他又是一位歷史學家，著有十多本歷史專著。

這次採訪正值「修例風波」演變成大規模暴亂。厄本一上來就質問，中國是否依然遵守《中英聯合聲明》？我告訴他，香港回歸後，《中英聯合聲明》就完成了它的使命。如果說《中英聯合聲明》今天還有什麼作用的話，那就是為國際社會提供了國家之間通過和平方式解決爭端的一個典範。但《中英聯合聲明》沒有使英國政府對香港擁有任何權力，無主權、無治權、無干涉內政的權力。我們還談了新疆和華為問題。

088

厄本：今天來到我們演播室的是二〇一〇年起即擔任中國駐英國大使的劉曉明。劉大使，你常駐英國的時間真是不短。我們先談談《中英聯合聲明》，中國是否依然承諾遵守這個條約？

劉曉明：中國承諾在香港實行「一國兩制」，這不僅是對世界的承諾，也是對包括香港同胞在內的全體中國人民的承諾。香港回歸後，《中英聯合聲明》就完成了它的使命。「一國兩制」在香港的實踐非常成功。

厄本：你說《中英聯合聲明》完成了它的使命，而兩年前中國外交部發言人稱，《中英聯合聲明》已經不具有現實意義了，它只是一個歷史文件。

劉曉明：它是一個歷史文件，已經完成了其使命。

厄本：它與今天已經無關了嗎？

劉曉明：《中英聯合聲明》今天的作用是為國際社會

提供了國家之間通過和平方式解決爭端的一個典範，國際社會仍可以參照這個很好的成功模式。但《中英聯合聲明》沒有使英國政府對香港擁有任何權力，英國無主權、無治權、無干涉內政的權力。

厄本：英國對香港的主權一九九七年就結束了，這是明確的。但是香港成千上萬的民眾依然認為英國根據《中英聯合聲明》有責任捍衛他們的權利。

劉曉明：英國政府有義務保護自己的公民，但並沒有保護香港人的義務，香港是中國的一部分，根據《基本法》，港人管理自己的事務，他們有權保持與中國內地不一樣的社會制度。但這與英國政府無關。

厄本：姑且不說英國政府。你可以看看香港民意，數以萬計的香港人，有人說香港人口的十分之一，他們走上街頭，他們感到不滿，他們認為北京不尊重他們選擇體制的權利。

劉曉明：這是錯誤的，整個事件被歪曲了，香港修訂條例是為了完善法律，堵塞現行法律體系的漏洞。

厄本：是誰在歪曲事實？

劉曉明：一些媒體，我認為，包括BBC。BBC把事件曲解成香港特區政府修例是受中央政府指使的。事實上，中央從未指示香港修例，此次修例是香港特區政府自己發起的，起因是一起發生在中國台灣的兇殺案……

厄本：對不起，鑑於爭議很大，你是否建議香港特區政府放棄修例？

劉曉明：我們為什麼要要求香港特區政府放棄修例呢？

厄本：你也看到，剛才節目中甚至有立法會成員說，警察把市民打得要離開香港。

劉曉明：你應該記得，開始時是和平遊行，但後來變得很惡劣。警察被襲擊，他們也要自衛，警方必須維持秩序，你不能責備警察。我認為，香港內部和外部的一些勢力在利用此事來挑起事端。讓我再接着講……

厄本：但這是香港草根民眾自發的運動。

劉曉明：事實上，一百萬的數字被誇大了，警方的估計大約有二十萬人。而且你們忽視了有八十萬人簽名支持修例。在英國，BBC並未報道那些支持修例的沉默大多數。

厄本：你說得有道理。

劉曉明：香港特區政府就修例徵求了民眾的意見和建議，收到的四千五百份反饋中，三千份支持修例，只有一千五百份反對。

厄本：我們再談一兩個其他問題。中國對待新疆維吾爾族的方式，對港人會產生什麼影響？估計有一百萬穆斯林受到不公正待遇。

劉曉明：你又在誇大其詞，不知你哪來的一百萬。

厄本：這是聯合國的估算。

劉曉明：聯合國從來沒有這樣的報告。新疆為了幫助受極端思想蠱惑的群眾回歸社會，獲得謀生技能，設立了職業技能教育培訓中心，提供職業技能和語言技能培訓，還提供法律知識教育，幫助學員維護自己的權益。

厄本：我們能去培訓中心看看嗎？能看看裏面到底什麼情況嗎？

劉曉明：當然可以，我們邀請了記者和外交官去參訪。

厄本：但是有報道說那裏面的穆斯林信仰得不到尊重。

劉曉明：這種說法是完全錯誤的。

厄本：還有報道說，不允許他們禱告，還說他們的信仰落後，等等。

劉曉明：這完全是歪曲捏造，是假新聞。中國尊重公民的信仰自由，人民有信仰宗教的權利。問題的關鍵是，你忽視了大局。教培中心設立的初衷是教育年輕人，清除極端主義流毒。新疆採取相關措施以來，已經連續三年沒有發生極端主義事件，這正說明相關措施是成功的。

厄本：我認為任何人都能理解中國防範恐怖主義和去極端化的初衷，在這一點上中國與世界上其他政府和社會有着共同之處。但是仍不斷有報告稱，教培中心規模巨大，人數非常多，大約有一百萬，聽起來很

恐怖。

劉曉明：我真不知道你哪來的一百萬這個數字。

厄本：你估計有多少人？

劉曉明：教培中心的學員有進有出，具體人數隨時變化，很難統計，關鍵是要認識到中心設立的目的。設立中心不是為了拘押，而是為了幫助年輕人通過接受教育和培訓過上更好的生活。

厄本：你是說目的不是消滅宗教？

劉曉明：絕對不是。

厄本：華為，這是一個大問題，我想也是你作為駐英國大使非常關心的問題。英國政府暫時決定在 5G 網絡建設中使用部分華為設備。你也知道，美國對此施加了很大的壓力，要求不使用華為的任何設備。從中

方的立場看，如果英國決定不使用華為設備，會面臨什麼樣的後果？

劉曉明：首先，我認為華為是一家好企業，是 5G 技術領軍者。華為與英國企業開展互利合作，不僅對英國的電信業作出了巨大貢獻，而且創造了五點一萬個就業機會。從雙贏角度來看，如果英國選擇與華為合作，雙方都將有一個十分光明的前景。

厄本：華為的技術非常先進，沒有人對此抱有懷疑。但如果英國不選擇使用華為會有什麼後果呢？

劉曉明：我認為這將向華為和其他中國企業釋放一個非常糟糕的信號。如果這樣，英國還能為中國企業提供友善的營商環境嗎？這將是非常負面的信號。

厄本：對貿易會產生消極影響嗎？

劉曉明：是的，不僅對貿易，對投資也會造成不好的影響。過去五年，中國對英國投資數量超過了此前三十年對英國投資的總量。中國對英國的投資正在快速增長，去年增長了百分之十四。如果英國對華為關門，必將向其他中國企業釋放非常糟糕的負面信號。

厄本：好的，大使，非常感謝你接受今天的採訪。

劉曉明：不客氣。

接受英國 BBC 世界新聞台
主持人霍金斯現場直播採訪

二〇一九年六月十三日，我接受英國 BBC 世界新聞台（World News）主持人露西·霍金斯（Lucy Hockings）現場直播採訪，就中國香港「修例風波」闡述中方立場。

世界新聞台是 BBC 二十四小時向全球兩百多個國家和地區滾動播放的新聞頻道，受眾近一億人。霍金斯是記者、製片人、媒體培訓師，擔任世界新聞台主持人十餘年。

採訪中，她反覆糾纏為什麼要修例。我告訴她，中國香港特區政府為的是解決現行法律體系中的缺陷，使香港免於成為「避罪天堂」，使香港變得更好。她藉「修例風波」質疑中國的司法制度。我強調中國是法治社會，法律體系在不斷完善，特別是中國在人權保護方面取得巨大進步。針對她懷疑中國是否遵守「一國兩制」，我指出，我們嚴格遵守「一國兩制」。香港回歸以來，「一國兩制」取得巨大成功，香港二十年來保持了繁榮和穩定。

霍金斯：關於香港問題，我們請中國駐英國大使劉曉明談談中國政府的看法。謝謝劉大使來到我們演播室。

我們看到成千上萬香港人走上街頭，他們中間有專業人士，還有律師，都在反對香港特區政府修例。為什麼中國要修例？

劉曉明：並不是所有人都反對。還有八十多萬香港人簽名支持香港特區政府對條例進行修訂。

霍金斯：中國中央政府支持修例嗎？

劉曉明：我們當然支持。香港特區政府的這些努力是為了解決現行法律體系中的缺陷，使香港免於成為「避罪天堂」，使香港變得更好，為什麼不支持？

霍金斯：走上街頭的那些人不反對把香港變得更好，但是他們擔心如果向中國內地移交政治犯，那麼異見活動分子、人權律師、記者、社工等將面臨安全風險，你能否解決他們的關切？中國中央政府能否承諾不會發生這樣的事？

劉曉明：這種說法是完全錯誤的。事實上，涉及移交的三十七項罪行與新聞、言論、結社、出版自由等完全無關，還特別規定涉及政治等罪行不會移交，而且相關罪行必須是香港和有關司法管轄區兩地法律均認定為犯罪的。最重要的是，修例不是向中國內地移交罪犯，而是面向所有尚未與香港簽訂移交逃犯長期安排的國家和地區建立特別移交安排。

霍金斯：但是，你能保證修例不會被當作對付政治對手的工具嗎？

劉曉明：絕對不會。這不是修例的目的。我認為事情被歪曲了，有人懷着不可告人、別有用心的目的。

霍金斯：誰懷着不可告人的目的？

劉曉明：那些不願看到香港繁榮穩定的勢力。

霍金斯：他們是誰？

劉曉明：對香港滿懷敵意的勢力。

霍金斯：是外國勢力，還是香港內部勢力？

劉曉明：有的外國勢力對香港的遊行示威表示支持，對修例表達所謂的關切。人們有理由質疑其背後的動機。

霍金斯：外界以及其他國家之所以關心這個問題，是因為中國內地司法體系被指責存在諸如酷刑、強迫認罪、任意逮捕等嚴重缺陷，令人擔心如果被移交到中國內地將不會得到公正的審判。

劉曉明：我斷然拒絕這些毫無根據的指責。中國是法治社會，法律體系在不斷完善，我們也在不斷改革。

霍金斯：但是大使先生，中國定罪率高達幾乎百分之一百。

劉曉明：我不同意這種說法。這是對中國法律體系的錯誤描述。我覺得你真應該好好看看、認真了解中國每天都在進步，特別是中國在人權保護方面取得了巨大進步，正在努力建設一個健全的法律體系。我認為在背後挑起事端的勢力，不光企圖詆毀香港特區政府，同時也想詆毀中國內地的司法體系。這就是我說的的「別有用心」。

霍金斯：就是說在中國內地可以得到公正的審判。

劉曉明：當然是，這是肯定的。

霍金斯：世界上很多人可能不這麼認為。最近新西蘭法官就不想把嫌犯交還給中國。我們繼續探討下一個問題。許多示威者稱，香港的體制被侵蝕，你是否承諾中國仍然遵守「一國兩制」？

096

劉曉明：我們嚴格遵守「一國兩制」。香港回歸以來，「一國兩制」取得了巨大成功，香港二十年來保持了繁榮和穩定。這個政策也保障了港人示威的權利。在修例問題上應當進行文明協商、文明辯論，應給立法會時間來進行討論。街頭暴力不利於建設香港文明社會。

霍金斯：修例讓許多商界領袖擔心，投資者的信心將受到影響，許多跨國公司擔心在香港的經營。

劉曉明：我覺得恰恰相反。如果香港繼續成為一個「避罪天堂」，你認為那就安全了？那能確保香港繁榮嗎？我聽到一些外國企業家……

霍金斯：人們真正的擔憂是，如果有人在香港做了中國政府不喜歡的事情，可能會被移送到中國內地，面臨不公平司法體系的審判。

劉曉明：這完全是曲解。我告訴你一些數字。過去

二十年裏，香港只對外移交了一百名罪犯，也就是說，每年五起移交逃犯案件。還有一個數據，自二〇〇六年以來，內地向香港移送了兩百四十八名罪犯，而香港沒有向內地移送任何罪犯。你認為這種關係可持續嗎？內地提出了移交請求，但是因為這種安排上的缺陷和漏洞，沒有一名逃犯被移交到內地。

霍金斯：目前，街頭示威群眾和各種請願給了林鄭月娥特首前所未有的壓力，示威者說他們大約有一百萬人。

劉曉明：你的數字不對。按照警方統計，人數約為二十萬。過去四個月左右，香港特區政府就修例法案徵詢公眾意見，收到的四千五百份書面意見中，其中三千份支持修例，只有一千五百份反對。

霍金斯：我們掌握的數字確實不一樣。但我們都看到了，上街的人出乎想象的多，他們來自社會各界。

劉曉明：你們媒體的問題在於只關注那些上街的人，而忘記了沉默的大多數。

霍金斯：中國人，特別是內地的中國人，對香港修例了解多少？

劉曉明：是的，我來這兒的目的之一，就是要告訴人們故事的另一面。

霍金斯：所以我們要請你來告訴我們故事的另一面。

劉曉明：人們認為，香港特區政府修例是正確的行動，香港特區政府正在努力採取措施使香港成為「正義天堂」，而不是「避罪天堂」。這將為香港繁榮發展提供保障，中國中央政府堅決、全力支持香港特區政府。

霍金斯：我一直在關注新華社今天的報道，作為國家媒體的新華社對香港的情況沒有報道。為什麼不報道？

霍金斯：感謝劉大使接受 BBC 世界新聞台的採訪。

劉曉明：不客氣。

劉曉明：我昨晚剛剛接受了 BBC《新聞之夜》的採訪，中國各大網站廣泛刊發了這次採訪的全部內容。

霍金斯：我想請你看一下屏幕。這是新華社網站，首頁沒有香港的消息。

劉曉明：我不評價新聞通訊社自己的報道政策。但我

接受英國 BBC《安德魯·馬爾訪談》欄目主持人馬爾現場直播採訪

作者手記

二〇一九年七月七日，我在英國 BBC 總部演播室，接受英國 BBC 旗艦高端訪談欄目《安德魯·馬爾訪談》（The Andrew Marr Show）主持人安德魯·馬爾（Andrew Marr）現場直播採訪。

採訪主要圍繞三個問題：香港「修例風波」、華為、新疆。他問我如何評價英國外交大臣同情香港示威者，提出所謂華為設備安全風險，稱新疆到處都是「集中營」，並突然插播一段視頻讓我評價。

我指出，英國外交大臣威脅要對中國實施制裁，這完全是冷戰思維；華為是一家優秀的企業，拒絕華為只會讓英國錯失巨大機遇；所謂新疆問題，完全是西方媒體對新疆真實情況的歪曲報道。

馬爾：最近，圍繞香港修例引發的示威遊行，中英之間發生了外交爭論。示威者認為修例是對人權的侵蝕，英國外交大臣亨特對示威者表示同情。中國駐英國大使劉曉明罕見地舉行了記者會，對英方干涉中國內政表示強烈譴責。今天我邀請劉曉明大使作客訪談節目，這是他自記者會後首次接受採訪。歡迎大使先生！記者會上，你確實感到十分憤怒吧？

劉曉明：是的，中方堅決反對英方干涉香港內部事務。我們認為，修例決定是合理的，香港特區行政長官和政府為的是使香港成為更好、更安全的地方，而不是「避罪天堂」。然而，英國政府高官卻支持示威者。更惡劣的是，當發生暴力衝擊立法會的行動，英方依然表示支持，不僅不譴責暴力衝擊立法會的行動，反而批評香港特區政府處置暴力事件。

馬爾：亨特外交大臣只是表示「心與示威者同在」，但並不贊同暴力行動。很多人認為，香港回歸中國時，中方承諾對香港政策將保持五十年不變，但修例

將侵蝕這一承諾。在他們看來，如果香港人能夠輕易被移交到中國內地，那麼很多人就不敢隨便說話了，言論自由將被逐漸壓制，這意味着「一國兩制」開始走向終結。

劉曉明：安德魯，看來你對修例的實際內容缺乏了解，有關條例並不只是要把罪犯從香港移交到內地。香港與超過一百七十個國家簽訂了刑事司法協助協定，但香港與三十個國家或地區還沒有簽訂相關協定。如果有人在香港以外地方犯罪，逃到香港，香港就無法對其依法懲治。修例就是為了堵住漏洞。一些人有意利用此事在香港民眾中煽動恐慌。

馬爾：北京需要移交罪犯的權力，是嗎？

劉曉明：我不這麼認為。修例的提議由特區政府發起，正如行政長官所說，特區政府從未收到來自中央政府的指示或命令，這完全是特區政府的提議，是為了完善香港的法律體系。

100

馬爾：我們都看到了立法會受衝擊的視頻，香港警方似乎無法阻擋抗議的示威者。如果中方認為形勢失控、特區政府無法控制局面，中國中央政府會直接介入嗎？

劉曉明：你提到了「一國兩制」五十年不變，我們完全遵守這項承諾，這是毫無疑問的。從這件事開始一直到現在，中國中央政府從未進行任何干預，每個階段都是特區政府在處理。對你的問題，我的回答十分明確，我們對特區政府有信心，而且事實已經證明它有能力應對事態。

馬爾：無論如何，修例將使向內地移交罪犯變得更加容易。末任港督彭定康稱，事態正在逐步惡化，持有不同觀點的人不能參加政治活動，媒體和大學言論自由被削弱。一些人在香港被劫持，然後被帶回內地。

劉曉明：我斷然拒絕彭定康的指責。作為香港末任港督，他身體已經進入二十一世紀，但腦袋卻仍留在舊殖民時代。修例並不會使從香港移交罪犯變得更容易，修例有保障條款，三十七種罪行以外的不屬於移交範圍。比如，涉及宗教和政治類的不在移交之列，而且罪行必須在香港、內地兩地都成立。假設一個極端的例子，如果謀殺在香港不構成刑事犯罪，那麼殺人犯就不會被移交。

馬爾：近期中英之間爭吵十分激烈。亨特甚至威脅要對中國實施制裁，中英關係出現危機了嗎？

劉曉明：我不這樣認為。我們對與英國進行外交爭論不感興趣，中方仍致力於與英國發展強勁有力的夥伴關係。我還記得上次接受你的專訪，是在習近平主席二〇一五年對英國進行國事訪問前夕，那次訪問開啟了中英關係「黃金時代」。

馬爾：我當然記得。

劉曉明：中方一直致力於推進中英關係的「黃金時代」。但我不同意英國某些政客所謂對華保持「戰略模糊」的說法，它不屬於中英關係的詞彙，而完全是冷戰思維語境。

馬爾：英中關係另外一個爭議很大的話題，就是華為參與英國 5G 電信網絡建設。我想問的是，中國會允許西方國家，比如英國或美國的企業直接參與你們的安全領域基礎設施建設嗎？

劉曉明：中國仍在不斷發展中。對你的問題，簡而言之，我不認為華為會直接參與涉及英國安全的基礎設施建設。

馬爾：華為將能夠監聽涉及英國人民日常生活的方方面面。中國的法律也規定了，企業有義務配合政府，提供政府需要的信息，這是讓人們最為擔心的事情。

劉曉明：絕對不會發生這樣的事情。首先，華為不存

在任何「後門」。其次，還有很多其他的安全措施。

馬爾：你可以在我的節目上向所有觀眾保證，即使華為擁有進入英國 5G 網絡的全部權限，華為也不會將有關信息傳遞給中國政府嗎？

劉曉明：我可以保證，這樣的事絕不會發生！華為是一家優秀的企業，是 5G 建設中的領軍者。拒絕華為只會讓英國錯失巨大機遇。華為來英國是為了互利合作，而不是為了監聽任何人。

馬爾：好吧，讓我們轉到兩國關係中另一個具有爭議的話題，即中國西北的維吾爾族受到的待遇。據報道，那裏到處都是「集中營」。根據聯合國統計數據，近一百萬人被關押。BBC 也報道了兒童被迫與家人分開，被送到專門的「兒童營地」。那裏究竟發生了什麼？

劉曉明：我認為這是你們的媒體對新疆真實情況的歪

曲報道。在中國，新疆經濟發展相對落後，全國三十多個省級行政區中，新疆地區國內生產總值（GDP）排名位列第二十六名。自二十世紀九〇年代以來，新疆遭受了恐怖主義、分裂主義和極端主義「三股勢力」的嚴重破壞。十年前的七月五日，新疆發生了非常嚴重的暴力恐怖襲擊事件，一百九十七人遇難。

馬爾：但「培訓營」不是解決問題的答案。英國在北愛爾蘭使用過類似方法，用鐵絲網圍起來，不允許人員自由離開。這種做法損害了英國的形象。

劉曉明：沒有什麼「培訓營」，我們稱為「職業技能教育培訓中心」。極端思想在貧困地區更易傳播滲透，要使人們擺脫極端思想的毒害，就要使貧困地區的人民脫貧。

馬爾：那為何中國政府否認它們的存在？

劉曉明：我們從未否認它們的存在，我們甚至邀請外

國外交官和包括BBC在內的外國媒體去參訪，BBC記者與學員見面並採訪了他們。我認為，人們應該從積極的角度看待這件事，設立職業教培中心的目的就是預防恐怖活動，從源頭上消除恐怖極端思想的侵害。自從這項措施實施以來，新疆已有三年未發生恐襲事件。

馬爾：不管怎麼說，這也是嚴格管理的地方。在這些「集中營」，人員不能離開，是嗎？

劉曉明：他們當然能離開，他們能自由會見他們的家人親屬，這絕不是所謂「監獄」或「集中營」。

馬爾：BBC採訪了一些在土耳其的新疆人，他們稱自己的孩子被迫與他們分開，他們表示很擔心。我可以放一段視頻，讓我們聽聽他們說了什麼。這些孩子現在在哪裏？（馬爾播放視頻）

劉曉明：我們先來談談這些人是什麼人。這些人都是

反對中國政府的，你期待他們會說中國政府的好話嗎？教培中心學員的孩子們得到政府精心照顧。

馬爾：在新疆，他們的孩子被迫與他們分離？

劉曉明：絕不是這樣。這些人如果想見自己的孩子，完全可以回中國。

馬爾：所以這些都是謊言嗎？

劉曉明：當然是謊言。根本沒有所謂「強制父母和孩子分離」的情況。

馬爾：BBC 記者去新疆採訪了一次，稱有四百個家庭的孩子失蹤。

劉曉明：你可以把失蹤孩子的家庭具體信息告訴我。關於人員失蹤，有許多信息是錯誤的，我們需要甄別處理。比如，某國稱新疆一位維吾爾族音樂家被殺

害，但這位音樂家很快公開露面，活得好好的。如果你掌握所謂失蹤孩子的信息，請你告訴我，我們會盡力幫助尋找，我們會告訴你，他們是誰，他們現在在幹什麼。

馬爾：大使先生，謝謝你接受我的採訪。

劉曉明：不客氣。

接受英國天空新聞台《今夜天空新聞》欄目主持人莫納罕現場直播採訪

作者手記

二○一九年十月一日，我在英國天空新聞台演播室，接受該台旗艦欄目《今夜天空新聞》（Sky News Tonight）主持人德莫特‧莫納罕（Dermot Murnaghan）現場直播採訪。

《今夜天空新聞》是天空新聞台旗艦新聞訪談欄目。莫納罕是該台資深主持人，二○一一至二○一六年曾創辦、主持天空新聞台《莫納罕訪談》欄目。二○一五年十月，習近平主席對英國國事訪問前夕，我曾接受莫納罕的採訪，我們算是「老相識」了。

採訪當天正值中華人民共和國成立七十週年，莫納罕的第一個問題就是，中國在閱兵式上展示包括洲際彈道導彈在內的先進軍事裝備，是否會讓世界感覺受到威脅？我告訴他，中國無意主導世界。中國仍然是一個發展中國家。我們還討論了中國香港、新疆、華為問題。

接着，他問中國是否希望在未來七十年取得世界主導地位？我告訴他，中國無意主導世界。中國仍然是一個發展中國家。我們還討論了中國香港、新疆、華為問題。

莫納罕：今天，我邀請中國駐英國大使劉曉明來到天空新聞台。大使先生，很高興見到你。我們首先來看今天在北京舉行的中華人民共和國成立七十週年的慶祝活動。我們看到中國展示了包括洲際彈道導彈在內的先進軍事裝備，以及成千上萬的軍隊。習近平主席說，沒有任何力量能夠阻擋中國的前進步伐。世界是否應該感覺受到一些威脅？

劉曉明：絕對不會。習近平主席在講話中強調，中國將堅持和平發展道路。我們願與世界各國分享中國的發展機遇。我認為，外界特別是英國媒體在談到中華人民共和國成立七十週年慶典時，只關注閱兵，閱兵只是慶祝活動的一部分。今年參加慶祝活動的既有一點五萬名各軍種官兵，也有十多萬名普通民眾，還有七十組彩車組成的方陣，展示了中華人民共和國成立七十年來的發展成就。

莫納罕：中國從農業經濟發展成為世界最先進的經濟體之一，成就確實十分震撼。

劉曉明：不僅僅是農業經濟的變遷。中華人民共和國成立之初，中國剛經歷了一百多年的戰亂（莫納罕：確實是。）和外來侵略與欺凌。

莫納罕：大使，我想問一下，中國經歷了外國欺凌、佔領及其引發的戰爭歷史，這讓中國對於未來的態度會產生什麼樣的影響？中國下一個七十年的目標是什麼？有人說，中國不僅要求得到世界的尊重，而且希望在未來七十年取得世界主導地位。

劉曉明：完全不是這樣。中國無意主導世界。中國仍然是一個發展中國家，中國的發展仍然面臨嚴峻挑戰。因此，習近平主席說，要把我們的人民共和國鞏固好、發展好，這是中國領導人和中國人民面臨的最根本的任務。正如我所說，中國曾飽受外來侵略、欺凌、羞辱，因此永遠不會將之施加給其他國家。

莫納罕：剛才我們報道了今天香港的局勢，一位示威者被近距離射中胸部，人們認為中國的鎮壓是對民主

106

權利的不尊重。

劉曉明：我不能同意你的說法，香港的情況根本不是鎮壓。我們強烈譴責暴徒的暴力行徑。香港的暴力活動已經持續了數月，嚴重挑戰了「一國兩制」的底線，嚴重破壞了香港法治，嚴重威脅到香港安全……

莫納罕：香港特區政府為什麼不就示威者提出的民主訴求進行接觸、展開對話？

劉曉明：你應該將和平示威者和暴徒區別開來。你談到警察使用真槍實彈，因為他們的生命受到了嚴重威脅。那名左肩受到槍擊的暴徒，當時正用鐵棒攻擊警察。我想問的是，如果同樣的事發生在英國會怎樣？英國警察會如何應對這樣的暴徒和暴行？

莫納罕：那也不會用實彈射擊未攜槍支的示威者。

劉曉明：如果你的生命都受到嚴重威脅呢？

莫納罕：英國警察是不帶槍的。

劉曉明：我認為你說的不是事實。假如英國議會大廈被一群暴徒衝擊，英國警察會如何應對？我們應該譴責這些暴行。香港是建立在法治基礎上的，法治和「一國兩制」是香港未來繁榮穩定的保障。

莫納罕：你能告訴我，如果抗議示威持續下去，雙方暴力繼續升級，香港特區政府會使用更多實彈嗎？

劉曉明：我希望事態會逐漸平息。

莫納罕：如果不能平息會怎樣？

劉曉明：我不回答假設性問題。過去幾週，香港局勢已有所好轉，特別是林鄭月娥特首開始與各界人士進行真誠對話，還成立對話辦公室。民眾應給予香港特

區政府機會來解決他們的關切。我們承認，香港存在一些根本的、深層次的問題，如住房、年輕人就業機會等，但示威特別是暴力活動不可能解決這些深層次問題。

莫納罕：我想問一下新疆維吾爾族的問題。天空新聞台記者車德明報道，有數百萬維吾爾族人被關押在「集中營」。

劉曉明：這不是事實。新疆是中國最大的省級行政區，經濟發展迅速。

莫納罕：但新疆有許多人被關進「集中營」。

劉曉明：那不是「集中營」，正確的說法是職業技能教育培訓中心。這項措施主要是為了預防恐怖主義，過去二十多年新疆深受恐怖主義之害。

莫納罕：我們看到視頻中這些人被捆綁雙手、蒙着眼睛，被警察押送。他們是自願被送進培訓中心的嗎？

劉曉明：這是完全不同的兩回事。視頻中是押送服刑人員的正常司法活動，一些媒體有意炒作。這與教培中心沒有任何關係。我們採取的措施是為了新疆絕大多數人的安全，是對聯合國《防止暴力極端主義行動計劃》的具體落實。

莫納罕：教培中心學員完成培訓後，可以自由離開嗎？

劉曉明：當然可以。培訓的基本目的是教育年輕人，幫助他們消除恐怖極端主義思想、學習謀生技能，避免受到極端主義思想的毒害。

莫納罕：最後，我想問關於華為的問題。包括美國在內的許多國家都認為華為與中國政府關係密切，所以美方禁止華為參與其網絡建設。但華為仍在參與英國的5G網絡建設。我們今天剛採訪了美國商務部部長

108

羅斯，他說英國應對華為保持高度警惕。如果英國也禁止華為，中國會持什麼態度？

劉曉明：首先，我完全拒絕針對華為的所謂指控。華為是一家很好的公司，是一家民營企業，與中國政府沒有關係。華為是5G技術的領軍者，它到英國來是為了與英國合作夥伴實現雙贏，它為英國電信行業發展作出了貢獻。我希望英國政府根據自身國家利益作出明智抉擇。

莫納罕：我們都知道，美國特朗普政府給英國約翰遜政府施加了很大壓力，英美就華為問題進行了討論。如果英國真的禁止華為，那麼在英國脫歐後與中國簽自貿協定時，中國將採取什麼態度？

劉曉明：我認為，如果英國政府禁止華為，會發出非常錯誤、消極的信號。英國一直被認為是非常開放、宜商的國家，禁止華為會向世界發出消極信號，也將向中國企業發出錯誤信號，影響中國對英國投資。因

此我希望，英國政府能根據自身國家利益和中英合作的共同利益作出決定。

莫納罕：謝謝劉大使。

劉曉明：不客氣。

接受英國BBC《新聞之夜》欄目
主持人沃克現場直播採訪

作者手記

二〇一九年十月四日，我接受英國BBC旗艦欄目《新聞之夜》（Newsnight）主持人柯絲蒂·沃克（Kirsty Wark）現場直播採訪。

沃克一九七六年進入BBC，一九九三年加入《新聞之夜》欄目團隊，是該欄目任職時間最長的主持人；曾獲多項新聞大獎，包括英國電影和電視藝術學院獎。

採訪正值中國香港「修例風波」演變成社會動亂，沃克指責香港警察對示威者使用真槍實彈，並問如果香港的暴力活動升級失控，中央政府會怎麼辦。她還藉香港動亂指責中國在新疆的政策。我闡述了中方原則立場，並批駁BBC和西方媒體對新疆問題的歪曲報道。

沃克：我們邀請中國駐英國大使劉曉明來到節目。歡迎你，大使先生。首先，今晚香港局勢再次升級，有更多的香港人佩戴面罩，你是否對這種公然違抗禁令的行為感到震驚？

劉曉明：完全沒有。我認為《禁止蒙面規例》的出台十分及時而且非常必要。這項禁令的目的是制止暴力、恢復秩序以及震懾新的暴力行為。

沃克：可是從今天晚上看，禁令並未奏效。

劉曉明：現在就下結論還太早。禁令生效才剛剛幾小時，現在就說禁令未奏效為時過早。香港特區政府決心要止暴制亂。

沃克：但是自香港特區政府宣佈禁令以來，香港民眾的反應是，我們不會容忍這些，我們還是要上街，還是要戴面罩，我們不需要誰告訴我們該怎麼做。

劉曉明：我認為你確實需要將和平示威者和兇惡暴徒區別開來。特區政府之所以要訂立規例，是因為形勢已經升級到了危險的程度。正如林鄭月娥特首所說，到了需要頒佈禁令的時候了。

沃克：林鄭月娥是否已對局勢失去了控制？

劉曉明：我不這麼認為，我認為局勢仍然可控。我們對此充滿信心。

沃克：可是形勢看上去並不可控。

劉曉明：如果林鄭月娥特首已對局勢失去控制，她怎麼能宣佈禁令？

沃克：香港警察開始使用實彈，又有一個青少年被打中腿部，之前還發生槍擊事件，看上去政府已不能掌控局面。

劉曉明：警察之所以開槍是因為他們的生命受到嚴重威脅。讓我們來看看英國警察是如何應對類似情況的。英國首席警監西蒙‧徹斯特曼稱，「訓練有素的武裝警察可以開槍，以消除威脅，保護公眾和警察自身安全」。

沃克：可是公眾就是街上的示威者。我想問的是，你是否仍對林鄭月娥有完全的信任？

劉曉明：是的，對此我非常肯定。

沃克：BBC 記者剛才說，根據路透社的報道，中國人民武裝警察部隊人數已從三千至五千名增加到一萬至一萬二千名，這是否屬實？如果香港的暴力活動升級，超出林鄭月娥的控制，中國中央政府是否還將增加部隊人數？

劉曉明：我們當然希望情況會好轉，但我們也要作最壞的打算。正如我在記者會上所說，如果事態發展到特區政府無法控制的地步，中央政府不會坐視不管。這仍是我們的立場。

沃克：但你們會怎麼做？路透社報道說，香港有一萬至一萬二千名武警部隊，比之前翻了一番，你能證實嗎？

劉曉明：我能證實的是，現在事態仍然可控。我們對特區政府和林鄭月娥特首完全有信心。

沃克：但如果本週末出現更多的示威者，數千人上街呢？是否會達到臨界點？

劉曉明：我們應該給特首時間來實施「面罩禁令」。現在下結論還為時過早。

沃克：你們會部署更多的部隊嗎？

劉曉明：如果事態發展到特區政府無法控制的地步，

我們不會坐視不管。正如林鄭月娥特首所說，她的政府不會讓事態一直惡化下去。

沃克：但總不能把所有香港人都關起來吧？

劉曉明：我對特區政府有信心。我相信這項禁令可以有助於改善香港局勢。我希望香港大多數民眾能對特區政府的努力作出積極反應。

沃克：但整個夏天事態都在發酵，你們還會容忍多久？如果到聖誕節還控制不住抗議活動，你們會怎麼應對？

劉曉明：如果你將現在與幾個月前作對比，就應看到香港局勢整體呈轉穩趨緩態勢。英國乃至西方媒體的問題在於，你們只關注暴徒和暴力。

沃克：我們關注的是街頭發生的事。如果林鄭月娥為平息街頭抗議而取消「面罩禁令」，你會支持嗎？

劉曉明：我認為，她決心實施禁令。我們尊重林鄭月娥特首和特區政府。我們理解和支持她的決定。我們對她應對事態完全有信心。

劉曉明：香港示威者稱他們是在為生存而戰，因為當他們看到你們如何對待內地的新疆維吾爾族人時，比如「再教育中心」等，他們擔心香港也會那樣。

劉曉明：我認為這是你們媒體捏造的故事。

沃克：怎麼捏造？

劉曉明：中國新疆的職業技能教育培訓中心是為了預防恐怖主義而設立的，此項措施實施三年以來，新疆沒有發生過一起恐怖事件。此前的二十多年裏，新疆發生過數千起令人髮指的恐怖事件，我們沒有看到BBC和西方媒體對此有任何報道。請你告訴我，新疆發生恐怖事件的時候，你們在哪裏？！

沃克：劉大使，你說到中國在新疆實施反恐措施，而進駐香港的中國武警也具有這樣的職能。

劉曉明：你是在混淆視聽！香港沒有中國武警，目前香港的局勢是由香港警方處理的。

沃克：我們知道中國在香港派駐了武警，而且數量在增加。

劉曉明：這不是事實。

沃克：港人因此感到恐懼，他們沒有別的選擇，他們想要林鄭月娥特首下台，要求調查警方暴力執法，還要求實行普選。香港能實現普選嗎？

劉曉明：中國堅定奉行「一國兩制」。習近平主席在慶祝中華人民共和國成立七十週年招待會上強調，中國政府將繼續全面準確貫徹「一國兩制」、「港人治港」、高度自治的方針，這是中國政府堅定不移的

政策。

沃克：這是否意味着中國中央政府絕對不會介入並接管香港？

劉曉明：「一國兩制」五十年不變，我們會堅定奉行這一政策。

沃克：非常感謝大使。

劉曉明：不客氣。

接受英國BBC《尖銳對話》欄目
主持人薩克現場直播採訪

作者手記

二○一九年十一月二十六日，我在英國BBC總部演播室，接受BBC旗艦訪談欄目《尖銳對話》（HARDtalk）主持人斯蒂芬·薩克（Stephen Sackur）現場直播採訪。

《尖銳對話》是BBC旗艦訪談欄目，聚焦國內外熱議、敏感話題，邀請各國政要、商界領袖、社會名流、知識精英與主持人進行一對一的「尖銳對話」。欄目以深度挖掘、唇槍舌劍、激烈交鋒、充滿火藥味著稱。節目通過BBC新聞頻道、世界新聞台、國際廣播電台等平台，向全球兩百多個國家和地區播放，受眾達四億多人次。

薩克是BBC著名節目主持人，曾擔任BBC外事記者，常駐中東和北美。他主持過廣播四台和世界新聞台等，擔任《尖銳對話》主持人七年多，曾採訪過多國總統和總理，獲多項新聞大獎，包括「國際電視年度人物」。他的採訪風格以直率、敏銳、犀利、執着著稱，提問刁鑽、尖銳、咄咄逼人，曾引起一些被採訪者的抱怨。他的一句名言是：「好的採訪，從深度調研開始，通過激烈交鋒，達到揭示真相。」

這次採訪聚焦中國香港暴亂。剛好十二天前，習近平主席在巴西出席金磚國家領

導人會議期間就香港問題發表講話。我在第一時間通過英國電視台向世界解讀習主席的重要講話，指出這是中國政府發出的最權威的聲音，那就是，止暴制亂、恢復秩序是香港當前最緊迫的任務。

我們談到香港的民主、自由、普選，談了中國的發展、法制、人權、新疆、中國的戰略目標等問題。

薩克： 劉曉明大使，歡迎來到《尖銳對話》欄目。

劉曉明： 謝謝！

薩克： 很高興你能接受我們欄目的邀請。讓我們從香港問題開始。香港持續動亂，這是否是習近平主席就職七年以來面臨的最大挑戰？

劉曉明： 中國政府的立場十分清楚。十二天前，習近平主席出席金磚國家領導人會議期間發出最權威的聲音，那就是，止暴制亂、恢復秩序是香港當前最緊迫的任務。

薩克： 中方幾個月來一直在講這些話，但香港的暴力局面從初夏開始到現在仍在持續。除了暴力局面，還有上週日香港區議會選舉結果所體現的民眾普遍的政治呼聲。香港民眾投票讓民主派取得絕對多數席位，明確表達了對香港特區政府和中央政府的嚴重不滿。

劉曉明： 首先，我認為你需要將和平示威者與暴力犯罪分子區別開來。你提到最近區議會選舉，這正說明習近平主席闡述的嚴正立場產生了積極影響。只有在

和平的環境下，民眾才能行使民主權利。

薩克：那麼這次選舉的結果意味着什麼？候選人中既有很多是建制派，也有不少是代表反對派和街頭民主抗議者的觀點，選民們是可以選擇的。此次選舉投票率高達百分之七十。結果是，反對派贏得四百五十二個議席中的四十個，取得壓倒性多數，在十七個區議會中，十七個被他們控制。

劉曉明：首先，我認為你不應過度解讀所謂反對派取得「壓倒性多數」勝利。雖然看上去反對派贏得十八個區議會中的十七個，但從得票率上看，是百分之六十比百分之四十，百分之四十的選民沒有把選票投給反對派。其次，在任何國家包括在西方國家選舉中，在暴亂、動亂和經濟放緩等背景下，當政者總是容易失去更多選票。而這些正是暴力犯罪分子造成的，他們給香港帶來了巨大麻煩。

薩克：可是，劉大使，你和許多中國官員這幾個月來

一直在對我們說，香港「沉默的大多數」並不支持民主抗議示威，他們擁護中央政府。我們現在知道事實並非如此。

劉曉明：我認為目前下結論還為時過早。我剛說了百分之四十的選民沒有把選票投給反對派。根據媒體報道，建制派候選人受到騷擾、干擾、威脅，一些人甚至遇刺，比如何君堯先生。這些暴力極端分子製造恐怖氣氛，讓一些選民無法前往投票站投票，我稱之為「黑色恐怖」。

薩克：大使先生，你和我一樣在電視上看到了香港發生的一切，香港警察近幾個月來對抗議示威者實施了野蠻的暴力「鎮壓」，但未奏效。林鄭月娥行政長官最終代表的是中國中央政府的利益。她開始的應對策略是用撤銷修例平息民主抗議，但不管用。之後，她明確指示警察要更強硬，但也不管用。中央政府現在要做什麼？

劉曉明：我認為你沒能看到事情的全貌。問題不在於香港警察。我認為香港警察是世界上紀律最嚴明、最專業、最文明的警隊。我認為如果香港警察是世界上紀律最嚴明、最專業、最文明的警隊。如果和英國作一個比較，你認為如果類似的暴力事態發生在英國會持續多久？

薩克：但你看到警察近距離向抗議者開槍的畫面了嗎？

劉曉明：警察開槍是為了自衛，是為了維護法治。我在接受 BBC《新聞之夜》欄目採訪時曾引述英國首席警監西蒙·徹斯特曼的話，他說「訓練有素的武裝警察可以開槍，以消除威脅，保護公眾和警察自身安全」。英國媒體的問題是，你們只盯着警察的應對行動，而對暴徒的暴力行徑視而不見。這些暴徒向一位持不同意見的香港市民潑灑易燃液體並對他縱火焚燒，你們仍然稱暴徒為抗議者。

薩克：劉大使，我們也採訪了抗議活動的頭目，就他們使用的一些暴力策略提問，包括為什麼使用汽

油彈和其他武器，這些問題我們都提了。但現在的問題是，中國政府面臨巨大的困境，暴力和動盪仍在繼續，林鄭月娥的策略失敗了。下一步，比較現實的策略是是否讓林鄭月娥下台？

劉曉明：首先我要說，林鄭月娥特首工作做得很好。她的政府和管治團隊仍然獲得中央政府的全力支持。

薩克：這可太有意思了，林鄭月娥過去半年來的執政狀況很失敗。

劉曉明：我不這樣認為。我有許多理由。如果外部勢力不在幕後操縱，激進的暴徒不破壞特區政府與民眾的對話，她就不會失敗。林鄭月娥特首和她的團隊作了許多努力，他們以開放的態度與民眾接觸、溝通。自「修例風波」發生五個多月以來，林鄭月娥特首和特區政府與民眾進行了一百多場對話交流，但極端分子不給他們機會。

薩克：你是位資深大使，你知道外交如何運作取捨。林鄭月娥現在可以作出選擇。她可以讓步，成立真正獨立的調查委員會，對警方近幾個月的行為進行調查；她也可以推動下屆特首選舉實現全民普選。否則，香港警察將沒有能力重建秩序，特首將不得不依靠一點二萬駐軍實施更加嚴厲的鎮壓。你有沒有認真考慮過這種前景？

劉曉明：林鄭月娥特首及其團隊為解決問題竭盡全力。一開始，她擱置了逃犯條例修訂草案，後來撤銷了草案。她還提出四項行動，包括與民眾進行一百多次溝通。全民普選不可能一蹴而就，需要經過法律程序。中央政府致力於在香港實現普選。如果反對派在二○一五年沒有投票否決普選方案，早在二○一七年就可以實現普選。

薩克：行政長官這樣關鍵崗位的選舉並不是普選。行政長官候選人由北京提名，由約千人組成的選委會來選。我認為，中國內地同胞正在密切關注香港人追求

真正的自由民主最終會得到什麼樣的結果，這才是你們擔心的事。

劉曉明：你又忽略了另一個更大的問題。你提及的問題太多，讓我一個一個解釋。首先是全民普選，如果反對派在二○一五年沒有投票否決普選方案，二○一七年就可以實現特區行政長官普選。雖然那不是百分之百的全民普選，但是全民普選要一步一步來。

薩克：大使先生，你是一位外交官，不應粉飾普選。

劉曉明：全民普選涉及兩個選舉：一個是特區行政長官，另一個是香港立法會。如果反對派沒有否決二○一五年普選方案，明年的香港立法會選舉將是全民普選，七百萬人一人一票。

薩克：這些都不會發生，香港沒有全民普選。不久前北京宣佈香港高等法院有關《禁止蒙面規例》不符合《基本法》的判決無效，這是在侵蝕「一國兩制」的

基礎。

劉曉明：你的說法是完全錯誤的。你沒有給我時間回答你提出的問題。你談到中國的根本性問題，你還說中國擔心香港事態氾濫影響內地。事實並非如此。如你所知，我們剛剛慶祝了中華人民共和國成立七十週年，你應該看到中國在過去七十年取得了怎樣巨大的成就。中國人民的生活更加美好，更加幸福，壽命也更長。七十年來，中國人民預期壽命從三十五歲提升至七十七歲。請你告訴我，世界上哪個國家取得了這樣的成就？改革開放四十多年來，中國從世界經濟排名第十一位躍居第二大經濟體，七億人實現脫貧。中國人民熱愛中國共產黨，中國共產黨是中國的脊梁！你說香港事態會在中國其他地方引起外溢效應，引發大規模示威，這樣的情況根本不存在。

薩克：你描繪了一幅美妙的畫卷。

劉曉明：我沒有作任何粉飾，這些都是事實。

薩克：你的話題已脫離香港，我們可以討論。

劉曉明：是你把我帶入香港以外的話題。

薩克：沒有人懷疑中國政府過去幾十年來取得的驚人經濟成就。如果你堅持認為中國人民的生活非常幸福，那中國政府為何如此害怕不同意見？

劉曉明：我們不害怕任何不同意見。

薩克：中國有多少政治犯？

劉曉明：中國沒有政治犯。

薩克：大使先生，這不是事實。

劉曉明：沒有人是因為不同政見入獄。入獄服刑者都是因為違反了中國法律。

薩克：中國的法律事實上阻止政治反對派存在，誰不和黨保持一致，就是違法。

劉曉明：根本不存在你說的情況。

薩克：不僅如此，過去兩三年，中國加大了對社會各種思想、行動的監控。

劉曉明：我來問問你，英國有多少監控探頭？

薩克：沒有中國那麼多。

劉曉明：但人均……

薩克：英國並不是世界上擁有監控探頭最多的國家。

劉曉明：你怎麼解釋英國人均監控探頭數量非常多這種情況？

薩克：我可以解釋，但中國……

劉曉明：我在問為什麼英國有這麼多監控探頭。

薩克：我想說，中國監控探頭數量達到每兩人一個，中國人口有十四億，這是一個難以想象的被監控的社會。為什麼要進行監控？

劉曉明：你去過中國嗎？

薩克：去過。

劉曉明：最近一次去中國是什麼時候？

薩克：大約三年前。

劉曉明：在中國，你會感到人們是很自由、很幸福的。難道你沒有感受到嗎？你認為中國人民處於被壓迫、被恐嚇的狀態並且有很多不滿嗎？在中國，你到

處都能看到人們的笑臉。當然，任何社會都會有人有不滿，但中國人民有表達意見的渠道。我們有人民代表大會和政治協商制度。你認為中國沒有街頭政治，所以中國就沒有民主。但是，中國的民主是中國特色的民主。你們不能用自己的標準去評判別的國家，就像我們不用自己的標準來評判你們。

薩克：我們討論一下中國西部的自治區新疆。

劉曉明：你去過新疆嗎？

薩克：還沒有。如果中方邀請，我很樂意去。

劉曉明：當然可以。中國有句話：不到新疆，不知道中國之大；不到新疆，不知道中國之美。新疆是和睦、繁榮的好地方，但自二十世紀九〇年代至二〇一六年，發生了很多讓人不願看到的事情，新疆某種程度上變成了「戰場」，發生了數千起恐怖襲擊事件，成千無辜群眾遇難。僅二〇一四年，每三天就發

生兩起恐襲事件。民眾無法安全出行，紛紛呼籲政府採取應對措施。所以，政府依法設立了「職業技能教育培訓中心」，目的是去極端化。

薩克：大使先生，你們的確遇到了問題。我們剛才討論了香港局勢和新疆問題。美國國會剛剛通過了《香港人權與民主法案》，準備制裁帶頭鎮壓示威者的香港官員。你本人也被英國外交大臣拉布「召見」了。中國處於守勢，是否反映出你們的外交面臨巨大壓力？

劉曉明：我不這樣認為。相反，我認為西方國家應該為干涉中國內政而感到巨大壓力。如果中國全國人大通過一項與英國某地方有關的法律，表達我們的關切並制裁你們的政客，你們會怎麼想？現在是二十一世紀，不是「炮艦外交」時代。中國不會再任人欺凌。

薩克：你認為西方國家政府是任意欺凌中國嗎？你擔任大使時間很久了，不久前，你和英國政府還常常提

到中英關係「黃金時代」。而現在，英國外交大臣告訴你，英國政府對英國駐香港總領事館僱員鄭文傑被逮捕並遭酷刑感到震驚和震怒，對中國在香港和新疆的做法提出批評和譴責。美國聯邦調查局負責人稱，「中國的目標看起來是要取代美國成為世界頭號超級大國，為此不惜違反法律」。中英關係「黃金時代」是否已因互相譴責和競爭而不復存在？

劉曉明：現在該輪到我講話了？

薩克：是的。

劉曉明：希望你不要再打斷我的講話。你們的《尖銳對話》欄目應該是話題尖銳，而不是總聽你一個人講，不讓別人講。首先，關於英國外交大臣拉布和我的會見，他的確提到鄭文傑案，但並沒有談及新疆問題。是我向他指出，中國對英國干涉中國內政、干涉香港事務表示堅決反對。關於鄭文傑案，鄭因涉嫌嫖娼違反了中國法律，他對違法事實供認不諱。

薩克：他在警方酷刑下當然會認罪。

劉曉明：請你不要總打斷我。你提了很多問題，我需要逐一回答。關於所謂中國警方對鄭使用「酷刑」，我們完全拒絕這種無理指責。我們絕不接受英方指責，鄭沒有遭受所謂「酷刑」，他在被收押和被釋放時均接受了體檢，身體狀況很好，沒有任何問題。這只能說，你們對中國充滿偏見。

我們已經對英國外交部作出了回應，我們絕不接受英方指責，鄭沒有遭受所謂

薩克：大使先生，你已講清楚了你的觀點。我們剩下的時間不多了。還有一個大問題。美國一位高級官員稱，「中國的目標是取代美國成為頭號超級大國」。美國和英國現在都持這種觀點。這是北京的終極戰略目標嗎？

劉曉明：絕對不是。我們根本沒有興趣取代誰，也沒有興趣挑戰誰。儘管中國是世界第二大經濟體，但是我們依然是一個發展中國家，人均 GDP 不到一萬美

元，在世界上排名靠後。這是我第三次擔任駐外大使，在我擔任駐埃及大使後，我曾到中國西北部貧窮省份甘肅掛職。在偏僻的西北地區，人們連喝水都很困難，要靠挖水窖收集雨水、淨化雨水，人畜都得依靠這種淨化窖水。對於中國政府和中國領導人來說，解決這些問題都是很艱巨的任務。對內，我們要保障中國人民的溫飽，使中國人民更幸福、更長壽；對外，中國奉行和平發展的外交政策。

薩克：鄧小平有句名言：中國的戰略是「韜光養晦、絕不當頭」。這顯然不是習近平的戰略。

劉曉明：中國堅持奉行和平發展戰略，因為我們從和平發展中受益。中國四十多年發展的奇蹟是在和平的環境中取得的，只有繼續努力營造和平環境，才能取得更大發展。這就是為什麼習近平主席提出構建人類命運共同體的倡議。這是我們的目標，是我們堅定不移的目標。

薩克：劉曉明大使，非常感謝接受《尖銳對話》的採訪。

劉曉明：不客氣。

接受英國 BBC《安德魯‧馬爾訪談》欄目主持人馬爾現場直播採訪

作者手記

二○二○年七月十九日，我在英國 BBC 總部演播室，接受 BBC 旗艦訪談欄目《安德魯‧馬爾訪談》（*The Andrew Marr Show*）主持人安德魯‧馬爾（Andrew Marr）現場直播採訪。

這是我在英國十一年期間第四次，也是最後一次接受馬爾的採訪。當時，《香港國安法》剛剛頒佈實施，我們圍繞中國香港、華為、新疆等問題進行了激烈的辯論。

馬爾一上來就指責《香港國安法》違反了中國關於「一國兩制」的承諾，他還質問香港人是否有自由。

關於華為，他問英國政府將為禁用華為設備付出什麼代價。

關於新疆問題，馬爾使用他的慣用伎倆，當場播放一段囚犯被押上列車的視頻。

我闡述了中方在香港問題上的原則立場，批駁了西方情報機構和媒體關於新疆的虛假信息。關於華為問題，我提及英國歷史學家雅克的一段話，即乾隆皇帝在一七九三年告訴英國國王，「天朝物產豐盈」，不稀罕英國的東西。結果這成了中國此後一百五十年衰落的開端。我說，二百二十七年後的今天，英國對中國說，「我們

不需要你們的 5G 技術」。我真不知道接下來的一百五十年將會發生什麼。

訪談節目播出後，一些英國友人來信祝賀，稱中國大使給英國大牌主持人、歷史學家上了一堂生動的歷史課。

馬爾：歡迎大使先生。我想首先談談中國香港的情況，在香港，表達不同意見的權利和言論自由是否仍然得到尊重？

「一國兩制」的承諾。

劉曉明：完全得到尊重。有人拿《香港國安法》說事，事實上，《香港國安法》旨在恢復香港的正常社會秩序，保護的是絕大多數人的權利，針對的是極少數危害國家安全的犯罪分子。

馬爾：我想提醒觀眾《香港國安法》實際上說了些什麼。它說：什麼行為屬於違法將由北京而不是香港決定；抗議者僅因使用標語牌就可能被捕；警方無需搜查令即可進入建築物進行搜查；審判可以在沒有陪審團的情況下秘密進行。這些法律條款顯然違反了中國

劉曉明：這些信息是完全錯誤的。我不知道你是否讀過《香港國安法》。首先，《香港國安法》開宗明義指出，中國將堅定不移並全面準確貫徹「一國兩制」、「港人治港」、高度自治方針。為什麼要實施國家安全法？《基本法》第二十三條授權香港特區就維護國家安全自行立法，即我們常說的第二十三條立法。但二十三年來，由於反對派的干擾和麻煩製造者的恐嚇，相關立法遲遲未能完成。維護國家安全歷來是中央政府的職責所在。

馬爾：你提到麻煩製造者，但是根據我們節目觀眾所尊重的「大赦國際」組織稱，隨着香港當局逐步

126

採用中國內地模糊且包羅萬象的國家安全定義，香港人享有的和平集會、言論、結社自由的權利迅速受到侵蝕。

劉曉明：「大赦國際」沒有任何信譽可言，因為它製造了大量污衊中國的不實之詞，對中國從來沒有說過一句好話，從來沒有一句客觀的評論。這就是它的問題。去年我曾和你討論過香港形勢，面對當時的動盪和暴亂，任何負責任的政府都必須採取措施予以制止。

馬爾：香港現有的法律相當有力了，難道還不夠嗎？如果真的有人在香港製造麻煩、擾亂香港，可以用現有法律對付他們。

劉曉明：這恰恰就是為什麼香港需要一部國家安全法。現有的法律不足以遏制打砸搶燒以及衝擊立法會等暴力行為。這種行為就如同衝擊搶燒以及衝擊英國議會。過去二十三年，香港始終沒有一部維護國家安全的法律。

馬爾：真正的問題是，你們不希望香港人談論民主，不是嗎？特朗普總統說過，香港人的自由和權利已被剝奪；沒有特殊待遇，就沒有香港，因為香港將無力與任何自由市場進行競爭。很多人會離開香港，前往澳大利亞、美國和英國。這些人可以自由離開嗎？

劉曉明：人們當然可以自由進出。回歸祖國二十三年來，香港人享受到前所未有的自由。回歸前，他們有什麼自由？他們可以自由選舉港督嗎？末任港督還是英國政府任命的。但過去二十三年中，香港人已經自由選舉了五任行政長官。

馬爾：一個根本性的事實是，在你們新領導人的領導下，中國更具民族主義傾向，更加咄咄逼人。中國還能否與世界上的自由市場國家建立一種完全開放的關係？這是真正的問題所在，而香港是問題的「震中」。

劉曉明：我認為，你們對中國真實情況的認識是非常錯誤的。我可以給你提供最新情況。你們常常不

相信中國的表態，認為那是一種宣傳。你們更相信美國人，認為他們的話不是宣傳。那麼好，我可以告訴你美國人如何看中國。最近，哈佛大學肯尼迪政府學院發佈了一份報告，這份報告涵蓋了過去十三年的調查，結論是，中國民眾對中國共產黨和中國政府的滿意度高達百分之九十三，遠遠高於任何西方政府和任何西方國家領導人。這才是中國的真實情況。

馬爾：下週，英國政府將就香港問題作出反應，據報道，英國政府很可能會採取類似《馬格尼茨基法案》的措施，禁止中國某些個人入境英國，也可能廢除英國和香港之間的移交逃犯協議。如果真是那樣，中國將如何回應？

劉曉明：那將是完全錯誤的。我們歷來反對單邊制裁。只有聯合國才有權力實施制裁。如果英國政府走出對中國任何個人實行制裁這一步，中國必將作出堅決有力的回擊。你已經看到中美之間的情況。美國制裁中國官員，中國就制裁美國參議員和官員。我不願

看到這種針鋒相對的情況發生在中英之間。英國應該有獨立自主的外交政策，而不是隨美起舞，就像對待華為問題一樣。

馬爾：說到針鋒相對或是報復措施，我們來談談華為。在有關華為的決定宣佈後，中國外交部稱此舉將嚴重削弱互信，要付出代價。請問是什麼代價？

劉曉明：英國的決定是一個非常錯誤的決定。我們正在評估其影響和後果。在這一決定宣佈那天，我說這對華為是黑暗的一天，對中英關係也是黑暗的一天，對英國則是更黑暗的一天，因為英國失去了成為5G領軍者的機會。我和英國歷史學家馬丁‧雅克的看法不約而同。

馬爾：他很了解中國。

劉曉明：他是很了解中國，寫了一本名為《當中國統治世界》的書。他有一段精闢論述：中國的乾隆

128

皇帝在一七九三年告訴英國國王「天朝物產豐盈，無所不有，原不藉外夷貨物以通有無」。結果這成了中國此後一百五十年衰落的開端。歷史總在輪迴。

二百二十七年後的今天，二〇二〇年，英國對中國說，「我們不需要你們的 5G 技術」。我真不知道接下來的一百五十年將會發生什麼。

馬爾：有媒體報道，抖音近日作出擱置在英國設立全球總部的決定。中國政府是否會對捷豹路虎等在華經營的英國企業進行懲罰？

劉曉明：我們無意將經濟問題政治化。這種做法是十分錯誤的。英國迫於美國的壓力對中國企業採取歧視性措施是十分錯誤的。有些人大談所謂「國家安全風險」，卻拿不出華為對英國構成「風險」的確鑿證據。華為已在英國經營二十年，它不僅為英國電信產業發展作出了巨大貢獻，而且認真履行企業社會責任，助力英國發展。約翰遜首相制訂了雄心勃勃的計劃，要在二〇二五年實現全英 5G 網絡覆蓋。華為有

實力，本可以大力相助，但英國現在卻要把華為「踢出去」，用你們媒體的話，是在美國的壓力下「清理門戶」。美國領導人近日表示，這都是他們的功勞。

馬爾：讓我們談談新冠疫苗研發。現在，英國指責俄羅斯試圖竊取英國疫苗研發機密。我採訪與特朗普總統關係非常密切的美國佛羅里達州聯邦參議員里克·斯科特時，斯科特說美國情報機構有證據表明，中國正試圖破壞或遲滯美國疫苗研發。你對此怎麼回應？

劉曉明：這些「逢中必反者」對中國的無端指責數不勝數。我不想浪費我們的時間去駁斥他們的無端指責。中國在疫苗研發上非常開放，包括正與英國在內的各國科學家開展研發合作。習近平主席在第七十三屆世界衛生大會上明確表示，中國新冠疫苗研發完成並投入使用後，將作為全球公共產品，特別是要實現非洲最貧窮國家等發展中國家的可及性和可擔負性。

馬爾：讓我們談談中國維吾爾族的境況，這也是目前

中國和西方國家之間最大的問題。首先，讓我們看一段無人機拍攝畫面。這段非常令人不安的視頻已在世界各地廣泛傳播，幾乎可以肯定發生在中國新疆。你能告訴我們視頻裏是什麼情況嗎？（馬爾播放視頻）

馬爾：沒有，我從未去過新疆。

劉曉明：我不同意你的觀點。這已不是你第一次給我播放視頻，我記得去年你採訪我時也播放過所謂新疆情況視頻。你本人去過新疆嗎？

劉曉明：新疆被認為是中國最美麗的地方。中國有句俗語：不到新疆，不知道中國之大；不到新疆，不知道中國之美。

馬爾：大使先生，這個視頻可是一點也不美。

劉曉明：這正是我要告訴你的。自一九九○年以來，新疆共發生數千起恐怖襲擊事件，人們無法……

馬爾：那是十年前的事了。我想問，在中國北方地區為什麼有人跪在地上、被蒙上眼睛、剃光鬚髮、被帶上火車？那裏到底發生了什麼事？

劉曉明：我不知道你從哪裏得到這段視頻。要知道，不論哪個國家，都有需要正常轉移監獄囚犯的時候。

馬爾：但是大使，這視頻裏到底發生了什麼事？

劉曉明：我不知道你從哪裏得到這段視頻。

馬爾：這段視頻已經傳遍全球。西方情報機構和澳大利亞專家都已確認其真實性。澳大利亞專家說這是維吾爾族人被帶上即將出發的火車。

劉曉明：西方情報機構不斷對中國進行虛假指控。他們誣稱有一百萬人或更多的維吾爾族人遭到迫害。新疆維吾爾族有多少人口？四十年前，新疆維吾爾族人口為四百萬至五百萬人，現在是一千一百萬人。這些

人謊稱，我們搞「種族清洗」，但四十年間新疆維吾爾族人口翻了一番……

馬爾：抱歉打斷你。根據中國地方政府的統計數據，二○一五至二○一八年間，新疆維吾爾族聚居區的人口增長率下降了百分之八十四。

劉曉明：這個數據不對。我以中國大使的身份給你最權威的官方數據：過去四十年新疆維吾爾族人口翻了一番。沒有所謂人口控制，也沒有所謂強制絕育。

馬爾：但是從中國逃出來的人說，目前新疆正在實施強迫維吾爾族婦女絕育的政策，這一政策已經實施很長時間。一位勇敢的女士在 BBC《新聞之夜》欄目上公開作證。你可以看看視頻，的確有人在中國經歷了強制絕育。（馬爾播放所謂維吾爾族婦女視頻）

劉曉明：這種污衊指控不值一駁。一小撮反華分子和組織不遺餘力地從事損害中國利益的活動。但是

大多數新疆人民對新疆的發展變化感到滿意。過去三年多，新疆沒有發生過一起恐怖襲擊。包括維吾爾族在內的新疆人民享受和諧生活，各民族和平、和諧地共處。維吾爾族僅佔中國人口的一小部分，即使在穆斯林中也是如此。他們與其他民族幸福、和平、和諧共處。中國的民族政策非常成功，各民族一律平等。

（馬爾重播所謂維吾爾族婦女視頻）

首先，不存在所謂針對維吾爾族的大規模強制絕育，這絕非事實。其次，中國政府的政策是，堅決反對這種做法。但個別違反政策的情況不能排除，這在任何國家都是如此。

馬爾：你不能完全排除個案，但總的看法是……

劉曉明：總的看法是這絕不是中國政府的政策，在中國各民族一律平等。

馬爾：西方民眾收看這個採訪，看到人們被蒙上眼睛押解到火車上，送往「再教育營」的視頻，就會想起

二十世紀三四十年代的德國。

劉曉明：這種說法是完全錯誤的。正如我過去向你指出，新疆沒有所謂「集中營」。現在我們已進入信息時代，反華勢力可以用各種手段編造各種污衊中國的虛假信息。

馬爾：我讀一段聯合國《防止及懲治滅種族罪公約》的內容。公約說，種族滅絕行為包括：殺害該團體的成員；致使該團體的成員在身體上或精神上遭受嚴重傷害；故意使該團體處於某種生活狀況下，以毀滅其全部或局部的生命；強制施行辦法，意圖防止該團體內的生育；強迫轉移該團體的兒童至另一團體。據稱，中國存在所有這些情況，將在聯合國面臨指控。

劉曉明：這不是事實。恰恰相反，新疆人民享受着幸福生活，他們要求在新疆恢復良好的社會秩序。中國堅決反對酷刑以及迫害、歧視任何少數民族。中國不存在這樣的情況。如我所說，中國政府的政策是，每一個少數民族在中國都得到平等對待，這是中國少數民族政策的成功所在。

馬爾：對於西方國家來說，還有沒有可能與一個篤信民族主義、由共產黨領導的國家打交道？

劉曉明：你對中國的描述是不對的，中國並沒有變得「更加民族主義」，這種說法大錯特錯。中國沒有變，是以美國為首的西方國家對中國發起了所謂「新冷戰」，制裁、抹黑、污名化中國。以新冠肺炎疫情為例，這些人仍將新冠病毒稱為「中國病毒」「武漢病毒」。對這種非常錯誤的言行，我們必須作出回應。我們從不惹事，但也不怕事。如果有人挑釁，我們必須回擊。

馬爾：劉大使，非常感謝你參加我們今天的訪談節目。

劉曉明：不客氣。

新冠肺炎疫情

新冠肺炎疫情是百年來全球發生的最嚴重的傳染病大流行，也是中華人民共和國成立以來我國遭遇的傳播速度最快、感染範圍最廣、防控難度最大的重大突發公共衛生事件。在以習近平同志為核心的黨中央堅強領導下，我國迅速打響疫情防控的人民戰爭，奪取了全國抗疫鬥爭的重大戰略成果。我們同時與世界各國攜手合作、共克時艱，第一時間向世界衛生組織、有關國家和地區組織主動通報疫情信息，第一時間發佈新冠病毒基因序列等信息，第一時間公佈診療方案和防控方案，同許多國家、國際和地區組織開展疫情防控交流活動，毫無保留地同各方分享防控和救治經驗。我們以實際行動幫助挽救了全球成千上萬人的生命，彰顯了中國推動構建人類命運共同體的真誠願望。

然而，一些西方國家自己疫情防控不力，卻將矛頭指向中國，極力污名化中國，甚至要求中國「道歉」和「賠償」，以此「甩鍋」，逃避責任和轉移視線。一些西方媒體也罔顧事實，顛倒是非、混淆黑白，炒作各種「陰謀論」。

面對這種惡劣的輿論環境，我不懼風險挑戰，迎難而上，利用各種機會發表演講，在英國主流大報上發表文章，接受各大電視台採訪，包括上 BBC 的直播訪談欄目《安德魯·馬爾訪談》和《尖銳對話》，澄清事實，説明真相，戳穿謊言，批駁謬論，激濁揚清，大講中國抗疫故事，大講中外合作抗疫故事，向世界展示中國人民和中華民族的偉大力量，展現中國負責任大國的貢獻和擔當。

接受英國BBC《安德魯·馬爾訪談》欄目主持人馬爾現場直播採訪

二○二○年二月九日，我就抗擊新冠肺炎疫情接受英國BBC旗艦訪談欄目《安德魯·馬爾訪談》（The Andrew Marr Show）主持人安德魯·馬爾（Andrew Marr）現場直播採訪。

我介紹了中國的抗疫情況，指出中國政府已經採取了最全面、最嚴格的防控措施。中國人民不僅是在保護自身的生命安全和健康，也是在為保護世界人民的生命安全和健康作出貢獻。

我們還討論了華為問題，馬爾稱，美國對英國施加了巨大壓力。我說，「不列顛」只有堅持獨立自主的外交政策，才能成為「大不列顛」。我希望英國政府能堅持接受華為的決定，這符合英國的利益，也有利於中英合作，更重要的是，有利於維護英國全球最開放、最自由的市場經濟形象。

馬爾：劉大使，歡迎你。首先，可否請你介紹一下最新的病毒感染病例的數據，包括不幸病亡的病例數字？

劉曉明：根據最新數據，截至北京時間二月八日二十四時，死亡病例八百一十一例，治愈病例兩千六百四十九例，治愈病例數是死亡病例數的三倍多，這是令人鼓舞的，說明治療是有效的。此外，確診病例數首次超過疑似病例數，說明醫院的收治率在上升。你也看到我們用十天時間新建的兩家醫院已投入使用，有效地提升了收治率和醫療救治能力。

馬爾：同時給人的印象是感染率仍在上升？

劉曉明：是有新的感染，但我認為是沒有必要恐慌。可以比較一下，這次病毒的致死率是百分之二左右，與埃博拉的百分之四十、SARS的百分之十相比低得多，因此沒有必要恐慌。中國政府已經採取了最全面、最嚴格的非常規防控措施。

馬爾：中國政府採取了不同尋常的措施，在城市周圍設置路障，實際上是對整個城市實施了防疫隔離。隔離期間大部分的交通關閉，經濟活動暫停。這種狀態還要持續多久？

劉曉明：目前很難預測拐點何時到來，我們當然希望能早點到來。隔離防疫措施是非常有效的，目前大部分的病例仍集中在湖北和武漢。湖北的面積相當於英格蘭加上蘇格蘭，人口相當於英格蘭加上威爾士，涉及相當大的範圍。

馬爾：受到影響的大約共有六千五百萬人吧？

劉曉明：是五千九百萬人，但中方採取的措施是有效的，否則病毒很容易擴散到中國其他地區。中國人民不僅是在保護自身的生命安全和健康，也是在為保護世界人民的生命安全和健康作出貢獻。

馬爾：的確如此。中國政府是否準備在中國其他地區

和城市實施同樣的隔離措施？

劉曉明：這要視情況而定。湖北以外的中國其他地區也在採取防控措施。中國各地情況不同，雖然百分之八十的感染病例發生在湖北省內，但全國人民都要提高警惕，所以其他地區也採取了相關預防性的防控措施。

馬爾：關於年輕醫生李文亮，他是最先對未知新病毒可能帶來的威脅發出警告的人。然而中國政府逮捕了他，對他進行了嚴厲警告，稱他要是不悔改、繼續從事非法活動，他將受到法律的制裁。然後，令人悲傷的是，他去世了。你是否認為中國政府在這件事上做得不對？

劉曉明：我要糾正你的說法，不是中國政府，是地方政府相關部門。事實上，國家監察委員會已派出調查組赴湖北省武漢市，就群眾反映的涉及李文亮醫生的有關問題進行全面調查。人們對李醫生的去世感到悲痛，我也通過推特表示哀悼和致敬。李醫生是位英雄，人們會永遠記住他的勇氣和他為抗擊疫情作出的貢獻。我們還有成千上萬的醫護工作者，李文亮是他們中間的一員，他們都將生死置之度外，戰鬥在抗疫第一線。

馬爾：他們中的很多人都是英雄，但是李醫生公開談及信息公開的必要性。此時此刻中國政府是否已經意識到，面對這樣的形勢，中國需要信息更開放、反應更迅速？

劉曉明：我們非常開放，我們分享了所有的信息，包括治療情況、病例情況，同時我們也歡迎國際合作。我們認為這次的病毒是人類共同的敵人，全世界應該並肩作戰。同時，我們與英方也正在進行良好合作。中國駐英國使館正在盡我們所能，協助中英兩國科學家合作研發治療藥物和疫苗。

馬爾：如果以中國的實力和所採取的所有措施，依然

無法阻止病毒——現在中國以外已經有感染病例，疫情是否將蔓延到全世界所有地區？

劉曉明： 我們會竭盡全力，但是我仍然要提醒人們不要恐慌。我們認為，病毒是可防、可控、可治的。我們相信，有中國中央政府的堅強領導，有全國人民眾志成城，有國際社會廣泛支持，我們一定能戰勝疫情，打贏疫情防控阻擊戰。

馬爾： 你也知道，中國對世界經濟至關重要。包括蘋果、汽車製造商、時尚產業在內的許多公司已經面臨供應鍵的問題，這些公司關心的是工廠何時重新開工。

劉曉明： 經濟當然會受到一定影響，但我認為影響是暫時和短期的，中國政府正在採取措施，推動企業復工復產。你在節目開始時也提到，中國正在打一場「人民戰爭」，舉國上下都動員起來了。我認為，對中國經濟應該保持信心，因為中國經濟的基本面依然

良好。世界銀行、國際貨幣基金組織及國際知名經濟學家普遍認為，長期看，中國經濟仍極具韌性。

馬爾： 但是短期影響將是非常嚴重的。很多公司都在擔心，希望知道中國的工廠何時復工。什麼時候能恢復生產蘋果手機。

劉曉明： 我不能替蘋果公司回答這個問題，但據我所知，華為手機的生產仍在加班加點。我知道，你可能還要問關於華為的問題，它現在在中國做得很好。中國有句話……你會說中文嗎？

馬爾： 你可能已經注意到，我不會說中文。

劉曉明： 在中文裏，「危機」是由「危」和「機」兩個字組成的。我們始終認為，危機裏面蘊含着機遇，因此我們正努力化危為機。

馬爾： 說到機遇，我想問個問題。疫情最初暴發時，

就有人說中國政府試圖隱瞞，他們對中國政府釋放的種種信息表示高度懷疑。那麼，中國共產黨和中國人民看到當前的情況，是否意識到中國需要比以往更加開放，到了該改變的時候了？

劉曉明：我們沒有任何隱瞞。世界衛生組織（WHO）總幹事譚德塞高度評價中方的應對行動。我們與WHO以及包括英國在內的相關國家和地區分享信息，它們對中國體現出的開放和透明給予了高度評價。

馬爾：我打斷一下，一月二十二日，約兩千萬人在得到疫情暴發的消息後離開了湖北。換句話說，在疫情暴發初期，地方政府反應並不迅速，卻對李醫生採取了行動。地方政府是否會因此受到懲罰？

劉曉明：這是一種新病毒，我們對它並不十分了解，認識它需要一個過程。但一旦意識到它的危害和風險，人們就會迅速動員起來，採取正確的措施。李醫

生做得很好，人們向他表示敬意。我剛才說了，中央政府已經派出工作組進行調查。有了調查結果之後，我會向你反饋。在對此事的處理中，任何人有任何不當行為都將承擔後果並受到懲罰。

馬爾：大使先生，你說我會問關於華為的問題。是的，我是一定要問的。現在有五位保守黨重量級議員在英國議會呼籲撤銷英國政府的相關決定，確保華為被排除在英國5G網絡之外。他們認為華為毫無疑問與中國政府有着緊密的聯繫，在數據傳輸問題上是不可信賴的。他們說，5G網絡是關係到國家安全的基礎設施，中國政府同樣絕對不會允許任何英國公司參與其國家安全基礎設施核心建設。

劉曉明：這些議員的說法是完全錯誤的，這與中世紀歐洲的「獵巫行動」如出一轍，可謂「欲加之罪，何患無辭」。華為是一家民營企業，與中國政府沒有任何關係。它唯一的「問題」就是它是一家中國公司。改革開放以來，中國越來越開放。中國現在實行市場

經濟，民營企業在國民經濟中佔三分之一，外資和中外合資企業佔三分之一。華為是完全獨立的公司，它是電信領域的領軍者。英國首相之所以選擇華為，是因為他對英國的發展有雄心勃勃的計劃，希望在二○二五年前在英國實現 5G 網絡全覆蓋，而華為為可以為之作出重要貢獻。

馬爾：這一決定的代價就是，美國總統特朗普火冒三丈、暴跳如雷，對約翰遜首相大發雷霆，對此你怎麼看？對首相站到中方一邊，你是否感到滿意？

劉曉明：英國首相和特朗普總統之間的事還是交給首相去處理吧。正如我常說，「不列顛」只有堅持獨立自主的外交政策，才能成為「大不列顛」。我希望約翰遜首相能堅持他的決定，這符合英國的利益，也有利於中英合作。更重要的是，這有利於維護英國全球最開放、最自由的市場經濟形象。當然，我們對英方決定並非百分之一百滿意，因為英方給華為設定了百分之三十五的市場份額上限，這不符合英國自由經濟和自由競爭的原則，但英方的決定仍是值得歡迎的。

馬爾：非常感謝劉大使接受我們的採訪。

劉曉明：不客氣。

接受英國天空新聞台外事編輯海恩斯採訪

二〇二〇年二月十八日，我接受英國天空新聞台（Sky News）外事和國防編輯黛博拉・海恩斯（Deborah Haynes）採訪。

採訪當天，習近平主席與英國首相約翰遜通了電話。我重點闡述了兩國領導人通電話的重要意義，介紹了中國抗擊新冠肺炎疫情的最新進展和相關國際合作。

這次採訪在天空新聞台《晚間新聞》（Nightly News）欄目和《十點新聞》（Sky News at Ten）欄目播出，並在該台整點新聞時段滾動播放。該台網站和推特對採訪進行了報道。

海恩斯：劉大使，你有消息要跟我們分享？

劉曉明：是的，是一個好消息。習近平主席剛剛同約翰遜首相通了電話，這是約翰遜首相連任後中英兩國領導人首次通話。兩國領導人談得非常好，討論了中國抗擊新冠肺炎疫情的最新進展情況。習主席強調，中方已經採取了最全面、最嚴格的防控措施，全國上下都動員起來，我們的措施已開始顯現積極成效。我們有信心、有能力打贏這場疫情防控阻擊戰。約翰遜首相高度肯定中方的努力和貢獻，對中方反應的迅速和措施的全面、有力、高效表示讚賞。雙方表示中英應「肩並肩」共克時艱。

習主席表示，中方始終堅持公開、透明的態度，與包括英國在內的國際社會保持密切合作。中國政府不僅對中國人民的健康與生命安全負責──這是政府工作的首要任務，而且也正在為保護全世界人民的生命安全和健康、維護全球公共衛生作出貢獻。我們對英方的支持表示感謝，約翰遜首相表示英國願進一步提供幫助。

通話中，兩國領導人還談及引領中英全面戰略夥伴關係新的十年再出發，進一步推進中英關係「黃金時代」，雙方達成廣泛共識。約翰遜首相向習主席表示，他喜歡中國，他和他領導的英國政府願與中方共同努力，將中英關係推向更高水平。習主席也重申了中方重視發展中英關係，中英同為具有全球影響力的國家，都是聯合國安理會常任理事國，兩國在雙邊和多邊事務上擁有巨大共同利益。約翰遜首相還提到《生物多樣性公約》第十五次締約國會議（COP15）和《聯合國氣候變化框架公約》第二十六次締約國會議（COP26），認為中英面臨諸多機遇，應該合作推進全球事務，應對包括氣候變化在內的全球性挑戰。

在當前關鍵時期，兩國領導人通話不僅為中英關係定了調，也為兩國關係未來發展指明了方向。這就是我想第一時間向你傳遞的好消息。

海恩斯：謝謝！通話時有沒有談及何時能夠談判達成英中自由貿易協定？

142

劉曉明：通話涉及廣泛議題。在自貿協定問題上，中方的態度是開放的。英國離開歐盟盟後，希望與中國達成新的自貿協定，我們也始終持開放態度，中英已成立工作組進行可行性研究。英國政府去年專注於脫歐，今年成功脫歐，首要任務當然還是與歐盟貿易夥伴談判。中方也已做好準備，爭取與英方達成自貿協定。

海恩斯：由於脫歐等原因，去年工作組暫停工作，目前有沒有恢復？

劉曉明：我們隨時準備好與英國合作。英方仍處於政策調整之中，政府也剛剛重新組閣，尚不知誰是負責雙邊貿易的國務大臣。我們準備好進行接觸，英方表態也很積極。但目前中方正在全力抗擊疫情，仍需要一些時間，我們才能開始討論具體問題。雙方都有進一步加強接觸的積極意願。

海恩斯：兩位領導人是否談到安全、華為、5G 等

問題？

劉曉明：我尚未掌握更具體的信息。習主席指出，中英應相互尊重，重視彼此的核心利益和重大關切。雙方應合作建設開放經濟，堅持自由貿易和多邊主義。我認為中方傳遞的信息是清晰的。

海恩斯：坦率地說，如果英國政府沒有作出允許華為參與英國 5G 網絡建設的決定，是不是就不會有這次通話？

劉曉明：不能將這次通話與某個具體問題聯繫起來。此次通話涉及廣泛議題。我認為約翰遜首相希望直接向習主席了解中國抗擊疫情的情況，相信他聽了習主席的介紹，對中國防控舉取得的積極成效更有信心了。我想，天空新聞台的廣大觀眾也希望了解疫情防控最新積極進展。根據我剛剛收到的數據，今天我們實現了「三個首次」：全國新增確診病例首次降至兩千人以內；全國新增死亡病例首次降至一百人以內；

湖北省以外新增確診病例首次降至百百人以內，這些數字說明隔離防控舉取得了良好效果。通話還談及中英雙方如何合作應對疫情。用首相的話說，要「肩並肩」抗擊疫情。此次疫情對中國和整個世界都是一次嚴峻挑戰，所以國際社會應團結應對。英方向中方提供了援助，並表示願繼續幫助中國。我們對此表示感謝。我想強調，華為只是中英關係的一個議題、一個局部。

海恩斯：英國能在哪些具體方面向中國提供幫助？

劉曉明：首先，我們感謝英國人民給予的同情和支持。女王陛下通過約克公爵安德魯王子向習主席和中國人民轉達了慰問，習主席在通話中對此表示感謝。約翰遜首相也向李克強總理致信表達同情和支持。我們收到了英國工商界乃至普通民眾的捐贈，特別是最急需的醫療物資。許多英國普通民眾也致信我們使館表達慰問或提供捐款，我們十分感謝。英國政府還向中方援助了兩批醫療物資，我們對此表示感謝。

海恩斯：你認為中國的感染病例已經達到峰值了嗎？

劉曉明：我很難確定地說已經達到峰值。每天還有新增確診病例和死亡病例，但數量已經明顯下降。十七日，湖北以外其他省市新增死亡病例只有五例，目前絕大多數死亡病例還是集中在湖北。治愈病例大幅增加，現在治愈病例數是死亡病例數的七倍，證明我們對患者的治療是有效的。我無法預測何時出現拐點，希望拐點盡快到來。但我想，如果我們繼續採用這些有效做法，疫情就能達到峰值，就能盡早實現死亡病例的大幅減少。

海恩斯：中國政府是否行動太慢，在初期試圖掩蓋真相？

劉曉明：不存在這個問題。中國中央政府十分重視疫情防控。習主席強調，始終要把人民的生命安全放在政府工作的第一位，他三次主持召開中共中央政治局常務委員會會議，部署防疫工作。中央成立應對疫情

工作領導小組，領導全國防控工作，軍隊也動員起來了。但這是一種新病毒，一開始人們並不了解。世界衛生組織最近才正式命名了這種病毒，這說明認識和應對它需要一個過程。約翰遜首相讚賞中國防控措施的速度和效果。我可以十分肯定地說，中國政府全力以赴應對疫情，同時堅持做到公開透明，並與世界衛生組織和包括英國在內的相關國家分享信息。中國和英國科學家還在合力研製治療藥物和疫苗，希望他們早日取得成功。

海恩斯：關於疫情對中國經濟的影響，你在不久前的中外記者會上提到，疫情雖對交通運輸、旅遊等行業影響較大，但未對中國經濟產生嚴重負面影響。近日，韓國政府表示疫情可能對今年韓國經濟發展產生連帶不利影響。蘋果等大型跨國企業也表示在華業務受到影響。關於疫情對中國經濟的負面影響，你能否提供更多信息？比如影響到底有多嚴重？是否會給世界經濟帶來風險？

劉曉明：短期內會有一些影響。近日，BBC 或天空新聞台的電視節目也談到中國來英國的遊客減少，不少商店、購物村被迫關閉，景區遊客也不多。但我想強調，這種影響只是短期的、暫時的，中國經濟韌性強勁，基本面是好的。中國全面深化改革、擴大對外開放的步伐並未停滯。今年一月一日，《中華人民共和國外商投資法》正式生效。當前，中國政府正一面抗擊疫情，一面領導各行業復工復產。整個國家都被動員起來，全力完成這兩大任務。中國經濟長期向好的基本面並未改變，正如習主席在同約翰遜首相通話時指出的，我們有信心、有能力實現今年經濟社會發展目標。今年是中國發展的關鍵一年，我們將實現第一個「百年目標」，全面建成小康社會，完成脫貧攻堅。

海恩斯：對近期有關新疆的「洩密文件」，你有何評論？

劉曉明：有關報道純屬捏造。我曾多次指出，新疆問

題的實質不是人權問題，更不是什麼民族、宗教問題，而是防範打擊宗教極端主義和恐怖主義的問題。新疆人民享有充分的宗教信仰自由，並受到法律的保護，各族人民安居樂業。

海恩斯：謝謝劉大使接受我的採訪。

劉曉明：不客氣。

接受英國 BBC《尖銳對話》欄目
主持人薩克在線直播採訪

作者手記

二〇二〇年四月二十八日，我接受英國 BBC 旗艦訪談欄目《尖銳對話》（HARDtalk）主持人斯蒂芬・薩克（Stephen Sackur）在線直播採訪。

這是我第二次上《尖銳對話》欄目接受薩克的採訪。採訪主要圍繞新冠肺炎疫情展開。我重點介紹了中國抗疫情況，批駁了美西方對中國的污衊和不實之詞。

BBC《尖銳對話》欄目團隊稱，這次採訪非常成功，有助於人們，特別是西方公眾全面、準確了解中國的抗疫情況和中國政府的基本立場。BBC 在線直播此次採訪後，又在新聞頻道向英國國內播放兩次，通過世界新聞台和國際廣播電台等平台，向全球兩百多個國家和地區播放五次，受眾達四億多人。BBC 還在黃金時段新聞節目滾動播放採訪片段，並通過 BBC 網站和新媒體平台進行了延伸報道。

薩克：劉曉明大使，歡迎來到《尖銳對話》。

劉曉明：謝謝！很高興再次接受你的採訪。

薩克：很高興你能在這艱難時期接受我們的採訪。先問一個簡單、直接的問題：你是否同意新冠肺炎病毒源自中國？

劉曉明：武漢最早報告病毒，但不能說病毒起源於武漢。根據多方信息，包括 BBC 的報道，病毒可能源自任何地方，在航空母艦甚至潛艇中可以找到，在一些與中國很少聯繫的國家中也可以找到，在從未去過中國的人群中也可以找到。所以我們不能說它源自中國。

薩克：這個回答讓我有些困惑。顯然這是一種新病毒，它起源於某個地方。根據免疫學家和病毒學家的說法，病毒由動物傳播給人類，先出現一個病例，然後迅速傳播。毫無疑問，第一起病例發生在中國。你

剛才說，病毒傳播到了世界各地，一些從未到過中國的人也被感染，顯然病毒已引發全球大流行病，但至關重要的問題是，它最初來自何處？

劉曉明：我認為這個問題應交由科學家來解答。據我了解，中國的首起病例是由張繼先醫生於二○一九年十二月二十七日向中國地方衛生主管部門報告的。我還看到報道，稱中國以外有些病例甚至遠早於此。昨天英國報紙上的報道稱，英國的科學家、醫學專家在去年早些時候就曾警告政府，可能存在一種未知病毒。因此，我只能說中國第一例報告的病例於二○一九年十二月二十七日發生在武漢。

薩克：我認為不容置疑的是，專家們確信在武漢及其周邊地區發現了首例確診病例。你是否也認為我們必須搞清楚疫情暴發初期到底發生了什麼，以及哪些地方做得不對、哪些步驟走錯了，才導致病毒演變成全球大流行？

148

劉曉明：爭論了半天，我們只能各持己見。我還要強調，病毒是在中國武漢首次報告的，但不能說它起源於武漢。讓我給你介紹一下中國抗疫時間表。張繼先醫生首先於二〇一九年十二月二十七日上報了不明原因肺炎病例。中國衛生部門和疾控中心在四天後，也就是十二月三十一日，以最短的時間通知了世界衛生組織並與其他國家分享信息。中國還第一時間同世界衛生組織和其他國家分享病毒原體，在第一時間同世界衛生組織並與其他國家分享病毒基因序列。

薩克：大使先生，讓我打斷一下，你忽視了非常重要的一點。十二月三十日，武漢醫生李文亮在微信群裏告訴他的同事，武漢出現了一種非常令人擔憂的新疾病，建議他的同事們必須穿防護服，以避免被感染。幾天後，他被公安局傳喚並被迫供認散播虛假信息、嚴重干擾社會秩序。從那以後一直到一月份，中國政府一直在試圖掩蓋真相。

劉曉明：現在我明白為什麼一些人要鼓吹進行所謂獨

立調查了，其實就是試圖羅織藉口來指責中國掩蓋真相。但事實是，李文亮醫生不是「吹哨者」，如我剛才說的，張繼先醫生比李醫生早三天向衛生部門報告，武漢市衛生部門隨即向中央政府報告。四天後，也就是李醫生發出微信信息後一天，中國政府與世界衛生組織及其他國家共享了這一信息。完全不存在所謂掩蓋事實。

薩克：大使先生，實際上中方共享的信息非常有限。

根據《華盛頓郵報》和美聯社獲得的內部信息，中國國家衛生健康委員會主任馬曉偉曾在二〇二〇年一月十四日的內部會議中對形勢作出了非常嚴峻的評估，他說複雜、聚集案例表明病毒正在「人傳人」。但是第二天，中國疾病預防控制中心對外稱持續「人傳人」的風險很低，疫情是可防可控的。因此，我再次強調，有充足的證據表明中國在好幾個星期內沒有說實話。

劉曉明：你都沒有給我足夠的時間回答問題，我還沒

有說完關於李文亮的問題。你所謂「掩蓋事實」是不

存在的。張繼先醫生通過正常渠道向衛生部門報告，

但李文亮則在朋友圈傳播相關信息。在任何國家，如

果出現極其危險的未知病毒等情況，都可能引起恐

慌。我認為警方傳喚李醫生，向他提出警告，要求他

停止網上傳播，這不能稱為「隱瞞」。疫情已經通過

正規渠道上報，這種情況下要盡量避免恐慌。目前，

英國政府也在打擊利用假消息製造恐慌以達到個人目

的的做法。有關李文亮醫生的事已經有結論，中國中

央政府接到報告後，即向武漢派出調查組，武漢市公

安局決定撤銷對李醫生的訓誡書。李醫生被追認為烈

士，被授予很高的榮譽。

薩克：李醫生去世的時候的確被中國人民視為英雄。

劉曉明：不僅是中國人民，中國政府也是一樣，你不
能將兩者分開。

薩克：我認為中國人民很清楚，政府對他們和世界

其他國家並不坦率。一月十四日，中國衛健委的內
部文件稱存在人傳人、聚集性感染的證據，形勢嚴峻
複雜，並要求有關內容不公開、不上網。對此你如何
解釋？

劉曉明：我想你們的所有信息都來自《華盛頓郵
報》，你們過於依賴美國媒體。我真希望你們能採納
世界衛生組織的信息。我們與世界衛生組織分享了所
有信息。我看了你對世界衛生組織新冠特使大衛·納
巴羅（David Nabarro）博士的採訪，中國始終堅持
公開、透明，第一時間與世界衛生組織分享信息。一
方面在中國國內，我們必須保持高度警惕，採取最嚴
格的防控措施，當時對這個病毒並不十分了解。另一
方面我們與世界衛生組織和其他國家分享了信息和我
們對病毒的認知。

薩克：劉大使，你是一位資深外交官，應該了解目
前世界上很多人並不相信中國的故事版本。幾個小
時前，特朗普稱對中國的立場並不滿意，說中國完全

薩克：自一月底以來，情況發生了很多變化。中國說，我們做了很多好事，向世界各國提供了醫療物資援助，但在外界眼裏則是中國最近幾週正在全世界掀起一場假消息和宣傳攻勢。中國外交部官員在社交媒體上散佈「陰謀論」，稱美國軍人將病毒偷帶到中國。為什麼中國要掀起假消息攻勢？

劉曉明：我認為你選錯了目標。不是中國散佈假消息，如果將中國領導人、中國外交官和中國大使的表態與美國領導人、美國外交官和美國大使作一個比較，你就會發現誰在散佈假消息。

薩克：你同意趙立堅關於「美國軍人將新冠病毒偷帶到中國」的說法嗎？你相信嗎？

劉曉明：趙立堅是轉推一些媒體的報道。我不明白你為什麼抓住中國某個個人的言論，卻對美國國家領導人、高級官員，特別是美國最高級別外交官、國務卿發佈的假消息視而不見？只要這位國務卿談到中國，

可以把疫情控制在源頭，他還說美國正在進行徹底調查。美國副總統彭斯也列出一系列理由證明，中國沒有對世界說實話，應對疫情在全世界蔓延並造成大規模死亡和經濟損失負有責任，中國現在面臨巨大的問題。

劉曉明：我不同意這種說法。這只是一些西方國家的說法。疫情發生後，中國第一時間與世界衛生組織和其他國家通力合作，我們派出技術援助和醫療專家組，並向一百五十多個國家提供醫療物資援助，受到這些國家的高度評價。我認為，美國不能代表全世界，即使不少西方國家，包括英國、法國、德國，也對中國表示讚賞。你引用了特朗普總統的表態，我也想引用幾句他有關中國的表態。一月二十四日，在中國通報疫情大約一個月之後，特朗普總統說，「美國高度讚賞中國的努力和透明度」。六天後，他表示「中國正全力以赴抗疫，美國與中國進行了緊密合作」。二月初，他又表示「習近平主席工作出色，疫情處理得很好」。

就沒有一句好話；中國在抗疫鬥爭中向美國伸出援手，卻成了惡人。我實在不能理解。

薩克：你認為，目前由於疫情引起的各種指責給中美關係帶來的外交危機有多嚴重？

劉曉明：我們當然希望與美國保持良好關係。我曾兩次常駐美國，我始終認為中美和則兩利、鬥則俱傷，我們有充分的理由與美國保持良好關係，但這應該建立在相互信任、合作而不對抗的基礎上，雙方需要相向而行。疫情發生以來，習近平主席和特朗普總統保持了密切溝通，通了兩次電話，討論抗疫合作。正如習主席與約翰遜首相通電話一樣，中國致力於與國際社會一道，攜手戰勝疫情。我在此特別要告訴美國人，中國不是美國的敵人，美國的敵人是新冠病毒，美國應該找對目標。

薩克：你發出了非常重要的信息。那麼針對美國以及澳大利亞、英國等許多國家提出的中方應永久，而不是臨時關閉從事野生動物交易的「濕貨市場」的要求，中方是否將作出一些積極姿態，從而改善與這些國家的關係？

劉曉明：首先，我不同意你關於中國與許多國家關係出現問題的說法，中國的朋友多，對手少。正如我所說，少數西方國家不能代表整個世界。中國擁有良好的對外關係，正在積極推動國際抗疫合作。正如習主席所說，團結合作是國際社會戰勝疫情最有力的武器。我現在回答你所謂「濕貨市場」問題。

薩克：大使先生，我們時間不多了，你能不能就「濕貨市場」問題給出具體明確的回答？市場是關了還是沒關？

劉曉明：事實上，在中國根本不存在所謂「濕貨市場」，這個說法對很多中國人都很陌生，是西方、外來的說法。人們常說的是農貿市場和「生鮮」市場，主要銷售新鮮的蔬菜、海鮮等農副產品，也有極少數

市場銷售活禽。我想，你所談到的應該是非法銷售野生動物的市場，這類市場已經被徹底禁止。中國全國人大已經通過決定，全面禁止非法野生動物交易。

薩克：這是否意味着中國政府已經意識到這些野生動物市場的危險性，即它們確實造成病毒從動物傳給人類？

劉曉明：我們終於達成了一項一致。請注意，這裏所說的是非法野生動物市場已完全被禁止，在中國獵捕、交易、食用野生動物都是非法的。

薩克：如果中國能在新冠病毒蔓延之前早點下達禁令，就不會給世界造成這麼大的傷害。中國是否將為此表示歉意？

劉曉明：你又回到了採訪開始時的問題。我要說，不能因為疫情在中國發現就指責中國，這是錯誤的。中國發現了疫情，在很多與中國毫無聯繫的地方也發現了疫情。不能因為中國暴發疫情就指責中國，要看到中國正在竭盡全力抗擊疫情。中國是疫情受害者，中國不是病毒製造者，中國也不是病毒源頭。對於這一點，必須明確。

薩克：但一些英國政界要員稱中國應為疫情負責，比如，議會下院外委會主席表示，中國政府實行的是蘇聯式、有害的體制，這種體制損害中國人民的健康和福祉，背叛了中國人民，也背叛了世界。他們呼籲英國、美國和其他一些國家切斷與中國的緊密經濟聯繫。在英國，這一問題的核心是，華為不應被繼續允許參與英國5G網絡建設。作為中國駐英國大使，你是否擔心對華經濟脫鉤？

劉曉明：既擔心，也不擔心。你所談到的那位政界要員，他的觀點並不能代表英國政府的官方立場。我相信，在約翰遜首相領導下，英國政府仍致力於發展強勁的中英關係。在與習主席的兩次通話中，約翰遜首相重申將致力於推進中英關係「黃金時代」。疫情期

間，中英除了緊密溝通之外，還積極開展合作。我出任中國駐英國大使十年了，從未見到兩國領導人和高層保持如此密切的聯繫，除了習主席與約翰遜首相兩次通話外，中央外事工作委員會辦公室主任楊潔篪、國務委員兼外長王毅同英國首相國家安全事務顧問塞德維爾、外交大臣拉布在倫敦，我也與外交大臣拉布、衛生大臣漢考克，商業、能源和產業戰略大臣夏爾馬保持着密切接觸，中英關係十分強勁。至於你提到有人將中國比作蘇聯，這完全是「冷戰」思維。我們已經生活在二十一世紀第三個十年，而這些人還停留在過去「冷戰」時期。中國不是前蘇聯。中英之間的共同利益遠大於分歧，我對中英關係充滿信心。

薩克： 劉大使，今天的採訪只能到此結束。我再次對你在這樣一個艱難時刻作客《尖銳對話》表示真誠的謝意。

劉曉明： 不必客氣。

接受英國天空新聞台《新聞時間》欄目主持人奧斯汀在線直播採訪

二〇二〇年五月十四日，我接受英國天空新聞台《新聞時間》（*The News Hour*）在線直播採訪。

欄目主持人馬克·奧斯汀（Mark Austin）在線直播採訪。

《新聞時間》是英國天空新聞台旗艦欄目，時長兩小時，包括滾動新聞、一對一訪談和專家分析評論，在每天十七至十九點黃金時段播出。

奧斯汀是英國著名記者、時事評論員，曾擔任英國獨立電視台旗艦欄目《十點新聞》主持人，二〇一八年九月起擔任《新聞時間》欄目主持人。曾獲多項新聞大獎，包括英國電影和電視藝術學院獎和國際艾美獎。

採訪的主題是新冠肺炎疫情。針對奧斯汀的提問，如「國際社會」似乎不相信中國關於新冠病毒的解釋、中國為什麼拒絕國際獨立調查、中國的數據是否真實、英國抗疫的問題出在哪裏等，我介紹了中國的抗疫情況及與世界衛生組織和相關國家的合作，批駁了美國等少數西方國家對中國的毫無根據的指責。

奧斯汀：數月來，全世界越來越多的人呼籲中國就新冠病毒的蔓延作出解釋。大多數科學家都認為病毒最早在武漢開始擴散，包括美國總統在內的一些人認為病毒源於實驗室洩漏而非自然界。到今天，中國仍拒絕邀請來自世界衛生組織的科學家參加對該病毒來源的調查。問題還有很多，今天我們有難得的機會向中國駐英國大使劉曉明提出這些問題。大使先生，晚上好，感謝你接受採訪。

劉曉明：晚上好！感謝邀請。

奧斯汀：首先，你是否同意中國面臨信任危機？就目前來看，全世界似乎並不信任中國。

劉曉明：我認為並非如此。中國做得很好。中國是首個報告該病毒的國家，在第一時間甄別出病原體，並在第一時間與世界衛生組織及其他國家分享病毒基因序列資料。你提到全世界不信任中國，我不同意你的看法。我認為只有少數幾個國家在對中國進行毫無根據的指責和挑釁。

奧斯汀：我們從頭梳理一下為何一些國家不信任中國。據新華社報道，張繼先醫生於二〇一九年十二月二十七日向中國地方衛生主管部門報告了其接診三例不明原因肺炎患者的情況，她懷疑存在「人傳人」，一對夫婦傳給其子。但直到一月二十二日，即近四個星期之後，中國才向世界衛生組織通報了病毒的人際傳播。為何會有這樣的延遲？

劉曉明：這不是事實。張繼先醫生於十二月二十七日向當地衛生部門報告。四天後，中國衛生部門即通知世界衛生組織駐華代表處。一月三日，即七天後，中國政府衛生主管部門國家衛健委正式通知世界衛生組織。這是一種新病毒，不論是對世界還是對中國，這都是未知病毒，我們必須採取謹慎、負責任的態度，全力以赴應對。因此，在十一天後，我們甄別出病原體，並與世界衛生組織及其他國家分享病毒基因序列資料。所以我認為上述指責是不公平的。

156

奧斯汀：但是世界衛生組織的時間線清楚地表明，中國衛生部門於一月二十二日才通告稱有證據表明病毒存在人際傳播。張繼先醫生告訴新華社：「一家人病狀基本相同，可以確定是人傳人了。」她於十二月二十七日上報了武漢當局，為何直到次年一月二十二日，世界衛生組織才確認病毒的人際傳播。

劉曉明：正如我所說，這需要過程。即使這樣，我們在獲知了病毒人際傳播的風險後沒有絲毫延誤就通知了世界衛生組織。鍾南山院士是這一領域的權威。他在一月二十日的發佈會上表示，目前非常肯定地證實出現了人傳人現象，這比你說的時間線要早。那時，中國僅有不到二百個確診病例。對任何國家而言，確定某種傳染病都需要一定程序和時間，這才是負責任的處理方式。

奧斯汀：可以理解。但為什麼李文亮醫生在社交媒體上表達了對疫情擴散的擔憂之後就被警方逮捕並被噤聲呢？

劉曉明：首先，李醫生沒有被捕，媒體報道有誤。他是被警方傳喚訓誡。對任何國家包括英國來說，給傳染病定性都必須謹慎、負責，不能引發恐慌。李醫生在網上發帖的三天前，張繼先醫生已經向當地衛生部門報告了不明原因肺炎病例，當地衛生部門立即向中央政府報告了情況，中方隨後也就是李醫生在網上發帖的第四天就向世界衛生組織通報了，所以中方不存在任何隱瞞。中央政府對李文亮一事十分關注和重視，派調查組到武漢了解實際情況。最後李文亮被追認為烈士，被確認為英雄。

奧斯汀：我們談一下國際社會不相信中國的另一個原因。美國國務卿蓬佩奧稱，中國未能及時分享疫情信息，特朗普總統說有大量證據顯示病毒源於武漢實驗室，中方犯了錯並試圖隱瞞。我想問，中方犯了什麼錯誤，是否存在隱瞞？

劉曉明：根本不存在任何隱瞞。中方及時與世界衛生組織和國際社會分享了疫情信息，並早在一月三日通

報了美方。此後，中美雙方疾控部門均就疫情信息保持日常溝通。美國領導人和首席外交官的有關說法根本代表不了國際社會。要說特朗普總統說了些什麼，讓我告訴你，三月二十七日特朗普總統與習近平主席通話後，對外表示：「我們了解中國為抗疫作出的巨大努力，美中雙方一直保持密切溝通，中方向我們提供了很多資料，美方獲取了全部信息，中國的經驗對美國很有啟發。」而現在你引述的特朗普的表態與那時截然不同。

奧斯汀：國際社會不信任中國還有一個原因是中國拒絕國際獨立調查。如果沒有隱瞞的話，中國為什麼不允許國際社會對武漢的實驗室、「濕貨市場」進行調查？

劉曉明：這種國際調查不應含有政治目的。首先，當前國際社會的首要任務是抗擊疫情。我同意英國衛生大臣所說，目前國際社會應全力合作應對疫情。其次，中國是開放的、透明的，沒有任何隱瞞，也沒有

什麼好怕的。我們支持在適當時候對疫情進行回顧和總結，但必須由世界衛生組織牽頭開展，必須是國際性的。

奧斯汀：中國同意由世界衛生組織牽頭組織各國科學家到中國進行調查嗎？

劉曉明：是總結和評估，但應該在適當的時候，而不是現在。評估的目的是進行科學分析、總結經驗，在應對下次大流行病時怎麼能做得更好。這才是評估目的，而不是指責中國。

奧斯汀：恕我直言，源自中國武漢的病毒已導致全世界四百五十萬人感染，近三十萬人死亡，這是一場全球性悲劇，難道不應該由世界知名科學家盡快開展全球調查嗎？

劉曉明：目前，中國、美國、英國的科學家和專家們正在努力工作，尋找病毒源頭。疫情暴發，中國是第

一個報告病例的國家，但不能說中國就是病毒的源頭。這應該由科學家來決定，不是你，也不是我。

奧斯汀：我使用「源頭」一詞是因為中國發現了第一起病例。這不是第一次了，之前的 SARS，這次的冠狀病毒，我們不能允許這種情況再次發生。

劉曉明：當然不能。但科學家尚未弄清病毒的源頭，因此不能指責中國，中國是受害者，不是肇事者。病毒不是人為製造的，而是源自自然。我們應該堅持科學的態度，而不是像個別美國政客一樣，對中國污名化、利用假消息無端抹黑。

奧斯汀：那就讓科學家們進去調查，他們會發現真相。大多數發達、公正、公開和負責任的國家都會允許國際科學家盡快進去調查。

劉曉明：毫無疑問，我們與國際社會的科學家密切合作，但是這應與背後有政治動機的所謂「獨立調查」

區分開來。當你說世界各國呼籲進行獨立調查，那只是個別國家，美國、澳大利亞，你能說出十個國家嗎？我認為許多國家呼籲的是全球團結合作抗疫，而不是相互指責。當今的主題是聚焦如何戰勝病毒、挽救生命，而不是玩指責、甩鍋遊戲。

奧斯汀：根據情報機構所說，中國支持黑客組織竊取英美科學家關於新冠病毒的研究資料。中國為什麼要這麼做？

劉曉明：這種指控從何而來？你們有證據嗎？

奧斯汀：美國聯邦調查局聲稱「調查發現黑客組織試圖竊取公共衛生數據」。

劉曉明：這已經不是美國第一次對中國污衊抹黑，美國的企圖就是阻撓國際社會合作研發疫苗。疫苗是戰勝疫情的最終解決辦法。中國科學家正在爭分奪秒地工作，一是靠我們自己的努力，二是進行國際合作，

包括與美國科學家的合作。中英在疫苗研發方面也緊密合作，兩國領導人，習主席和約翰遜首相對兩國科學家的合作給予了大力支持。

奧斯汀：談到疫苗，如果中國比其他國家先研發出疫苗，中國會遵循「全球疫苗免疫聯盟」的原則，公平、公正地分享疫苗嗎？

劉曉明：中國當然願意分享疫苗，我們視之為全球科學家共同努力的結果，將助力全球抗疫，因此我們積極地與各國開展科研合作。

奧斯汀：根據「全球疫苗免疫聯盟」的原則，疫苗將首先提供給疫情暴發的中心地區，無論是在世界哪個地方，之後再提供給世界各地的醫護人員。中國會同意這一原則嗎？

劉曉明：我認為現在提這樣的問題為時尚早，因為各國尚未研發出新冠疫苗。現在討論疫苗如何使用，似

乎也有些超前。但正如我此前所講，中方本着一貫原則，願同其他國家分享相關科研成果和疫情防控經驗，不論是急需這些信息的國家，還是那些身處抗疫一線的醫護工作者。我們已向包括英國在內的一百五十多個國家和地區援助醫療物資，這些物資大部分被分配至一線醫護工作者手中。我們還向英方捐贈最急需的醫療物資，協助英國政府在中國採購呼吸機等設備。這些物資均已在英國抗疫中有效發揮作用。

奧斯汀：好。你剛才談到中國是開放的，那咱們再來談談「開放」這個話題。我的第一個問題是，中國為何要驅逐十三名美國記者？要知道他們中很多人曾嘗試在中國調查新冠病毒來源問題。此外，在中國疫情初期曾發佈相關視頻的當地記者陳秋實、方斌為何會失蹤？他們人在何處？

劉曉明：你應該首先問美國政府，為何要驅逐六十名中國記者？你還應該問，為何中方為美國記者在華採

160

訪提供了更多便利？由於美方驅逐中國記者在先，中方被迫採取了反制措施，這與新冠肺炎疫情無關。正如我所講，中國疫情防控是開放的、透明的……

奧斯汀：大使先生，據我所知，美國並未監禁記者，但中國去年拘押了四十八名記者，這個數字比世界其他任何國家都要多。你怎麼解釋中國的所謂「開放」？

劉曉明：在中國，沒有人因為從事記者工作被拘押，有些人被拘押是因為從事了違法活動。在中國，沒有人能凌駕於法律之上，法律面前人人平等。任何人不能以記者身份為掩護從事違法活動，回答就是這樣簡單。

奧斯汀：下一個問題，中國人口超過十億人，但你們官方公佈的因新冠病毒死亡人數不到五千人，這在很多人看來難以置信。這個數據是真實的嗎？

劉曉明：這是因為疫情發生以來中國採取了最全面、最嚴格、最徹底的防控舉措。我們願同世界其他國家分享這些經驗。武漢在面積上是倫敦的五倍，人口有一千一百萬人，超過倫敦和北愛爾蘭人口的總和。這座城市封城七十六天，當地民眾為此作出了巨大犧牲。但新冠病毒具有很強的人與人之間的傳染性，因此封城對防控病毒傳播是一種非常有效的手段。此外，我們採取了「四早」方針——「早發現、早報告、早隔離、早治療」。這些舉措都被證明是十分有效的。因此，不能因為中國死亡人數較少，就指責中國「掩蓋數據」或「隱瞞事實」。

奧斯汀：大使先生，我並未指責中國。我想再談最後一個問題，英國人口比中國少得多，但疫情導致的死亡人數卻超過三萬人。你認為英國的問題出在哪裏？

劉曉明：我無意批評英國的防疫政策。我想說，我們願同英方分享、交流疫情防控經驗。我在這裏向你提供一條第一手新聞：明天，中國衛健委主任馬曉偉及

中方專家將與英國衛生大臣漢考克及英方專家舉行視頻會議，會議預計持續兩個多小時，雙方屆時將就疫情防控進行深入交流。我認為，這才是我們現在要做的事情。我們需要認識到新冠病毒是人類共同的敵人，我們需要加強團結合作，攜手應對風險挑戰，共同抗擊疫情，直至最後勝利。正如習主席所說，團結合作是國際社會戰勝疫情的最有力武器。

奧斯汀：很好。劉大使，謝謝你。無論對病毒來源的國際調查何時開展，我都十分期待。再次感謝你今晚作客我們的欄目，回答我們的問題。

劉曉明：不客氣。

162

參加英國天空新聞台《疫情後我們的新世界》特別節目在線直播訪談

作者手記

二〇二〇年六月一日，我應邀參加英國天空新聞台特別節目《疫情後我們的新世界》（Live Panel Discussion—After the Pandemic: Our New World）在線直播訪談，與愛爾蘭前總統瑪麗·羅賓遜、英國前外交大臣戴維·米利班德、美國歷史學家尼爾·弗格森就疫情的全球影響、中國抗疫表現、涉疫情獨立調查、新冠疫苗研發、世界衛生組織改革、氣候變化、中國香港局勢等展開討論，並回答在線觀眾的提問。

英國天空新聞台著名主持人德莫特·莫納罕（Dermot Murnaghan）主持訪談節目。

該台電視、網站、新媒體全平台進行直播。

莫納罕：首先請嘉賓們談一談我們的世界面臨的機遇與挑戰？

劉曉明：疫情將帶來什麼樣的影響？世界是將走向團結，還是更加分裂？圍繞這一問題，有很多的討論。我認為，疫情會使世界更加團結。疫情再次證明人類生活在一個地球村。正如習近平主席所說，我們應努力構建人類命運共同體。我認為，疫情再次說明，國際社會應該加強合作。事實證明，凡是攜手抗疫、支持世界衛生組織、聽取世界衛生組織建議、支持多邊主義的國家，疫情都有效得到了控制；凡是拒絕國際合作、排斥世界衛生組織建議的國家，則付出了沉重代價。疫情證明，再強大的國家也不可能獨善其身，也不可能對病毒「免疫」，因為病毒不分國界、不分種族。

莫納罕：談到國際調查，核心問題是：中國是否為這次危機承擔責任？是否接受獨立調查人員進入中國領土進行實地調查？

劉曉明：我們當然歡迎國際審議。但審議的目的不是給哪個國家貼標籤，審議應覆蓋所有與疫情密切相關的國家。在世界衛生大會上，我們與世界衛生組織的一百二十個成員國共同支持國際社會在合適的時機對本次疫情進行審議，審議的目的是總結經驗教訓，以便今後更好地應對重大傳染性疾病。審議必須是獨立的，排除各種政治干擾，應該是以科學為依據，由科學家主導。

莫納罕：中國認為應該由誰領導這一審議？

劉曉明：應該由世界衛生組織主導。所有國家都應該參與，特別是主要國家。我不同意弗格森剛才的說法。他批評中國反應緩慢，這不是事實。弗格森講的許多信息都是錯誤的，包括他說武漢封城期間，仍有很多航班從武漢飛到其他國家。這不是事實。一月二十三日武漢封城後，所有航班都停飛了。沒有航班，也沒有火車，沒有任何對外交通。中國是第一個向世界衛生組織報告疫情的國家，第一個分離出病原

164

體，第一個與世界衛生組織和其他國家分享病毒全基因序列。中國沒有浪費任何時間與各國分享信息和防控經驗。

莫納罕：武漢封城後還有許多中國航班沒有停飛，導致疫情傳播到很多國家，這不是一個很嚴重的問題嗎？

劉曉明：你的信息完全不對。武漢封城後根本沒有任何航班飛行，已經與外部斷絕了聯繫。我很遺憾在這裏聽到弗格森的許多冷戰言論，我與弗格森相識，但不知道他為何對與中國進行冷戰這麼感興趣。中國不是前蘇聯。作為歷史學家，你應該認真研究中國的歷史。中方編寫了一份關於疫情的二十四個謊言與真相的材料，我可以寄給你看看。世界衛生組織讚賞中國的抗疫努力，不應因此就貶低世界衛生組織的作用。世界衛生組織是一個重要的國際組織，有一九十四個成員國。

莫納罕：中國是不是對疫情負有責任？中國在很長一段時間裏否認病毒從動物傳染給人、否認人之間的傳染，你們並沒有及時告訴世界真相。

劉曉明：我已經明確告訴你，中國第一時間向世界衛生組織進行了通報，沒有任何延誤。新冠病毒是一種全新的病毒。面對未知的全新病毒，我們必須採取負責任的態度，這需要科學家進行認真、負責任的研究。中國在發現首個病例十一天後，就完成了病毒鑑定，並立即向世界衛生組織通報，同時與有關國家分享信息。中國沒有任何隱瞞，也沒有任何延誤。中國抗疫記錄清清楚楚、一目了然，經得起時間和歷史的檢驗。我還要指出，中國首先報告疫情，並不意味着病毒的源頭問題需要科學家去研究探索。隨着形勢的發展，我們看到一些報道，美國、意大利等國發現了比中國更早的病例。因此，對待病毒溯源問題應當採取科學的態度。

莫納罕：中國會同意對世界衛生組織進行改革嗎？

劉曉明：當然。在這次疫情應對中，反映出世界衛生組織的一些不足，包括應對能力和資源不足，如何更快、更有效地應對，以及如何幫助最貧困和缺乏能力的國家抗疫。改革可以在我們戰勝疫情之後進行。當前，疫情仍在全球蔓延，當務之急是團結合作，支持世界衛生組織領導抗疫鬥爭。

莫納罕：作為世界上最大的碳排放國，中國將採取什麼舉措，以保持目前疫情期間排放暫時減少的局面？

劉曉明：中國堅定支持《巴黎協定》，認真履行義務。中國提前三年完成降低碳排放計劃，二〇一八年碳排放強度比二〇〇五年累計下降百分之四十五點八。二〇一九年中國單位 GDP 能耗同比下降百分之二點六。中國是全球新能源和可再生能源最大投資國。中國始終致力於應對氣候變化。中國原定於今年年底前舉辦《生物多樣性公約》第十五次締約方大會（COP15）。

莫納罕：COP15 還開嗎？中國計劃何時舉行？

劉曉明：因為疫情，具體時間尚未最後確定。今年本應是中英環境保護合作之年。英國已將第二十六屆聯合國氣候變化大會（COP26）會期調整至明年十一月，但我們仍與英國同事們在線上保持密切聯繫，交流溝通，確保兩場會議均取得成功。

莫納罕：我想問一個關於重建信任和新冠疫苗研發競賽的問題。我們看到中國和一些國家正領先疫苗的研發。如果中國研製出有效疫苗，從重建信任的角度，中國是否願意將疫苗以盡可能低的價格與全世界分享？

劉曉明：當然。習近平主席在世界衛生大會上莊嚴宣佈，中國新冠疫苗研發完成並投入使用後，將作為全球公共產品，特別是要實現疫苗在發展中國家的可及性和可擔負性。中國在疫苗研發上居於世界領先行列，我們有五支疫苗已進入二期臨床試驗，我們願與

166

世界各國分享。中國同時也在與包括英國、美國在內的各國科學家開展研發合作。

剛才，你展示了一個圖表，顯示所謂「中國的聲譽已經受損」，我不同意這個結論。這要看你從哪兒獲得信息。我可以向你提供一些信息。今年初，全球最大的獨立公關公司愛德曼根據它發佈的《全球信任度調查報告（Trust Barometer）》顯示，中國民眾對政府的信任指數高達百分之八十二，在所有被調查的國家中高居榜首。還有，根據近期新加坡獨立民調機構「黑箱研究」（Blackbox Research）民調公司對全球二十三個經濟體所做的調查，中國民眾對政府的滿意度最高，以綜合得分百分之八十五再次位居榜首。

莫納罕：我們剩下的時間不多了。最後，我想問一下劉大使關於民眾，特別是年青一代對政府缺乏信任的問題。在香港街頭可以看到這種情況：中國政府鎮壓要求民主的抗議者。

劉曉明：香港事態根本不是什麼「中國政府鎮壓民主

抗議者」，香港街頭上演的是持續不斷的違法暴力活動。這些活動危害中國國家安全。這些暴力激進分子衝擊香港立法會，甚至放火燒傷無辜民眾。請問，如果同樣的事情發生在倫敦街頭，如果暴徒衝擊英國議會，英國將作何反應？難道英國政府和警方會坐視不管、聽之任之嗎？我認為，任何一個負責任的政府都會採取行動。另一方面，人們應當看到，香港回歸二十三年來，「一國兩制」在香港取得巨大成功。

莫納罕：對不起，我們時間到了。我要感謝所有嘉賓。謝謝你，劉大使。

劉曉明：不客氣。

中日關係

二〇一三年十二月二十六日，日本首相安倍晉三冒天下之大不韙，悍然參拜供奉有十四名二戰甲級戰犯的靖國神社。這一事件引發中國、韓國等亞洲國家和國際社會的嚴厲譴責。七天後，即二〇一四年一月二日，英國主流大報《每日電訊報》在社論評論版刊登我題為《拒不反省侵略歷史的日本必將對世界和平構成嚴重威脅》的署名文章。我在文章中把日本軍國主義比作英國家喻戶曉的小說《哈利·波特》中的反面人物「伏地魔」。我說，伏地魔把自己的靈魂分藏在七個「魂器」中，消滅伏地魔的唯一方法是把七個「魂器」全部摧毀。如果把軍國主義比作日本的「伏地魔」，靖國神社無疑是藏匿這個國家靈魂最黑暗部分的「魂器」。

我在文章中指出，靖國神社一百多年來一直是日本軍國主義對外發動侵略戰爭的精神工具和象徵，至今仍供奉着對亞洲受害國人民犯下滔天罪行的二戰甲級戰犯。日本領導人參拜靖國神社這一問題絕不是日本內政問題和個人問題，也不僅僅是中日、韓日關係問題，它的實質是日本領導人能否正確認識和深刻反省其軍國主義對外侵略和殖民統治歷史，日本是否遵守《聯合國憲章》的宗旨和原則、走和平道路的根本方向問題，是關乎侵略與反侵略、正義與邪惡、光明與黑暗的大是大非問題。

文章發表後在英國和國際上引起很大反響，英國各大報，以及美國《紐約時報》《華爾街日報》等主流報紙，路透社、美聯社、法新社、合眾社等西方四大通訊社，英國各大電視台、電台和美國有線電視新聞網（CNN），紛紛報道和引用。英國電視台和電台也提出採訪我。對此，我來者不拒，並主動出擊。十天內，我對英國各大電視台和電台全覆蓋，其中一天接受兩次現場直播採訪。英國和西方主流媒體把我這一系列撰文和採訪稱為「中國大使在倫敦發起強大攻勢，狠批日本軍國主義」。還有英國評論說，「伏地魔」這個比喻通俗易懂，既鮮明表達了中國的立場，也易於被西方民眾接受。

接受英國獨立電視台《十點新聞》欄目
高級外事記者莊銳採訪

作者手記

二〇一四年一月三日，我接受英國獨立電視台《十點新聞》（ITV News at Ten）欄目高級外事記者莊銳（John Ray）採訪，揭批安倍企圖復辟日本軍國主義的本質，闡述中方在釣魚島及其附屬島嶼問題上的嚴正立場，呼籲國際社會共同努力制止日本軍國主義復活，維護地區穩定與世界和平。

莊銳曾任英國天空電視台政治記者，二〇〇〇年加入獨立電視台任高級外事記者，曾在中國、中東、非洲常駐，獲多項新聞大獎，包括國際艾美獎、英國電影和電視藝術學院獎。

獨立電視台在當晚黃金時段播放了此次採訪的主要內容，並在該台網站播放了採訪實錄視頻。

採訪實錄如下：

莊銳：能否先從「伏地魔」談起？你在《每日電訊報》上使用的這個比喻非常生動。為什麼把日本比作「伏地魔」這樣一個邪惡角色？

劉曉明：我認為日本軍國主義與「伏地魔」有一些共同之處。消滅「伏地魔」的唯一方法是把七個「魂器」全部摧毀。只要靖國神社還留存在日本人民的記憶之中，軍國主義就始終陰魂不散。一些人認為中國在參拜靖國神社這個問題上小題大做。但是日本領導人參拜的是一個供奉戰爭罪犯，特別是有十四名二戰甲級戰犯的神社。這些戰犯給各國人民，包括英國人民帶來重大傷亡和損失。東條英機是十四名二戰甲級戰犯之首。他不僅對中國發起戰爭，而且對美國、英國和荷蘭開戰。所以日本領導人參拜靖國神社是一個關乎日本未來發展方向的重大問題，是關乎和平與戰爭、正義與邪惡、光明與黑暗的大是大非問題。鑑於上述原因，中國對日本領導人參拜靖國神社提出強烈抗議。

莊銳：你認為日本什麼是邪惡的？是日本軍國主義嗎？

劉曉明：確實如此。我們對日本領導人背離和平的言論深感憂慮。你知道，安倍甚至否認日本發動過侵略戰爭，鼓吹所謂「侵略未定論」。日本副首相麻生太郎甚至揚言「日本可以學習納粹德國修憲的做法」。他們還蓄意煽動所謂「中國威脅論」，製造地區緊張，為擴充軍備尋找藉口。我們對安倍復辟軍國主義的企圖表示嚴重擔憂。今天的日本和二戰前的德國有不少相似之處，對此我們深感憂慮。

莊銳：在日本看來，過去二十年來中國不斷擴充軍備，正成為地區新興大國，日本需要防禦中國這個新的超級大國。中國軍費在過去二十五年中一直保持兩位數增長。

劉曉明：實際情況不是這樣。中國國防支出近年雖有所增加，但是中國的人均軍費和美國、英國、日本相

比都是最低的。中國是一個擁有十三億多人口的大國，擁有二點二萬公里陸地邊界線和三點二萬公里海岸線，國防任務十分繁重。中國的國防費用佔GDP和財政總支出比重近年來不斷下降。美國、英國、日本的人均軍費分別是中國的二十二倍、九倍和五倍。

最重要的是中國國防政策的性質，中國奉行的是防禦性國防政策。中國從沒有侵佔過別國一寸土地。事實上，中國百年近代史是被外國列強侵略瓜分的歷史，而日本恰恰相反。

莊銳：但從另一個角度來說，中國是侵略者而不是日本。比如釣魚島，中國劃設東海防空識別區，但國際法認定釣魚島屬於日本，不是嗎？而中國卻在宣誓主權，看上去是中國存在領土野心。

劉曉明：這種觀點是完全錯誤的。釣魚島自古以來就是中國的領土。一八九五年中日甲午戰爭後，釣魚島才被日本非法侵佔。根據中、英、美三國首腦發表的《開羅宣言》，日本必須向中國歸還所有通過戰爭竊

取的領土，包括台灣及其周邊島嶼，當然也包括釣魚島。二戰結束後，美國在冷戰中支持日本，向其移交島嶼行政管轄權。中國從未承認美日這種私相授受，並提出多次抗議。然而即便是美國，在釣魚島的主權問題上也保持中立。

釣魚島一直是中日之間的爭議問題。中日邦交正常化時，兩國領導人達成諒解，同意將釣魚島問題放一放，留待以後解決。一九七八年，中國領導人鄧小平訪問日本時，一位日本記者向他提出釣魚島問題。鄧小平回答說：這個問題我們同日本有爭議，可以把它放一放，也許下一代人比我們更聰明些，會找到實際解決的方法。

莊銳：但從目前看來，中國在釣魚島問題上似乎不會妥協，堅持認為島嶼是中國領土，歸中國所有。

劉曉明：現在的問題是，日本主動挑起了爭端。日本右翼勢力和日本政府製造了將釣魚島「國有化」的鬧劇，才引起領土爭端緊張，中國不得不作出反應。中

方一直在被迫回應日本的挑釁。中國是一個愛好和平的國家。但我們也是講原則的：人不犯我，我不犯人；人若犯我，我必犯人。

劉曉明：要想保證亞太地區的和平與繁榮，就必須消滅日本軍國主義。

莊銳：在外人看來，目前局勢令人擔憂。我想問你，局勢將向什麼方向發展？人們將中日爭議視為可能引發戰爭的「火藥桶」。你是否有同樣的擔心？

莊銳：中國政府表示中國不會允許日本重新走上擴充軍備之路，這是否意味中國將採取防禦性軍事行動來阻止日本？

劉曉明：我們同樣感到擔心。但我想強調，中國希望與日本發展睦鄰友好關係。四十二年前中日邦交正常化時，兩國領導人宣佈「中日永不再戰」。中日同為亞洲重要國家，中日關係對亞太地區和平至關重要。但日本右翼勢力及軍國主義蠢蠢欲動、再次抬頭，形勢的發展並不取決於中國。這也是我為什麼把日本軍國主義比作「伏地魔」。只有制止日本軍國主義，才能確保地區和平與穩定，避免戰爭。因此我們呼籲安倍政府不要在錯誤的道路上越走越遠。

劉曉明：正如我剛才所說，中國從不挑釁，但會反擊。我們對外闡明我們的立場，是希望引起國際社會的警覺。我在《每日電訊報》上發表文章正是希望英國民眾了解我們的擔憂。我們看重中英關係，也看重英方如何看待這件事。英國在維護歐洲及世界和平與穩定上發揮着重要作用。中英既是二戰盟友，也是戰爭受害者，兩國與國際社會一道共同承擔起維護戰後秩序的責任。這一秩序帶來了戰後七十年的和平與穩定。明年將迎來世界反法西斯戰爭勝利七十週年。我們在慶祝勝利的同時，也應關注二戰歷史是否會重演。如不制止日本軍國主義復活，另一場世界大戰的可能性就不能完全排除。我們希望以和平的方式解決

莊銳：在電影結尾，「伏地魔」最終被消滅了。

174

問題，但也要作最壞的打算。因此，最好的辦法是國際社會共同努力。我高興地看到，不僅中國抗議安倍參拜靖國神社，韓國、美國等國家也表達了嚴重關切和失望。我們希望國際社會共同制止日本軍國主義復辟。

莊銳：我們知道，日本侵華戰爭給中國人民造成了巨大的傷害，中國人民是否能夠原諒日本，還是在七十年後的今天仍然懷有仇恨？

劉曉明：日本侵華戰爭給中國人民帶來了巨大災難，造成了三千五百多萬人傷亡，直接和間接經濟損失達六千多億美元。我們希望彌合戰爭造成的傷痛，因此中日邦交正常化時，中國政府決定放棄對日本戰爭索賠。因為我們認為，犯下戰爭罪行的是日本軍國主義者，不是日本普通百姓。我們也不希望今天的日本年輕人為父輩曾經犯下的罪行承擔責任。中國希望與日本和平相處。但日本領導人通過參拜靖國神社、改寫歷史、篡改教科書、拒絕懺悔，不斷挑起新的仇恨。

日本當局不希望向下一代講述侵略歷史。日本和德國在對待歷史問題上採取了截然不同的態度。德國時任總理勃蘭特在猶太人紀念碑前下跪謝罪，現任總理默克爾訪問納粹集中營憑弔遇難者。而日本領導人從未作出類似政治姿態，甚至連向中國人民道歉的話都沒有，怎麼讓中國人民忘記歷史？日本政府和領導人的態度非常重要，我們希望他們改弦易轍，向中國、亞洲和所有遭受日本侵略戰爭苦難的人民真誠道歉、懺悔，從而翻開新的一頁。問題是，日本戰爭罪行從未得到徹底清算，因此軍國主義在日本總是蠢蠢欲動，國際社會應對日本軍國主義的危險動向保持警惕。

接受英國 BBC 國際廣播電台《週末》欄目
主持人沃里克現場直播採訪

作者手記

二〇一四年一月五日，我接受英國 BBC 國際廣播電台 (BBC World Service)《週末》(Weekend) 欄目主持人朱利安·沃里克 (Julian Worricker) 現場直播採訪，闡述中國在日本侵略歷史、釣魚島主權等問題上的嚴正立場，揭批安倍復辟軍國主義企圖，呼籲國際社會對此保持高度警惕。

BBC 國際廣播電台用四十多種語言向二百多個國家和地區廣播，聽眾達二點一億人次。《週末》是該台品牌欄目，聚焦一週重大事件，邀請英國和外國政要、社會名流、各界精英與主持人一對一對話。沃里克於一九八五年加入 BBC，先後任記者、編輯，在 BBC 多個頻道擔任主持人，創辦《沃里克星期日訪談》欄目，是《週末》欄目資深主持人。

在這次採訪中，沃里克還邀請英國《金融時報》政治編輯喬治·帕克和遠在新德里的印度記者喬蒂·馬豪特拉參加討論。

沃里克：日本首相安倍晉三參拜靖國神社的理由遭到中國政府的駁斥。中國駐英國大使劉曉明呼籲英國和國際社會對日本軍國主義復辟保持高度警惕。今天，劉大使來到了我們的演播室。大使先生，早上好。

劉曉明：早上好，朱利安。

沃里克：中國對安倍參拜靖國神社的具體關切是什麼？

劉曉明：我們對安倍參拜靖國神社表示嚴重關切。靖國神社一直是日本軍國主義對外發動侵略戰爭和殖民統治的精神工具和象徵，至今仍供奉着包括東條英機在內的十四名二戰甲級戰犯。東條英機不僅對中國發起戰爭，而且偷襲珍珠港，對美國、英國和荷蘭開戰。這是一個雙手沾滿了數百萬中國人民鮮血的戰犯。

沃里克：我理解中國人民為何對安倍參拜如此憤怒。

但這歸根到底不是日本的內政嗎？

劉曉明：這當然不是日本的內政問題。我們關注的不僅是日本領導人如何對待這些戰犯和歷史，更關注他們對未來的態度。

沃里克：你認為日本政府是什麼態度？

劉曉明：日本領導人參拜戰犯，顯示他們對日本侵略和殖民統治歷史毫無懺悔之意。日本副首相麻生太郎甚至揚言「日本可以學習納粹德國修憲的做法」。安倍本人也鼓吹所謂「侵略未定論」。

沃里克：我想進一步探討一下這個問題。中國也在不斷加大軍費開支，中國新一屆領導人表示還將繼續加大軍費投入。你們批評日本，這不是雙重標準嗎？

劉曉明：我不同意你的看法。我願談談中國的軍費開支。中國是一個大國。中國的國土面積是日本的

二十五倍，人口是日本的十倍，但日本的人均軍費開支是中國的五倍。就國防費在GDP中的比重而言，日本與中國差不多。

沃里克：但中國將會加大軍費投入，我想我們應該明確這一點。

劉曉明：那是因為中國經濟在不斷增長，中國的國防任務十分繁重。正如我剛才所說，中國有幅員遼闊的國土需要保衛。我們有十四個陸上鄰國和七個海上鄰國，擁有二點二萬公里陸地邊界線和三點二萬公里海岸線。

沃里克：我想討論一下中日在東海一些無人居住島嶼的爭端問題。中日都表示擁有這些島嶼的主權。作為爭端的一方，中國單方面宣佈在該地區劃設防空識別區。日本不可避免地會將這種行為視為「侵略」。

劉曉明：我們把這些島嶼稱作釣魚島。釣魚島及其附屬島嶼自古以來就是中國的領土。

沃里克：你知道日本對此有不同看法。

劉曉明：它會有不同看法，但我說的是事實。一八九五年中國在甲午戰爭戰敗後，釣魚島被日本非法侵佔。根據二戰期間中、英、美三國首腦發表的《開羅宣言》，日本必須向中國歸還所有竊取之領土，包括台灣及其周邊島嶼，當然也包括釣魚島。二十世紀五〇年代初，美國「接管」釣魚島。由於冷戰的原因，美國未向中國移交釣魚島及其附屬島嶼，因為美國需要日本。七〇年代，美國向日本「移交」釣魚島「行政管轄權」。但美國在釣魚島的主權問題上保持中立，並未承認日本對釣魚島擁有主權。

沃里克：除了加劇本已緊張的爭端外，你認為中方單方面劃設防空識別區能達到什麼目的？

劉曉明：請讓我把關於釣魚島的話說完。二十世紀

七〇年代中日實現關係正常化，兩國領導人達成諒解，同意將釣魚島問題先放一放，留待以後解決。

一九七八年，中國領導人鄧小平訪問日本時曾被問到釣魚島的歸屬問題。鄧小平回答說：這個問題我們同日本有爭議，可以把它放一放，也許下一代人比我們更聰明些，會找到實際解決的方法。因此兩國領導人決定擱置爭議。但近年來，日本多次單方面採取行動，發起了挑釁性的行為，製造了「購島」鬧劇，企圖將釣魚島進行所謂「國有化」。中國被迫對此作出反應。

劉曉明：你說的是劃設東海防空識別區問題嗎？

沃里克：我指的是更廣泛意義上的。

劉曉明：應當指出，日本早在四十五年前就已在該地區劃設防空識別區。過去四十五年裏，它不斷擴大防空識別區範圍，甚至劃到離中國領空僅有一百三十公里。

沃里克：你們用這來證明劃設東海防空識別區的合法性？

劉曉明：劃設防空識別區是國際通行的做法。

沃里克：但在某種程度上，雙方都必須從各自的立場上後退。

沃里克：我想邀請一位嘉賓喬治・帕克在線加入，他想問你一個問題。喬治，你一直在認真傾聽。

帕克：非常認真地聽。大使先生，我完全理解中日之間那段痛苦的歷史，以及你對安倍參拜靖國神社的憤怒。但如果對比一下中日的軍事實力，中國已遠遠超過日本。你仍然認為中國面臨日本的軍事威脅嗎？

劉曉明：你說的是包括軍費開支在內的一系列數字。但你忽略了一個事實：日本也在增加軍費開支。未來五年，日本的軍費開支將增長百分之五。目前日本的

軍費開支已達十八年來歷史新高。美國的國防預算比中國多四倍，人均國防開支是中國的二十二倍。即便英國，人均軍費開支也是中國的九倍。這只是其一。其二，軍費開支是衡量一國軍力的重要因素，但更重要的是看一個國家的國防政策，看它的歷史。中國是一個愛好和平的國家。如果你對比一下中日的歷史，就會知道日本與中國完全不同。

帕克：你是否認為日本仍是威脅？

劉曉明：歷史上，中國曾多次遭到侵略。一戰期間，日本強加給中國許多不平等條約。二戰期間，日本發動了侵華戰爭，中國人民傷亡和損失慘重。

沃里克：你認為日本仍然對中國構成軍事威脅？

劉曉明：當然。因為日本政府對待歷史的態度，因為日本領導人仍然參拜戰犯，並且企圖修改「和平憲法」。這些不能不使我們感到擔憂。

沃里克：下面我們連線在新德里的印度記者喬蒂·馬豪特拉。

馬豪特拉：大使先生，早上好。

劉曉明：早上好。

馬豪特拉：很高興在 BBC 節目裏與你對話。我是一名駐新德里的印度記者。在印度，我們認為中國是一個有着悠久歷史文明的偉大國家。中國很快就會成為世界第一大經濟體。但為什麼中國與包括印度在內的鄰國有着如此多的爭端？中印爭端的歷史可以追溯到印度獨立之前，雙方對一段長達四千公里的邊境線存在不同看法。你剛才說中國是一個愛好和平的國家，但就在幾個月前，中國軍隊越過實際控制線進入印度領土，並在那裏停留了三週時間。這是為什麼？

劉曉明：我想強調的是，我們希望與所有鄰國發展睦鄰友好關係。關於邊界爭端問題，需要說明的是，中國曾長期遭受帝國主義列強侵略。中國與一些鄰國的

邊界問題許多都是外國殖民者遺留下來的。但我們真誠地願意與爭議有關各方，包括印度，坐下來進行認真的談判。我高興地看到中印關於邊界問題的談判取得了積極進展。

馬豪特拉：大使先生，中印曾在二〇〇五年就解決邊界問題達成過協議。但幾年後，中國單方面退出該協議。目前兩國之間在邊界問題上不存在諒解。

劉曉明：我不同意你的說法。我今天主要是談中日關係問題。說到爭端，你不能只聽一面之詞。我們對印度方面的一些行動也是不滿的。但今天我不想與你爭論這個問題。我想強調的是，我們真誠希望雙方通過談判找到解決辦法。

沃里克：大使先生，非常感謝你參加本期節目。

劉曉明：不客氣。

接受英國 BBC 世界新聞台
主持人庫馬拉薩米現場直播採訪

二〇一四年一月五日，我在英國 BBC 總部演播室，接受 BBC 世界新聞台主持人詹姆斯·庫馬拉薩米（James Coomarasamy）現場直播採訪。

庫馬拉薩米曾任 BBC 外事記者，常駐蘇聯、波蘭、法國、美國，在 BBC 多個欄目擔任主持人。

我在採訪中揭批了日本首相安倍復辟軍國主義企圖，闡述了中方在劃設東海防空識別區、中國軍費等問題上的立場。

採訪內容除在 BBC 世界新聞台現場直播外，還在該台向全球一百多個國家和地區滾動播放，受眾近一億人次。

庫馬拉薩米：中國提醒國際社會對日本軍國主義保持警惕，中國的主要關切是什麼？

劉曉明：我們對安倍參拜靖國神社表示嚴重關切。靖國神社一直是日本軍國主義對外發動侵略戰爭和殖民統治的精神工具和象徵，至今仍供奉着包括東條英機在內的十四名二戰甲級戰犯。東條英機不僅對中國發起戰爭，而且偷襲珍珠港，對英國、美國和荷蘭開戰。日本領導人參拜這些戰犯，我們不能不對此感到擔憂。

庫馬拉薩米：你認為靖國神社所象徵的意義將把日本引向何方？

劉曉明：這正是我們所擔憂的。日本領導人參拜靖國神社並不是一個孤立事件，而是挑起地區緊張局勢的一系列行動的一部分。安倍上台以來，鼓吹所謂「侵略未定論」。他不承認日本是侵略者，甚至認為日本是戰爭的受害者。日本副首相麻生太郎還揚言「日本

可以學習納粹德國修憲的做法」。與此同時，日本不斷增加軍費。未來五年，日本軍費開支將增長百分之五。這應引起我們的警惕。

庫馬拉薩米：中國單方面劃設東海防空識別區，也引起了鄰國擔憂，這是否也是一種「侵略」行為？

劉曉明：我完全不同意你的說法。劃設防空識別區是主權國家的通行做法。英國、美國等許多國家都設有防空識別區。事實上，日本早在四十五年前就設立了防空識別區，並且不斷擴大，離中國海岸線最近距離僅一百三十公里。

庫馬拉薩米：但中國在當前局勢下宣佈劃設防空識別區，使緊張局勢升級，這難道不是「侵略」行為嗎？

劉曉明：我完全不同意你所謂中方「侵略」的說法。我想強調的是，東海防空識別區的劃設完全是為了防禦。它不是禁飛區，不會影響他國航空器依國際法享

有的飛越自由，只需向中方通報即可。自中國設立東海防空識別區以來，識別區內從未發生過衝突，一直保持着和平。中國的做法完全符合國際法和國際慣例。

庫馬拉薩米：中國在外交層面將採取什麼行動緩解兩國緊張關係？緩解緊張局勢也符合中國利益。

劉曉明：是日本挑釁在先。當務之急是制止日本軍國主義復辟企圖。我們要動員國際社會的力量，共同阻止日本在錯誤的道路上越走越遠。安倍參拜靖國神社後，不僅中國、韓國表達了強烈憤怒，美國也表示失望。我們只有建立國際統一陣線，共同防止日本重走軍國主義擴張的老路，戰後國際秩序才能得以維護。

庫馬拉薩米：你剛才說美國也對安倍參拜靖國神社表示失望，但這還不夠。因為這未能阻止日本領導人參拜靖國神社。我們是否需要外部干預？

劉曉明：日本侵華戰爭造成中國三千五百多萬人傷亡，直接和間接經濟損失達六千多億美元。韓國也在日本侵略戰爭中遭受慘痛損失。事實上，英國人民也是日本侵略戰爭的受害者。

庫馬拉薩米：如果當前緊張局勢無法緩解，會導致什麼後果？

劉曉明：我們希望日本領導人能傾聽國際社會的聲音，改弦更張，回到中日兩國領導人達成的共識和中日關係四個政治文件上來，對歷史罪行進行深刻反省和真誠懺悔。事實上，日本戰爭罪行從未得到徹底清算，因此軍國主義勢力總是蠢蠢欲動。我們決不能讓日本軍國主義再度復活。

庫馬拉薩米：但中國也在增加軍費開支，在地區部署航母，這不是對外發出錯誤信號嗎？

劉曉明：中日兩國不能相提並論。中國是一個幅員遼

闊的大國。中國人口是日本的十倍，國土面積是日本的二十五倍，但日本的人均軍費開支卻是中國的五倍。而且，中國的國防費用佔 GDP 和財政總支出比重近年來不斷下降。更重要的是，中國是愛好和平的國家，從未發動過侵略戰爭，相反卻屢遭外國列強侵略。而日本則完全不同，在歷史上多次發動對外侵略戰爭，包括侵華戰爭。

庫馬拉薩米：謝謝劉大使。

劉曉明：不客氣。

接受英國 BBC《新聞之夜》欄目
主持人帕克斯曼現場直播採訪

二〇一四年一月八日，我在英國 BBC 旗艦欄目《新聞之夜》(Newsnight) 演播室，接受該欄目主持人傑里米·帕克斯曼 (Jeremy Paxman) 現場直播採訪。

我在英國《每日電訊報》上發表文章，揭批日本首相安倍參拜靖國神社，並把日本軍國主義比作「伏地魔」後，日本駐英大使緊接着在同一報紙發表文章，狂妄地也把中國比作「伏地魔」。中日駐英大使在英國報紙上的公開論戰，引起英國媒體極大關注。BBC 第一個提出，大牌主持人帕克斯曼希望邀請兩國大使作客《新聞之夜》，就雙方各自立場進行辯論。我表示，沒有問題，願意赴約。然而，日本駐英國使館回絕了 BBC，說日本駐英國大使林景一可以接受帕克斯曼單獨採訪，但不與中國大使同台辯論。

英國是一個不愁創意的國度。BBC 並沒有因為日方的回絕而放棄，它提出能否請兩國大使同時作客《新聞之夜》演播室，可以不面對面地辯論，由帕克斯曼分別採訪。BBC 告之，《新聞之夜》演播室有兩個演播台，兩國大使可分坐兩個不同的演播台，相距十米，可以看到聽到，不必打招呼。帕克斯曼將分別採訪兩位大使。採訪

為現場直播，時長八分鐘，每位大使四分鐘。我方表示沒有問題，可以接受。但既然是同時到場，分別接受採訪，就有一個誰先誰後問題。為了掌握主動，我方提出後接受採訪。日方也要求後接受採訪。

英國也是一個講規矩的國度。BBC說，英方提出兩國大使同台辯論，中方同意，日方不幹，英方依了日方。現在中日雙方都要求後接受採訪，英方必須照顧中方，這才公平。

於是，一月八日，我和日本大使林景一同時步入BBC《新聞之夜》演播室，分別在兩個演播台坐下。帕克斯曼先採訪林景一，一連串的問題讓他招架不住。我在十米外靜聽，摩拳擦掌，準備逐一批駁他的謬論。四分鐘後，帕克斯曼移步我的演播台。這是他第二次採訪我，俗話說，「一回生，二回熟」，我們也算是「熟人」了。一見面，我們互致問候，氣氛與第一次採訪大不相同。我們談了安倍參拜靖國神社、釣魚島等問題，我闡述了中方在這些問題上的嚴正立場，揭批安倍企圖復辟日本軍國主義的行徑。

這場中日大使交鋒被媒體稱為「輿論甲午戰爭」，還有的媒體將兩位大使的表現作比較：日本大使語焉不詳，前後矛盾，被動招架；中國大使慷慨陳詞，有理有據，始終處於主動，可謂「完勝」。這一幕也被定格在六集大型政論專題片《大國外交》中。

帕克斯曼：大使先生，你好！非常感謝前來接受採訪。

劉曉明：你好，傑里米！很高興再次見面。

帕克斯曼：我也很高興見到你。你認為安倍參拜靖國神社問題有多嚴重？

劉曉明：非常嚴重。這是一個大是大非的問題。它事關日本如何看待其侵略歷史，溫斯頓·丘吉爾曾經說過，「不從歷史中吸取教訓的人註定重蹈覆轍」。如果日本不能正視其侵略歷史，人們不能不擔心日本今後將走什麼道路。

帕克斯曼：你提到參拜靖國神社的問題。二戰以來，日本首相參拜靖國神社共六十多次，但中國對其中二十多次都沒有表示反對。

劉曉明：這種說法是不對的。我知道這是日本駐英大使提供的數字。但事實是，一九七八年以後靖國神社才移入十四名二戰甲級戰犯的牌位。一九八五年，日本時任首相率領全體內閣成員參拜靖國神社，中國當即表示強烈抗議。此後，中國對日本領導人的參拜行為不斷提出嚴正抗議。

帕克斯曼：讓我們談談釣魚島問題。為什麼中國突然宣佈對該島嶼空域的控制？為什麼中國突然採取行動？

劉曉明：這個問題問得很好。過去四十年來釣魚島問題一直平靜，為什麼近來突然升溫呢？首先，我想強調釣魚島及其附屬島嶼自古以來就是中國的固有領土，一八九五年中國在甲午戰爭戰敗後，日本將其非法侵佔。根據《開羅宣言》和《波茨坦公告》，日本必須向中國歸還所有非法竊取之領土。這是中、英、美三國首腦共同達成的國際文件。

帕克斯曼：對不起，我不熟悉《開羅宣言》，請問那

是什麼時候？

劉曉明：一九四三年。

帕克斯曼：好的。你認為目前的問題與釣魚島及其海域蘊藏豐富的自然資源是否有關？

劉曉明：這一問題事關國家主權，事關領土完整。讓我繼續說明這一問題為何突然升溫。一九七二年中日實現關係正常化，兩國領導人達成諒解，同意將釣魚島問題先放一放，留待以後解決。一九七八年，中國領導人鄧小平訪問日本時曾被問及釣魚島歸屬問題。鄧小平回答說：這個問題我們同日本有爭議，可以把它放一放，也許下一代人比我們更聰明些，會找到解決的方法。因此兩國領導人決定擱置爭議。但近年來日本不斷單方面採取行動，企圖改變現狀，製造了「購島」鬧劇，企圖將釣魚島進行所謂「國有化」，迫使中國不得不作出反應。

帕克斯曼：對這一爭議，中國準備走多遠？

劉曉明：首先，日本要承認雙方在釣魚島問題上存在爭議。日本甚至拒絕承認存在爭議。

帕克斯曼：就在幾秒鐘前，坐在那裏的日本大使說有必要進行對話，這不是暗示承認存在分歧嗎？

劉曉明：事實上，是安倍破壞了中日關係的政治基礎，是安倍關閉了中日對話的大門。安倍拒絕就日本軍國主義向中國人民犯下的戰爭罪行表示真誠懺悔，在這種情況下怎麼可能要求中國同意與他對話！而且不僅中國表達了這一立場，韓國總統也因為安倍在歷史問題上的言行拒絕與他會見。

帕克斯曼：非常感謝你接受採訪。

劉曉明：不客氣！

後記

出使英國十一年，我接受了一百七十多次採訪，其中電視、電台採訪五十三次。所有主流電視台和電台都採訪過我。我被英國輿論界和外交界稱為「上鏡率最高」「被媒體引用最多」的外國駐英使節。我離任回國後，不少朋友和同事都說，看了我在英國電視台的採訪，印象深刻。他們希望我把這些採訪整理一下出本書，更希望我講講採訪背後的故事。

凡是故事，皆有源頭。採訪故事的源頭就是我們國家的崛起。隨着中國日益走近世界舞台的中央，世界更加關注我們，希望聽到我們的聲音，更多了解我們。與此同時，國際上的反華勢力極盡造謠污衊之能事，抹黑、詆毀中國，把西方涉華輿論環境搞得烏煙瘴氣。英國擁有大量媒體資源，是國際輿論中心，也

是西方輿論高地。在這樣的國度工作，我深感肩上沉甸甸的擔子，更感講好中國故事，傳播好中國聲音，是我義不容辭的責任。正是這種責任感，使我在嚴峻的輿論環境面前，不畏困難，不懼挑戰，敢於擔當。正是這種責任感，使我充滿自信，從容應對，努力展現中國大國風度，彰顯中華民族志氣和底氣。

許多人問我與西方媒體打交道有什麼經驗和體會，向我討教應對西方媒體的「秘訣」。我說，責任感和自信心是我最主要的經驗和體會，也是我制勝的法寶。說到「秘訣」，我倒有「三套武器」。每次上陣前，特別是接受現場直播採訪前，我都要認真仔細檢查這「三套武器」。一是「長矛」，二是「盾牌」，三是「匕首」。「長矛」用來主動出擊，積極闡述中

國立場和內外政策，講好中國故事，向世界展示真實、立體、全面的中國。「盾牌」用來防守，事先假設各種刁鑽問題，做足功課，備好預案，從容應對。「匕首」用來反擊。最好的防禦是進攻。短兵相接，特別是對方糾纏不休的時候，要伺機反問，打亂對方進攻節奏，轉守為攻，變被動為主動。比如二〇一九年十一月，我接受 BBC《尖銳對話》欄目現場直播採訪，主持人不停質問所謂中國人權問題。我問他：你去過中國嗎？他說三年前去過。我接着問：難道你沒有感受到中國人民是很自由、很幸福的嗎？你認為中國人民處於被壓迫、被恐嚇的狀態嗎？一連串的反問使他趕緊轉換話題。還是這次採訪，主持人一再糾纏新疆問題，而且不停打斷我，不給我介紹新疆情況的機會。我抓住機會反問：你去過新疆嗎？他一下愣了，沒想到我會問這個問題。他說還沒有去過，如果中方邀請，他很樂意去。我表示歡迎。接着向他介紹新疆情況，告訴他中國有句俗語：不到新疆，不知中國之大；不到新疆，不知道中國之美。但二十世紀九〇年代至二〇一六年，新疆變成另外一種景象，恐

怖襲擊事件頻發，成千無辜群眾遇難。中國政府對此必須採取措施，包括依法設立「職業教育技能培訓中心」。有力的反問打斷了對方糾纏，也為我說明新疆真相爭取了機會。反擊還要備足「炮彈」。也是在這次採訪中，主持人反覆糾纏所謂香港警察過度使用暴力「鎮壓」，甚至近距離向抗議者開槍。我引述英國首席警監的話：「訓練有素的武裝警察可以開槍，以消除威脅，保護公眾和警察自身安全。」主持人無言以對。

習近平總書記說，我們黨帶領人民經過幾代人不懈奮鬥，基本解決了「挨打」「挨餓」問題，但「挨罵」問題還沒有得到根本解決。我的體會是，解決了「挨打」問題，使中國人民站起來；解決了「挨餓」問題，使中國人民富起來；還沒有根本解決「挨罵」問題，說明我們國家仍面臨複雜嚴峻的國際輿論環境。要實現中華民族從站起來、富起來到強起來的偉大飛躍，必須要下大力氣加強國際傳播能力建設，解決「挨罵」問題。換句話說，解決「挨罵」問題將伴隨從站起來、富起來到強起來的全過程。這充分說明

解決「挨罵」問題的長期性和艱巨性，也說明加強國際傳播能力建設的重要性和必要性。在這一過程中，既要加強對國際傳播理論和規律的研究，也要用好外國主流媒體的平台和渠道，「借船出海」，「借台唱戲」，努力構建對外話語體系，提升對外發聲能力。

北京出版集團把我使英國期間接受英美電視電台採訪實錄彙編成《尖銳對話》，這既是一次有益的嘗試，也可謂恰逢其時。

在此，我要感謝北京出版集團董事長康偉、總編輯李清霞、副總經理趙安良，北京人民出版社總編輯呂克農、特邀譯審艾玫子和責任編輯馬群。由於他們的鼓勵和支持，特別是他們編輯和出版團隊的敬業精神和高效工作，使本書在較短的時間內順利出版。我還要感謝外交部的同事陳雯、曾嶸和王小晶，她們參與本書的審核、校對和聯絡工作，提出不少寶貴意見。

最後，我要感謝為本書寫推薦語的中英人士，特別是英國友人，他們中有前政府大臣、議員，有著名企業家、金融家、科學家，有知名學者、大學校長、教授，有公爵、男爵、勳爵。他們的肯定和鼓勵不僅充滿熱情，而且充滿智慧。他們是中英關係的見證者和參與者，也是中國聲音的傾聽者和建議者。我將珍視他們的友誼，不辜負他們的期望，接續努力，積極探索，讓世界更多的人聽到新時代中國聲音。

劉曉明

二〇二二年立秋

作者簡介

劉曉明

畢業於大連外國語大學，獲美國塔夫茨大學弗萊徹法律與外交學院碩士學位。一九七四年開始外交生涯，先後在非洲、美洲、亞洲、歐洲四大洲常駐，曾任外交部北美大洋洲司副司長、駐美國使館公使、駐埃及大使、甘肅省省長助理、中央外事工作領導小組辦公室副主任、駐朝鮮大使、駐英國大使。現任中國政府朝鮮半島事務特別代表、外交部外交政策諮詢委員會委員。

曾獲美國弗萊徹院長勳章、朝鮮民主主義人民共和國一級友誼勳章、美國弗萊徹一九四七屆紀念勳章、英國四十八家集團俱樂部中英關係傑出貢獻終身成就獎、英國諾丁漢大學榮譽法學博士學位、英國倫敦金融城榮譽市民、英國哈德斯菲爾德大學榮譽博士學位。

著有《大使講中國故事》（中信出版社，二〇二二年；三聯書店（香港）有限公司，二〇二三年）。

194

香港問題

目錄

保羅·納斯爵士

弗朗西斯·克里克研究所所長

英國皇家學會前會長

諾貝爾生理學或醫學獎獲得者

吉姆·奧尼爾勳爵

英國議會上院議員

「金磚之父」

英國財政部前商務大臣

英國皇家國際事務研究所前主席

《尖銳對話》彙集了劉曉明擔任中國駐英國大使期間，廣泛接受英國主流電視台和電台的採訪。他在採訪中思維敏捷、幽默風趣，有時還帶有火藥味，凸顯了一位成就卓著的外交官的氣質。他就當今世界一系列重要問題解釋中國的立場，使人們了解中國和西方國家在一些問題上並不總是意見一致。然而，要解決這些困難的問題，坐下來討論是非常重要的。閱讀本書，可以更好地了解中國，了解中國對當今世界問題的立場。

我很高興就劉曉明大使的系列採訪集談談感想，尤其是因為閱讀採訪集是在二〇一五年秋天，來白英格蘭「北部振興計劃」包括商界和其他名流在內的各界領軍人物，對中國進行了旋風式正式訪問。隨後，英國接待了習近平主席激動人心的國事訪問。作為曼聯的球迷，我直到今天仍無法理解為什麼自己當時未能阻止習近平主席訪問曼城俱樂部。為了給自己的懶惰尋找藉口，我總是說劉大使要為此負責。與劉大使面會進行了採訪，這一期事，尤其是回憶起我就全球化中存在的問題對劉大使會進行了採訪，這一期BBC廣播訪談節目內容也收錄在他的採訪集中。對於這次訪談我想談兩點。一個是訪談中劉大使在我和BBC的腦海中播下了一顆種子：我本可以沿着「絲綢之路」長途旅行並拍攝一部紀錄片，可惜這個絕妙的想法沒有實現。另一個更為重要：如果當初決策者們能夠聽取我和多位接受我訪談的人士關於全球化弱點的總體建議，那麼世界是有可能避免當前的一些混亂問題的，包括全球缺乏團結的問題——希望這種問題只是暫時的。

進，包括經濟和金融地位加強、基礎設施投資增加、對全球貿易的重要性提升、人民更加富足且吃苦耐勞、教育水平提高、軍事力量增強。我們見證了中國在全球市場上的驚人競爭力，以至於它在世界貿易中的份額已經上升到與美國相當。

此外，中國用四十年奇蹟般地使七億多人擺脫了貧困，醫療保險覆蓋率幾乎達到百分之百，人均預期壽命更長，人民生活更幸福。中國境外旅遊人數已增至一億左右。正是在此期間，劉曉明擔任中國駐英國大使，他以多種方式參與了這些進步的各個方面。正如時任英國首相戴維·卡梅倫所說，這一時期是「黃金時期——中英關係的黃金時代」。

在他擔任大使期間，中英之間的商品和服務貿易翻了一番，中國來英投資則增加了三倍。二〇一五年底，習近平主席對英國進行國事訪問之前，劉大使在二〇一五年十月接受英國獨立電視台（ITV）採訪，他表示，中國的崛起帶來的機遇遠大於威脅。兩國認為這個時代已經超越了浮華、客氣話和口號。人們希望並致力於深入發展兩國之間的關係。困難總是難免的，但總而言之，在劉大使任職期間，中英兩國關係迎來了黃金時期。

英國應當感謝劉大使所取得的所有成就，特別是使中英關係基礎更加堅實、牢固。

麥啟安
英國東亞委員會秘書長
全球化智庫國際理事會主席

雅各布‧羅斯柴爾德男爵
英國著名銀行家
英國科學院榮譽院士

二十一世紀地緣政治的核心挑戰之一，是「讓世界聽到中國的聲音」。

習近平主席自二○一二年擔任中共十八大報告起草組組長以來就認識到了這一需要。報告中包含推進如何「讓世界聽到中國的聲音」的政策。《尖銳對話》的巨大價值在於，它提供了一個獨特的案例研究：劉曉明大使如何在中國駐英國大使館作出最有價值的開創性努力，從而為「讓世界聽到中國的聲音」發揮最佳影響。劉曉明大使二○一○年抵達英國時，已在多國積累了豐富的交流經驗。他在美國擔任中國大使館公使（副館長）的經歷使他深刻認識到，中國需要在溝通方式上進行創新。仔細研究《尖銳對話》這本書中的採訪，可以看出他努力以最地道的英式英語在英國進行交流的價值。此外，他以一種對英國媒體產生最佳影響力的方式進行交流的技巧也令人印象深刻。從他接受如此之多的電台和電視採訪，以及撰寫的大量媒體文章中，人們能夠體會到他為「讓世界聽到中國的聲音」而不斷探索新方式的熱情。我希望這本訪談錄有助於讀者研究這位二十一世紀具有極高造詣的中國傳播者劉曉明大使。

祝賀劉曉明大使！

劉曉明大使於二○一○至二○二一年擔任中國駐英國大使十一年。在中國五千多年歷史的背景下，他的任期恰逢中國歷史及中英關係發生非凡的變革和進步。

自一九四九年中華人民共和國成立以來，中國國家利益得到顯著推

里士滿公爵

全英賽車俱樂部主席

義者致力於推翻資本主義。但事實並非如此。中國也擁有龐大的民營部門，同樣面臨與英國諸多相同的治理和共享問題。

在《尖銳對話》中，讀者可以了解到中國如何尋求共贏的成果，而英國的一些關切使取得這些成果變得困難。

《尖銳對話》表明，它不是在宣傳，而是在幫助人們看清事實，了解中國的歷史、中國的方式和中國的計劃。劉大使是在海外最早與西方媒體打交道的人之一，交流內容包括管控分歧甚至利益衝突。

只有打破繁文縟節，你才能觸及真正的問題。劉大使是來到英國願意以這種方式開展接觸的為數不多的中國人之一。

讓我們享受閱讀這些媒體訪談，跟隨劉大使穿越中英之間數百年缺乏交流的歷史，去真正了解彼此在關鍵問題上的立場。

與媒體公開交流的能力和意願，是劉曉明擔任中國駐英國大使期間的突出特點。正如《尖銳對話》書名所示，當中國問題以及後來的涉港、新冠肺炎疫情等問題成為全球關注的焦點時，劉大使認識到與BBC等新聞媒體進行公開對話的重要性。作為一個樂觀主義者，劉大使對全球化和中英雙邊關係等複雜問題有其獨到見解，這也是他在中國駐英國大使的崗位上取得巨大成功的重要因素。當前，中國在世界上的地位和影響幾乎佔據新聞頭條，《尖銳對話》一書讓我們有幸聆聽劉大使與不斷刨根到底的媒體進行交流時的雄辯口才。

劉曉明於二○一○至二○二一年擔任中國駐英國大使，這十一年是中英關係非同尋常的時期。二○一三至二○一六年，兩國享有有史以來最熱烈的關係。這個時期的亮點是二○一五年英國不顧奧巴馬政府的反對，決定加入亞洲基礎設施投資銀行，這一決定鼓勵了許多歐洲國家也採取同樣的行動。習近平主席於當年晚些時候訪問英國，這被廣泛認為是一次重大的成功訪問。這一時期在當時被稱為中英關係的「黃金時代」是有充分理由的，但是它並沒有持續下去。二○一六年，卡梅倫首相輸掉了脫歐公投並辭職，隨後中英關係開始惡化，直到二○一九年支持脫歐的鮑里斯·約翰遜政府上台，兩國關係達到了一個新的低點。「黃金時代」讓位於針對中國的越來越大的敵意和在香港問題上日益升級的緊張關係。劉曉明的文章和訪談為我們觀察這一時期中英關係的高潮和低谷提供了非常有價值的真知灼見。他一直是中國立場的有力支持者和能言善辯者，這使他成為英國政界非常知名和受人尊敬的人物。

馬丁·雅克

英國著名學者

政治評論家、作家

《尖銳對話》抓住了兩種文化和兩種體制之間的差異。劉曉明大使利用英國媒體幫助英國政府領導人、官員、商界和金融界了解中國，了解快速崛起的中國經濟和社會體系。

由於十九世紀劃定的分割線，許多西方人認為俄羅斯和中國的社會主

斯蒂芬·佩里

英國四十八家集團俱樂部主席

「中國改革友誼獎章」獲得者

《理智與情感》和《傲慢與偏見》均為英國著名女作家簡·奧斯丁的名著。

[1]

諸立力

英國倫敦大學學院理事會主席

世界經濟論壇國際商務委員會聯席主席

任何一位外國駐英大使，因此獲得了表達中國觀點前所未有的機會。

雖然他和他的中國同事謹記「每個人都有權擁有自己的觀點，卻無權擁有屬於自己的事實」這一格言，但是他展現出能言善辯者的智慧和鬥志，實在令人敬畏。他的語言能力非常出眾，反映出他在英國文學方面的深厚底蘊。他在一次採訪中曾告誡主持人：「我希望人們能多一些『理智與情感』，少一些『傲慢與偏見』。」[1]

總之，讀罷此書，人們對一位傑出的外交官應對媒體的專業能力，不能不表示欽佩。

劉曉明大使的書是對過去十年中英關係發展史的獨特貢獻。劉大使是在英國任職時間最長的中國大使，他長達十一年的任期與戈登·布朗、戴維·卡梅倫、特雷莎·梅和鮑里斯·約翰遜等四位首相領導的英國政府執政、英國脫歐公投以及最終退出歐盟的整個歷程重疊。

在英國的這段特殊時期，劉大使的長期任職使他對英國的政治、社會和經濟動態有着非凡的洞察力。他熱情廣泛地接觸各界人士，經常通過大眾媒體和多媒體講述中國故事。劉大使的做法非常有效——他從不迴避棘手和複雜的問題，總是以建設性的方式以及極具個性的雄辯和禮貌去應對這些問題。這本書是劉大使在英國期間的珍貴訪談錄，它代表了在這個關鍵的歷史節點，縮小中西方「了解赤字」的非凡努力。

已作為經典橋段而廣為傳播。《尖銳對話》一書不僅以採訪實錄的方式再現了這些經典場景，展現了作者與英國頂級媒體之間的精彩互動，具有強烈的現實場景感，而且充分展示了中國外交的豐富內涵，幫助我們從一個側面了解到國際形勢的風雲激盪、中國和平崛起的外部效應以及外交工作者對祖國的忠誠奉獻。本書將成為新時代中國外交和對外傳播的一個生動寫照。本書內容均為劉大使親身經歷，具有口述史的寶貴價值，可以成為深入研究國際形勢變化、中國外交、對外傳播以及對英外交等專題的重要參考資料。

劉曉明在擔任中國歷史上任期最長的駐英國大使期間曾發表一系列演講，並結集出版。現在他又將任內接受英國電視和電台採訪的內容彙編成冊，以《尖銳對話》為題出版。和他演講中的表現一樣，劉曉明在採訪中立場堅定、毫不留情。他的訪談直率、尖銳，具有說服力；他擅長反駁，對那些針對中國的虛假主張和指控作出回應，甚至可以用《帝國反擊戰》[1]給他的系列採訪加上詼諧的副標題。

採訪的主題從新冠肺炎疫情到香港，再到中國與英國的關係，涵蓋範圍廣泛。劉大使在採訪中與大多數英國最著名的電視主持人唇槍舌劍。值得稱讚的是，他從不迴避挑戰，這使他在電視和媒體上的曝光率遠遠超過

查爾斯‧鮑威爾勳爵
英國議會上院議員
英國前首相撒切爾夫人外事顧問

[1]《帝國反擊戰》又名《星球大戰二：帝國反擊戰》，是美國著名導演厄文‧克什納一九八〇年執導的太空歌劇史詩片，獲多項影視大獎。

崔洪建

中國國際問題研究院歐洲研究所所長

包括習近平主席訪英、新時代的中國、香港問題、新冠肺炎疫情、中日關係等等豐富內容。通讀下來，我的感受是：這無疑是一部「活」的中國外交史，不僅是專注中國外交崛起和外交話語權構建的學者的重要參考書，更是關心中國復興和中國走向世界舞台中心的所有讀者的必讀書。

如何清晰有力地向國際社會表達中國立場、形象生動地向世界講好中國故事，是中國外交和對外傳播在「百年未有之大變局」中的一道必答題。劉曉明大使的新著《尖銳對話》為這一難題提供了一個堪稱經典的答案。

劉大使在書中所涉及的重大國際、外交和內政問題上，堅定把握政治原則及政策立場，運用高超的敘事和應答技巧，充分闡釋中國看待上述問題的視角、制定政策的原則和採取行動的邏輯，既敢於鬥爭、不迴避尖銳問題，又善於鬥爭、不掉入話語陷阱。

英國是傳媒業最為發達、新聞集散最為活躍、輿論傳播能見度最高的西方國家之一，也是中國外交和對外傳播工作的重點與難點。劉大使在駐節英倫十一載的歲月中，為增進西方社會對中國國情和政策的全面真實了解，破解西方輿論對中國形象的曲解誤導，與當地媒體廣泛交流、持續發聲，在西方新聞傳媒業最為發達的心臟地帶成就了一系列精彩的對外傳播篇章。他與BBC節目主持人之間充滿睿智和機敏的唇槍舌劍，已經成為詮釋大國形象的經典場面；他將日本軍國主義形象地比作「伏地魔」等也

解振華

中國氣候變化事務特使

國家環境保護總局原局長

國家發展和改革委員會原副主任

鄭永年

前海國際事務研究院院長

香港中文大學（深圳）教授

《尖銳對話》反映了我國工作在一線的外交官在國際舞台上面對西方媒體諸多不確定性的挑戰，充滿自信，從容應對，發出中國聲音的現實故事，看後印象深刻。有此經歷和體會的人都清楚，每一次接受西方媒體新聞採訪或面對面訪談，甚至電視直播，對被採訪者的政策水平，以及其對國內外形勢的了解和判斷力、所涉專業知識的熟悉程度和水平、語言表達和應變能力，是一次真刀實槍的考驗。劉曉明大使駐英十一年，接受採訪一百七十多次，其中，電視、電台採訪五十三次，經常會面對很多不確定性或刁鑽問題，甚至不友好的挑釁，但他都能夠用事實、數據、法律、歷史、案例睿智地代表國家回答問題、申明立場、發表評論，講好中國故事，彰顯了中國外交官不懼挑戰、迎難而上、敢於鬥爭、善於鬥爭的責任擔當，彰顯了文明古國的大國風範。尤其面臨當前複雜的形勢，特別推薦《尖銳對話》。

劉曉明大使多年來活躍在中國外交舞台上，為世界外交界和政策研究界所矚目。我本人關注劉大使已經多年，這不僅僅是因為他在講好中國故事、做好國際傳播方面的國際影響力，更是因為我在思考這樣一個重要的問題：中國的崛起是如何賦能我國的外交官在國際舞台上展現中國風貌的？呈現在讀者眼前的這本書收錄了劉大使在任職駐英大使期間（二〇一〇至二〇二一年）接受電視和電台採訪實錄三十餘篇。書中重點回顧了二十一世紀第二個十年中英兩國共同關心的所有重大雙邊和國際事件，

重磅推薦

李肇星

外交部原部長

第十一屆全國人大外事委員會主任委員

我了解劉曉明戰友。他祖籍廣東，從小就知道三元里老鄉們愛國反帝的傳統；年輕時就敬佩老一輩革命家毛主席、周總理；在大西北掛職省長助理時，虛心學習老革命根據地的黨史；後來出任駐友好鄰邦朝鮮的大使，不負韶華。一九九九年美空軍悍然轟炸我駐南聯盟使館，我駐美使館在中央指揮和國內外輿論支持下，迫使美國時任總統寫下道歉詞時，他作為公使挺立在我身旁。

曉明同志在駐英期間，永記祖國天安門城樓上「中華人民共和國萬歲」「世界人民大團結萬歲」的口號和習主席「以人民為中心」的理念，特別注重與民間和新聞界交流……《尖銳對話》不妨說是真誠對話，記述了他為推動和平、正義和人類發展事業做的大量工作。

日前，他約我推介此書並謙虛地說，不用「吹捧」，寫「三百字」就行。我欣然從命。我想說的很簡約：此書難得，廣大中外朋友讀後會頗受啟迪，願為構建人類命運共同體多幹實事。

劉曉明

尖銳對話

讓世界聽見中國聲音